PEACEMAKING by
DEMOCRACIES

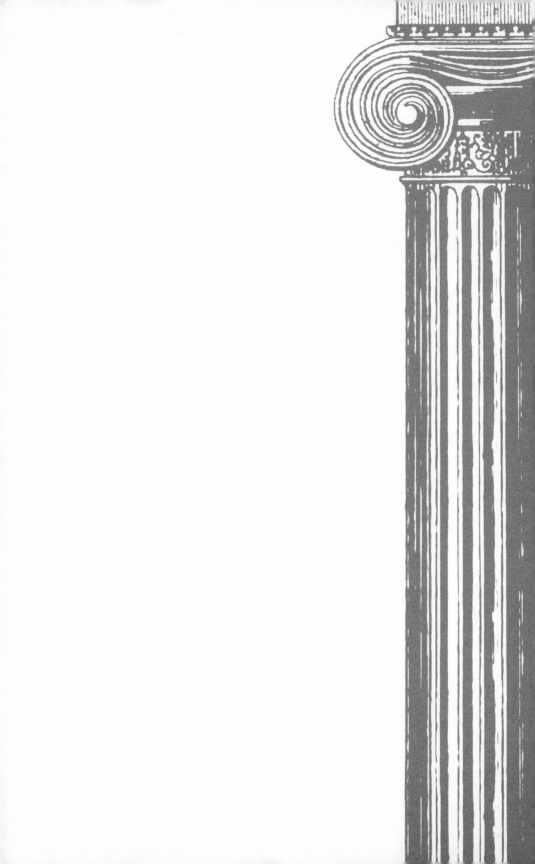

NORRIN M. RIPSMAN

PEACEMAKING by
DEMOCRACIES

THE EFFECT
OF STATE AUTONOMY
ON THE
POST–WORLD WAR SETTLEMENTS

THE PENNSYLVANIA STATE UNIVERSITY PRESS
UNIVERSITY PARK, PENNSYLVANIA

Library of Congress Cataloging-in-Publication Data

Ripsman, Norrin M.
    Peacemaking by democracies : the effect of state autonomy
on the post–World War settlements / Norrin M. Ripsman.
        p.   cm.
    Includes bibliographical references and index.
    ISBN 0-271-02222-1 (alk. paper)
    1. International relations—Political aspects. 2. Democracy.
    3. Peace treaties—History. I. Title.

JZ1251 .R57 2002
327.1′72—dc21   2002010315

Contents

Acknowledgments

I am indebted to many people whose comments, feedback, and encouragement helped me to complete this book. John Ikenberry, Daniel Deudney, and Marc Trachtenberg helped me to begin this odyssey. I am grateful to them for their probing comments, for stimulating my intellectual curiosity, and for accommodating my desire to marry international relations theory with rigorous archival research.

Many other friends and colleagues at the University of Pennsylvania, Lehigh University, the Hebrew University of Jerusalem, the Mershon Center at The Ohio State University, Dalhousie University, and Concordia University have made invaluable contributions to this manuscript with their incisive, often critical, but always supportive comments. In particular, I would like to thank Emanuel Adler, Steven Bernstein, David Black, Jean-Marc F. Blanchard, Thomas M. Callaghy, Raymond Cohen, Maria Fanis, Avery Goldstein, Chuck Gochmann, Maggie Hanson, Ted Hopf, Korina Kagan, Chaim Kaufmann, Mary L. Klingensmith, Ned Lebow, Oded Löwenheim, Ed Mansfield, Benny Miller, Csaba Nikolenyi, Galia Press Bar Natan, Randy Schweller, Tim Shaw, Denis Stairs, and Peter Swenson for their help. Two of these colleagues, Steven Bernstein and Jean-Marc F. Blanchard, deserve a special mention for enduring many drafts without complaint and providing me with insightful feedback. I am also indebted to David Auerswald, Deborah Avant, Daniel Drezner, Miriam Fendius Elman, Ben Frankel, Peter Katzenstein, John Owen, Susan Peterson, and Thomas Risse, who read and commented on related conference papers, journal articles, and/or portions of this book. The anonymous reviewers who read this manuscript also gave me comments and suggestions that improved the final product immeasurably.

Several institutions have provided funding to make this book possible. The archival research was made possible by a University of Pennsylvania

Penfield Traveling Fellowship in International Affairs and Belles-Lettres, a University of Pennsylvania School of Arts and Sciences Dissertation Fellowship, a research grant from the Harry S. Truman Presidential Library's Institute for National and International Affairs, and a research grant from Concordia University's General Research Fund. In addition, I am grateful to the Lady Davis Fellowship Fund at the Hebrew University of Jerusalem and the Mershon Center at The Ohio State University for providing me with postdoctoral fellowships in hospitable environments that enabled me to write this manuscript. Thanks are also due to the archivists and librarians at the Public Records Office of Kew Gardens, England, the archives of the Ministère des Affaires Etrangères and the Archives Nationales in Paris, France, the Harry S. Truman Presidential Library in Independence, Missouri, the Dwight David Eisenhower Presidential Library in Abilene, Kansas, the National Archives in College Park, Maryland, and the Seeley J. Mudd Manuscript Library in Princeton, New Jersey. I am particularly grateful to Mademoiselle Callu, custodian of the private papers of René Pleven, and to Madame Würms de Romilly for granting me special permission to consult them before they were available to the public.

Finally, I wish to thank several other people who contributed to this manuscript in important ways. My research assistants, Anna Kisielewska, Ara Karaboghossian, and Brian A. Vincent, worked above and beyond the call of duty in the final preparation of this book. Sandy Thatcher at Penn State University Press has been a very patient and helpful editor for this first-time author. Ron Wener, Jean-Marc F. Blanchard, and Pat Kozak have provided essential moral support throughout the research and writing process. My parents, Toba and Michael Ripsman, have been a source of love and encouragement throughout my life. Their contribution to this book is immeasurable. Above all, I could not have completed this book without the loving support of my wife, Nathalie. She has helped me in every possible way, serving as a friend, critic, typist, research assistant, and many other roles. Her inspiration fills every page.

Introduction

Not all democracies are alike. Some grant extraordinary powers to their heads of state or government to make policy, while others possess complex arrays of checks and balances among the various branches of government that limit such power. Parliamentary democracies vest power in a cabinet drawn from the legislature, and presidential systems place executive power in the hands of an independently elected president, while still others divide executive power. Some democratic electoral systems are based on proportional representation, while others are based on single-member constituencies and majority or plurality voting. Some are dominated by two political parties; others, by many. In addition to these and other institutional differences, their populations subscribe to different political attitudes and norms pertaining to the use of political power and the goals that the state should pursue.

Political scientists studying the domestic and foreign economic policies of democratic states have concluded that these differences between democracies affect both the policies they select and the autonomy that democratic executives have to choose policies when faced with public and legislative opposition. Surprisingly, however, international security scholars pay little attention to these differences and assume that they do not affect the way democracies choose their national security policies. Indeed, the conventional wisdom is that democracies react in similar ways to international threats and opportunities. This conventional wisdom is wrong.

In this book, I argue that the differences between democracies have profound effects on the way they conduct foreign security policy. In particular, they affect the ability of different democratic governments to choose foreign policies at odds with domestic preferences. Thus, for example, shortly after World War II, the Truman administration was able to commit American troops to Europe to serve its security interests, despite public pressure to bring the troops home. In contrast, the difficulties encountered by the Israeli governments led by Yitzhak Rabin, Shimon Peres, and Ehud Barak in implementing the 1993 Oslo Accords indicate that some democratic regimes must take domestic opposition seriously, even on security matters of the utmost importance. Clearly it would be useful to discover the conditions under which domestic opposition affects foreign security policy in different democratic states.

This book examines the institutional, procedural, and normative differences between democracies in order to determine how they affect the independence of democratic leaders from domestic opinion. It argues that domestic political structures that insulate the government from the public and the legislature increase its ability to pursue unpopular policies, but simultaneously weaken its position in international negotiations. Governments that are not structurally insulated can still achieve some independence when they are willing to deceive their domestic opponents, but this is a costly strategy that is of only limited utility.

I test this argument by examining the peacemaking policies of Great Britain, France, and the United States after both world wars. In each country, domestic opinion demanded punitive peace terms, while national leaders believed that some degree of moderation was warranted. Yet, they followed very different policies. The structurally insulated governments (the United States and Great Britain after World War II) opted for moderation, while the rest (all three democracies after World War I and France after World War II) made significant concessions to public and legislative demands.

Furthermore, the structurally weaker governments (all three democracies in 1919 and France after World War II) were able to parlay their democratic constraints into gains in international negotiations over the postwar settlements. Thus, the conventional treatment of democracies as a group of like states that behave similarly in the international arena is both inappropriate and misleading. We must, therefore, unpack this category in order to generate a richer understanding of the complex range of democratic arrangements and their effects on national security policy.

Unpacking Democracies: The Theoretical Argument

Do democratic states behave similarly in the international arena? The conventional wisdom in the international security literature is that they do. Both classical and contemporary theorists of foreign security policy have treated democracies as a coherent category of states, emphasizing that all democratic states—states that are characterized by popular sovereignty, where the ultimate source of authority resides within the people as a whole[1]—share certain constitutional, procedural, and normative features that affect their foreign security policies in similar ways. In particular, they assume: that democratic states are qualitatively different from other regimes because they allow their constituents a legitimate role in the foreign policy-making process; that public preferences are relatively uniform and predictable across states and over time; that they manifest themselves both directly and through their representatives in the legislature; and that, for better or for worse, all democracies are similarly constrained by public and parliamentary attitudes. Using this logic, traditional realists maintain that public involvement in the policy process puts democracies at a disadvantage in international politics, where balance-of-power policies are necessary.[2] Liberals contend that democratic control conveys certain advantages, particularly

---

1. V. O. Key, *Public Opinion and American Democracy* (New York: Alfred A. Knopf, 1961), 97; and Daniel Deudney, "The Philadelphian System: Sovereignty, Arms Control, and Balance of Power in the American States-Union, Circa 1787–1861," *International Organization* 49, no. 2 (spring 1995): 197–99.

2. The most eloquent expressions of the realist critique of democracies in the international arena can be found in Hans J. Morgenthau, *Dilemmas of Politics* (Chicago: University of Chicago Press, 1958); and George F. Kennan, "Foreign Policy and the Professional Diplomat," in Louis J. Halle and Kenneth W. Thompson, eds., *Foreign Policy and the Democratic Process: The Geneva Papers* (Lanham: University Press of America, 1978), 14–26.

in international bargaining, policy implementation, and the integrity of the policymaking process.[3] Moreover, as democratic peace theorists argue, shared political norms and common political procedures prevent democracies from waging war against other democracies.[4] Even neorealist critics of the traditional perspective assume that democracies—indeed all states—will behave in similar ways internationally, since they are compelled either to pursue the national interest in an anarchical international environment or to perish.[5]

This emphasis on the common features of democratic states has obscured important institutional, procedural, and normative differences between them, which could have profound consequences for the national security policies they choose. Moreover, the conventional assumption of democratic homogeneity is both surprising and unsatisfying in light of evidence by political economists that the impact of public and societal pressures on economic policy choices can vary significantly across democratic states depending on their domestic structures.[6] If some democratic states can act with

3. On bargaining advantages, see James D. Fearon, "Domestic Political Audiences and the Escalation of International Disputes," *American Political Science Review* 88, no. 3 (September 1984): 577–92; and Thomas Risse-Kappen, *Cooperation Among Democracies* (Princeton: Princeton University Press, 1995). On policy implementation, see David A. Lake, "Powerful Pacifists: Democratic States and War," *American Political Science Review* 86, no. 1 (March 1992): 30–31; and Aaron Friedberg, "Why Didn't the United States Become a Garrison State?" *International Security* 16, no. 4 (spring 1992): 109–42. On the incorruptibility of liberal states, see Baron de Montesquieu, *The Political Theory of Montesquieu*, Melvin Richter, ed. (Cambridge: Cambridge University Press, 1977).

4. Michael Doyle, "Liberalism and World Politics," *American Political Science Review* 80, no. 4 (December 1986): 1151–61; Bruce M. Russett, *Grasping the Democratic Peace* (Princeton: Princeton University Press, 1993); and John M. Owen, "How Liberalism Produces Democratic Peace," *International Security* 19, no. 2 (fall 1994): 87–125.

5. Kenneth N. Waltz, *Theory of International Politics* (New York: McGraw Hill, 1979). In an earlier book, Waltz attributes greater explanatory power to domestic politics, but concludes that "[c]oherent policy . . . is difficult to achieve in any political system, but no more so for democratic states than for others." Kenneth N. Waltz, *Foreign Policy and Democratic Politics: The American and British Experience* (Boston: Little, Brown & Co., 1967), 311. Defensive structural realists also pay attention to domestic political variables, but still conclude that democratic states behave like most other states in the international system. See Jack Snyder, *Myths of Empire* (Ithaca: Cornell University Press, 1991); Fareed Zakaria, "Realism and Domestic Politics: A Review Essay," *International Security* 17, no.1 (summer 1992): 177–98.

6. Peter J. Katzenstein, ed., *Between Power and Plenty: Foreign Economic Policies in Advanced Industrial States* (Madison: University of Wisconsin Press, 1978); Eric A. Nordlinger, *On the Autonomy of the Democratic State* (Cambridge: Harvard University Press, 1981); Stephen Skowronek, *Building a New American State: The Expansion of National Administrative Capacities, 1877–1920* (Cambridge: Cambridge University Press, 1982); Margaret Weir and Theda Skocpol, "State Structures and the Possibilities for 'Keynesian' Responses to the Great Depression in Sweden, Britain and the United States," in Peter B. Evans, Dietrich Rueschemeyer, and Theda Skocpol, eds., *Bringing the State Back In* (Cambridge: Cambridge

considerable independence in the construction of domestic and foreign economic policy, why should traditional realists and liberals assume that they cannot do so in the conduct of foreign security policy? Indeed, anecdotal evidence would suggest that some democracies *can*, at times, act with considerable autonomy in the international arena. For example, in the mid-1930s, despite strong public support for disarmament, the Conservative government in Great Britain began an unpopular rearmament program to keep pace with German remilitarization. In the late 1980s, although public revulsion against the South African apartheid regime was relatively consistent across the Western liberal democratic world, the governments of the United States and Great Britain were able to resist domestic pressure to impose sanctions on South Africa. Finally, as Thomas Risse-Kappen has demonstrated, although they confronted similar public opinion profiles, France, Japan, West Germany, and the United States followed sharply diverging nuclear strategies in the 1980s.[7] At the same time, some democratic regimes clearly must take domestic opposition more seriously than neorealists expect. The difficulty with which Rabin and Peres implemented the Oslo Accords, to which they were firmly committed, is a case in point. Similarly, widespread public pacifism in France made it difficult for Albert Sarraut's French government to take decisive action against Adolf Hitler's remilitarization of the Rhineland in 1936.[8] And powerful parliamentary opposition prevented Indian leader Jawarhalal Nehru from reaching an accommodation with Pakistan over Kashmir in the late 1940s. Clearly, if we categorize democracies as like regimes, we will sacrifice a richer understanding of the impact domestic political arrangements have on foreign security policy choices.

The central argument of this book is that treating democratic states as a homogenous group represents a fundamental misapprehension by the international security literature of the rich variety of democratic states that exist. While the similarities between democratic states may, at times, make it useful to study democracy as a category of regime, we must recognize that within this category lies a multitude of different institutional arrangements that can have profound and unique effects on the way different democracies

---

University Press, 1985), 107–68; and John B. Goodman, *Monetary Sovereignty: The Politics of Central Banking in Western Europe* (Ithaca: Cornell University Press, 1992).

7. Thomas Risse-Kappen, "Public Opinion, Domestic Structure, and Foreign Policy in Liberal Democracies," *World Politics* 43, no. 4 (July 1991): 479–512.

8. See Norrin M. Ripsman and Jean-Marc F. Blanchard, "Commercial Liberalism Under Fire: Evidence from 1914 and 1936," *Security Studies* 6, no. 2 (winter 1996–97): 38–39.

formulate foreign security policies. Democracies differ in the nature of democratic authority (parliamentary or presidential), the number of political parties that participate meaningfully in the system, the frequency of elections, the relationship of the foreign minister to the legislature, as well as a host of other institutional considerations.[9] Moreover, their foreign policy decision-making procedures vary markedly from country to country, and their populations subscribe to a myriad of different underlying values and political norms that govern the making of national security policy. It is, therefore, necessary to unpack this category of "democracy" to account for differences in what I call the *domestic decision-making environment* (encompassing these institutional structures, decision-making procedures, and procedural norms) and their impact on the *structural autonomy* of foreign policy decision makers.

I argue that the degree of structural autonomy a foreign policy executive derives from its domestic decision-making environment directly affects its policy independence from public and legislative opinion. Structurally autonomous (strong) executives are able to pursue their own policy preferences even when they face strong domestic opposition. Structurally constrained (weak) executives, though, can pursue an independent policy only with great difficulty and frequently are stymied by domestic opposition. Nonetheless, their very structural weakness grants these executives a unique advantage in multilateral negotiations amongst allies. It enables their leaders to resist compromise and secure concessions from their foreign counterparts by highlighting domestic hostility to compromise (*domestic constraint projection*). Structurally autonomous democracies cannot credibly make such claims, since their domestic decision-making environments insulate them from public and legislative opposition.

Structural differences are not the only source of variance, though, since the leadership strategies that democratic leaders pursue may also affect their policy independence from domestic opposition. In particular, even governments that are granted little structural autonomy by their domestic decision-making environments can employ independence-enhancing strategies to

9. Arend Lijphart, *Democracies: Patterns of Majoritarian and Consensus Government in Twenty-One Countries* (New Haven: Yale University Press, 1984); Alfred C. Stepan and Cindy Skach, "Constitutional Frameworks and Democratic Consolidation: Parliamentarism Versus Presidentialism," *World Politics* 46, no. 1 (October 1993): 1–22; and Juan J. Linz, "Presidential or Parliamentary Democracy: Does It Make a Difference?" in Juan J. Linz and Arturo Valenzuela, *The Failure of Presidential Democracy: Comparative Perspectives,* vol. 1 (Baltimore: Johns Hopkins University Press, 1994), 3–87.

free themselves from domestic constraints when conducting international negotiations. When states negotiate with each other under the shroud of secrecy that cloaks most international security negotiations, democratic leaders can conceal the aims that they pursue at these meetings (*hiding*), mislead the public and the legislature about their conduct and the content of any agreements that are reached (*misleading*), and attribute outcomes that diverge from domestic preferences to the positions of other states (*blaming*). Because these complementary strategies, which I collectively label *the politics of deception,* are available to even the most constrained national security executive, I expect even the least autonomous democratic executive to act more independently in foreign affairs than the traditional literature would suggest. Nonetheless, the political costs of deception and its unpalatable nature should prevent weak democratic executives from achieving the degree of policy independence that structurally autonomous executives enjoy.

This book is part of a small, but emerging, literature that attempts to rectify the uniform treatment of democracies by international security theorists.[10] It makes several important contributions to this literature. First, while some have suggested that institutional differences can affect the autonomy of different democratic states, they have not operationalized this concept well. Specifically, they have not systematically analyzed the sources of autonomy, nor have they specified how these factors affect the structural power of the state over foreign security policy. Conversely, this book examines the institutional, procedural, and normative determinants of structural autonomy in the foreign security policy issue area and constructs a model to explain their impact on actual policy independence in different democracies.[11] Second, by including the impact of procedural norms and

10. See Risse-Kappen, "Public Opinion, Domestic Structure, and Foreign Policy"; T. Clifton Morgan and Sally Howard Campbell, "Domestic Structure, Decisional Constraints, and War: So Why Kant Democracies Fight?" *The Journal of Conflict Resolution* 35, no. 1 (June 1991): 187–211; Norrin M. Ripsman, "The Conduct of Foreign Policy by Democracies: A Critical Review," paper presented at the 1994 annual meeting of the American Political Science Association, New York, September 1–4, 1994; Susan Peterson, "How Democracies Differ: Public Opinion, State Structure, and the Lessons of the Fashoda Crisis," *Security Studies* 5, no. 1 (autumn 1995): 3–37; Susan Peterson, *Crisis Bargaining and the State* (Ann Arbor: University of Michigan Press, 1996); Helen V. Milner, *Interests, Institutions, and Information* (Princeton: Princeton University Press, 1997); and Miriam Fendius Elman, "Unpacking Democracy: Presidentialism, Parliamentarism, and Theories of Democratic Peace," *Security Studies* 9, no. 4 (summer 2000): 91–126.

11. This distinction between autonomy, which is structural and calculated *a priori,* and actual policy independence demonstrated by a particular government is important. It allows us to examine the effect of a clearly defined independent variable (autonomy) on a clearly defined dependent variable (policy independence).

explaining how they can either amplify or restrict leaders' scope of action within a given institutional structure, this book yields a considerably richer understanding of structural autonomy than others. Third, it provides a theoretical framework and detailed empirical support for Robert Putnam's previously unverified suggestion that state autonomy should paradoxically undermine a state's bargaining position in international negotiations.[12] Moreover, it demonstrates that this logic applies even to negotiations over international security matters of the highest order. Fourth, it recognizes that nonstructural factors, such as a leader's ability to employ independence-enhancing strategies of deception, can also affect the policy independence of structurally constrained democracies. Finally, it tests the model developed here against the leading neorealist, traditional realist, and liberal alternatives by analyzing the construction and evolution of British, French, and American peacemaking policies toward Germany in 1919 and from 1945 to 1954, when they constructed postwar settlements. It pays particular attention to two dependent variables: the degree to which national leaders could make controversial decisions in the face of domestic opposition (*policy independence*), and their ability to use domestic political opposition as a means of securing concessions in international negotiations (*domestic constraint projection*).

The Problem of Democratic Peacemaking: Case Selection

Peacemaking after a major international war presents an excellent opportunity to study the impact of domestic structure on both an important disadvantage of democracies that traditional realists identify—their inability to conclude stable, conciliatory peace settlements with former enemies—as well as an important advantage that liberals herald—their ability to manipulate domestic opposition to their advantage in international negotiations. Furthermore, the strategic importance of the postwar settlements creates conditions favorable for testing my argument against the neorealist alternative, since all three states had powerful incentives to ignore domestic opposition on the grounds of national security.

12. Robert D. Putnam, "Diplomacy and Domestic Politics: The Logic of Two-Level Games," *International Organization* 42, no. 3 (summer 1988): 449. This is particularly important in light of Peter B. Evans's dismissal of Putnam's argument. "Building an Integrative Approach to International and Domestic Politics," in Peter B. Evans, Harold K. Jacobson, and Robert D. Putnam, eds., *Double-Edged Diplomacy: International Bargaining and Domestic Politics* (Berkeley and Los Angeles: University of California Press, 1993), 402–3.

Traditional realists have long charged that democratic states are incapable of concluding conciliatory peace settlements that reintegrate their former enemies into the international system on an equal basis when reconciliation would foster international stability and advance the national interest.[13] Instead, building upon their understanding of the Versailles Treaty ending World War I, they contend that strong public resentment of the defeated foe together with profound distrust of its future intentions will compel democratic victors to impose a punitive settlement even when a more conciliatory settlement would foster stability. Furthermore, since democratic peoples are stirred to war only with great propaganda efforts on the parts of their leaders, the public vilification intensifies the desire for vengeance. For these reasons, Reinhold Niebuhr laments, "(d)emocracies are indeed slow to make war, but once embarked upon a martial venture are equally slow to make peace and reluctant to make a tolerable, rather than a vindictive, peace."[14] Walter Lippmann maintains that this vengeance dynamic operated in all the Western democracies in 1919 and 1945:

When the world wars came, the people of the liberal democracies could not be aroused to the exertions and the sacrifices of the struggle until they had been frightened by the opening disasters, had been incited to passionate hatred, and had become intoxicated with unlimited hope. To overcome this inertia the enemy had to be portrayed as evil incarnate, as absolute and congenital wickedness.... As a result of this impassioned nonsense, public opinion became so envenomed that the people would not countenance a workable peace; they were against any public man who showed "any tenderness for the Hun," or was inclined to listen to the "Hun food snivel."[15]

13. Henry A. Kissinger maintains that conciliation is a prerequisite of a stable postwar peace and, therefore, always in the enlightened national interest. In his classic study of the Congress of Vienna, for example, Kissinger praises British Foreign Minister Castelreagh because "he recognized the precedence of integration over retribution in the construction of a legitimate order" even when his cabinet colleagues did not. *A World Restored* (Boston: Houghton-Mifflin, 1973), 325. Not all realists subscribe to his conclusions, though, and one can certainly imagine situations when punitive provisions would foster international stability and serve the national interest. Thus, for example, it was probably consistent with international stability to deprive Iraq of nuclear and chemical weapons after the 1991 Gulf War, and to enforce no-fly zones in the country.

14. Reinhold Niebuhr, *The Structure of Nations and Empires* (New York: Scribner, 1959), 197.

15. Walter Lippmann, *Essays in the Public Philosophy* (Boston: Little, Brown, 1955), 21.

When the political leadership believes that a severe peace would serve the national interest by curtailing a future challenge from the defeated foe, public vindictiveness does not present a problem. Conversely, when leaders believe that a more generous peace that rehabilitates the enemy would promote international stability and, therefore, national security, public rancor can be debilitating and dangerous.[16] Under these circumstances, as a consequence of intense democratic hostility toward defeated adversaries, unreasonable political, economic, and territorial penalties may be levied upon their vanquished foes, since democratic leaders must often subordinate the pursuit of the national interest to popular whims.[17] The result, as was the case in Germany after Versailles, is that bitterness will be sown into the hearts of the defeated nation, which will strive to overturn the new status quo, and cooperation between victor and vanquished in the interests of international security will be difficult.[18]

If this study of peacemaking after the two world wars indicates that some of the Western democracies were able to resist domestic pressure to punish the former enemy, as my model of democratic differences would predict, that would be powerful evidence against the traditional realists. Both of these colossal struggles have been termed "total wars" since the combatants mobilized all of their national resources—human, material, and economic—to serve their war efforts.[19] As a result, hardly a family in any of the belligerent countries escaped the hardship and privation of war. Moreover, these conflicts are notable for the unparalleled number of battle deaths suffered on all sides. Consequently, the degree of animosity between enemy nations was intense and public pressure for a vengeful settlement was high.[20] Thus, these are hard test cases of my argument vis-à-vis the

16. It is beyond the scope of this book to explain why some leaders prefer to impose harsh peace terms and others prefer to conclude conciliatory postwar settlements. Certainly, it could relate to the proximity of the state to the defeated foe, the relative military capabilities of the two states, the leaders' personalities, or even prevailing international norms. For our purposes, what matters is the degree to which leaders can pursue a conciliatory policy when they do favor one and domestic opinion opposes it.

17. Morgenthau, *Dilemmas of Politics*, 303.

18. Sir Basil H. Liddell Hart warns political leaders that "if and when you reach your military goal, the more you ask of the defeated side, the more trouble you will have, and the more cause you will provide for an ultimate attempt to reverse the settlement achieved by the war." *Strategy* (New York: Frederick A. Praeger, 1967), 370.

19. Raymond Aron, *The Century of Total War* (Garden City, N.Y.: Doubleday, 1954), 9–55; and Arthur Marwick, "Introduction," in Arthur Marwick, ed., *Total War and Social Change* (New York: St. Martin's Press, 1988), x–xix.

20. Béla K. Kiraly, "Total War and Peacemaking," in Béla K. Kiraly, Peter Pastor, and Ivan Sanders, eds., *Essays on World War I* (New York: Brooklyn College Press, 1982), 15–21.

traditional realist argument, since the conditions were most favorable for domestic hostility to shackle democratic leaders who counseled moderation. At the same time, since both of these peace settlements were negotiated and concluded by multiple democratic states—none of which was in a position to impose its preferred terms unilaterally—they allow me to examine the liberal proposition that democratic leaders can use their domestic weakness to their advantage in international negotiations.

Robert Putnam has observed that international bargaining can be modeled as a two-level game in which leaders must reach agreement not only with their counterparts in other countries, but also with their domestic populations.[21] Progress in Level I, the negotiation of international agreements with other chiefs of government, is directly affected by the prospects for success in Level II, national ratification of whatever agreement is reached. Leaders who are able to portray themselves as having their hands tied at home can often avoid making concessions at the international bargaining table and should be more successful at extracting concessions from their negotiating partners.[22] Liberals observe that democratic states should provide their representatives with a unique ability to exploit their domestic constraints. After all, the very nature of these regimes requires the participation of the public and its elected legislative representatives to legitimize political outcomes.[23] Therefore, as James D. Fearon has observed, democratic states face more powerful domestic audience costs than other regimes, making it far more difficult for democracies to compromise at the international negotiating table and encouraging their negotiating partners to make the concessions if an agreement is to be reached.[24] This reasoning leads one observer to conclude that, in the American context, "the astute American negotiator can employ the prospect of Congressional displeasure to explain why he cannot do what the other government wants him to do or why the other government had better do what *he* wants it to do."[25]

21. Putnam, "Diplomacy and Domestic Politics."

22. Andrew Moravcsik, "Introduction: Integrating International and Domestic Theories of International Bargaining," in Evans, et al., *Double-Edged Diplomacy,* 28.

23. Putnam observes, for example, that although treaty ratification is not a uniquely democratic phenomenon, it is far more meaningful in a democratic context. See "Diplomacy and Domestic Politics," 436–37. See also, Risse-Kappen, *Cooperation Among Democracies.*

24. Fearon, "Domestic Political Audiences and the Escalation of International Disputes."

25. Laurence I. Radway, *The Liberal Democracy in World Affairs: Foreign Policy and National Defense* (Glenview, Ill.: Scott, Foresman & Co., 1969), 120. Of course, as I discuss in Chapter 5, domestic constraint projection should be effective only when the democracy's bargaining partners value continued cooperation with it.

The postwar settlements present an excellent opportunity to test my structural autonomy model of democratic bargaining against this liberal alternative. Since the democratic foreign security executives in this study varied considerably in the structural autonomy they possessed,[26] I can examine whether successful domestic constraint projection depended on a low level of structural autonomy, as my model predicts, or whether all democracies could benefit from that tactic, as liberals predict.

Finally, the strategic imperatives of forging postwar stability and, after World War II, containing the growing Soviet menace provided leaders with strong incentives to ignore domestic concerns; hence, these cases also provide favorable conditions to test my model against the neorealist alternative, which assumes that international imperatives, and not domestic politics, determine national security policy. While most neorealists do not purport to explain foreign policies,[27] they do conclude that the foreign policies of all states—particularly on important security matters—tend to be determined by the international environment rather than domestic political considerations, since states are socialized to obey the dictates of the international system or risk annihilation.[28] Thus, Kenneth Waltz concludes that democracies perform no differently from other states in the realm of foreign affairs.[29] Defensive structural realists concur.[30]

Peacemaking after World War I was of critical importance to the three democracies, for if they failed, the threat of revolution and instability in Europe, as well as the potential for another international war, loomed large. Even more was at stake in the post–World War II settlement, forged as it was during the height of the Cold War, when the Western powers feared that Moscow would take military advantage of any mistake. The German rearmament question was especially sensitive.[31] After the outbreak of the

---

26. My detailed analysis of the domestic decision-making environments of the three Western democracies after the two World Wars (see Chapter 3) reaches the following conclusions. The United States and Great Britain had highly autonomous national security executives after World War II. The French post–World War II executive, however, was structurally constrained to the extreme in the field of foreign affairs. All three democracies after World War I also had weak national security executives, but not as weak as the French Fourth Republic.

27. For a recent exception, see Colin Elman, "Horses for Courses: Why *Not* a Neorealist Theory of Foreign Policy?" *Security Studies* 6, no. 1 (autumn 1996): 7–53.

28. Waltz, *Theory of International Politics.*

29. Waltz, *Foreign Policy and Democratic Politics,* 309–11.

30. Snyder, *Myths of Empire;* Zakaria, "Realism and Domestic Politics."

31. Indeed, Marc Trachtenberg contends that the German question was the most critical security question during the Cold War. *A Constructed Peace: The Making of the European Settlement, 1945–1963* (Princeton: Princeton University Press, 1999).

Korean War in 1950, all three Western democracies acknowledged the need to raise a German military contribution to Western defense or risk a Soviet attack in Central Europe, for which they were ill prepared. If domestic opposition prevented any of the three democratic executives from loosening the military restrictions on Germany in a timely manner in the face of these powerful systemic incentives, then the neorealist understanding of foreign security policymaking in democratic states would be undermined.

In addition to being appropriate test cases of my argument versus the traditional and neorealist alternatives, these cases offer other important advantages. First, they allow me to study the impact of public opinion in three different democracies with considerably different decision-making structures and political traditions. Second, by analyzing the experiences of the same countries in two different domestic contexts, negotiating peace after wars of similar magnitude, I can hold as much constant as possible in order to rule out alternative explanations for differences in policy outcomes, such as the possibility of learning, the influence of particular individuals, and the international imperatives for a peace settlement. Finally, an abundance of resource material is available to study these cases. There is a plethora of secondary source material as well as memoirs and declassified documents—both published and unpublished—on the Versailles settlement. While there is a relative dearth of secondary source literature on the post–World War II settlement process, there are ample memoir and documentary sources at government archives in Great Britain, France, and the United States.

The Design of the Study

In order to test the competing models of democratic foreign security policy, I employ the case study method, which, if done well, is the best method for establishing causation.[32] Furthermore, since the variables involved in this study (domestic decision-making environments, structural autonomy, policy

---

32. Bruce M. Russett, for example, maintains that quantitative research can discern patterns of correlation, but that qualitative case studies are necessary to establish causation. "International Behavior Research: Case Studies and Cumulation," in Michael Haas and Henry S. Kariel, eds., *Approaches to the Study of Political Science* (San Francisco: Chandler, 1970), 425–43. See also John Lewis Gaddis, "History, Science and the Study of International Relations," in Ngaire Woods, ed., *Explaining International Relations Since 1945* (New York: Oxford University Press, 1996), 32–48.

independence, etc.) all require contextual judgment, they do not lend themselves easily to meaningful coding for large N quantitative analysis. Therefore, the method of controlled comparison of a small number of cases is the most appropriate means for testing the argument empirically.[33]

I have drawn two hypotheses from each of three models of democratic foreign security policy—the neorealist model, the traditional realist/liberal consensus, and my own structural autonomy model—which reflect their expectations regarding: (1) the ability of democratic leaders to pursue policy options when faced with domestic opposition, and (2) their ability to project their domestic constraints as a means of influencing multilateral negotiations. I then generate a set of predictions about the postwar peace settlements that flow from each hypothesis. By comparing the three sets of predictions to the historical record, I can determine which theoretical alternative most accurately explains these important cases.

The neorealist hypotheses are as follows:

Neorealist Hypothesis I (N1)—*Policymakers in democratic states will be able to behave consistently with their own preferences (i.e., according to the dictates of the international system), regardless of domestic opinion.*
Neorealist Hypothesis II (N2)—*The outcomes of multilateral negotiations between democratic states will be determined primarily by the relative power of the states.*

Hypothesis N1 follows from the neorealist contention that democracies fare no worse than other states because the importance of foreign security policy makes them conform to international requirements rather than domestic politics. Thus, neorealists would expect that leaders in all three Western democracies should have been able to pursue moderate peace terms after World War I when they believed that moderation was necessary to prevent instability, revolution, and future war in Europe. Moreover, after World War II, all three democratic executives should have been able to promote German political and economic recovery as a counterweight to Soviet power, and especially German rearmament once they concluded that Western defense could not succeed without it. Domestic opinion should not have affected their decisions in any meaningful way.

33. See Arend Lijphart, "Comparative Politics and the Comparative Method," *American Political Science Review* 65, no. 2 (September 1971): 682–93; Alexander L. George, "Case Studies and Theory Development," in Paul Gordon Lauren, ed., *Diplomacy* (New York: The Free Press, 1979), 43–68.

Hypothesis N2 reflects the standard neorealist assumption that power is the currency of international politics, which determines all political outcomes. After World War I, neorealists would expect that leaders of the more powerful United States should have been able to dictate terms in negotiations with their war-weakened European allies. These expectations are even more pronounced during the post–World War II period, when the United States was by far the most powerful state and the British and French were heavily dependent upon the United States both economically and militarily. Neorealists would thus expect that American leaders should have been able to impose their preferences regarding the German settlement on the Europeans.

In stark contrast, hypotheses reflecting the traditional realist/liberal consensus—that democratic foreign security executives are necessarily constrained by domestic opinion—are as follows:

Traditional (Realist) Hypothesis I (T1)—*Policymakers in all democratic states will choose to pursue punitive postwar settlements, even if they believe that is contrary to national interests, because they will be unable to overcome domestic hostility toward the former enemy.*
Traditional (Liberal) Hypothesis II (T2)—*When democratic negotiators portray themselves as having their hands tied domestically, they should have some success in influencing multilateral negotiations by forestalling compromises and inducing their partners to make concessions.*

Hypothesis T1 is taken directly from the traditional realist criticism of democratic foreign security policy. It has two implications for the postwar peace settlements. First, there should have been tremendous support for punitive measures in all three countries and great opposition to rehabilitating and rearming the Germans. Second, this public hostility should have interfered with attempts by leaders in all three democracies to show leniency to the Germans, to restore the German economy, German territory, and German sovereignty, and to integrate German units into the Western defense effort, even when it was clearly in their national interests to do so.

Hypothesis T2 reflects the liberal argument that, because they are necessarily constrained domestically, democracies can project their constraints for gain at the international bargaining table. Since all three Western powers were democratic after both world wars, all three should have enjoyed comparable success with this bargaining tactic. Furthermore, because of this tactic's utility, liberals would expect that all three states should have attempted domestic constraint projection whenever they failed to achieve their goals through other means.

Alternatively, my model of structural autonomy suggests the following hypotheses:

Autonomy Hypothesis I (A1)—*In states whose domestic decision-making environments grant more structural autonomy to the national security executive, decision makers will be able to construct foreign security policies that are consistent with their own preferences, even when they face domestic opposition. In states whose foreign policy executives are granted little autonomy, domestic opposition will interfere with policy choices—even those that leaders believe are necessary to safeguard the national interest.*
Autonomy Hypothesis II (A2)—*The less autonomy afforded by a state's domestic decision-making environment, the more successful its representatives will be at projecting domestic constraints to induce concessions from their bargaining partners, provided that their negotiating partners place a premium on continued multilateral cooperation.*

Hypothesis A1 assumes that the level of structural autonomy a democratic executive possesses will determine how it manages competing domestic and international pressures. It implies that the more autonomous democracies (the United States and Great Britain after World War II) should have been able to resist domestic opposition when their leaders believed that German recovery was an important prerequisite for European stability and that German rearmament was essential to Western defense efforts. Conversely, the structurally constrained executive of the French Fourth Republic should have been hampered by domestic opposition to German rehabilitation and rearmament, even when its leaders recognized these measures as a strategic necessity. Similarly, all three democracies in 1919 should have had great difficulty overcoming domestic opposition to moderate territorial and reparations settlements.

As a corollary, we should expect the most structurally constrained democratic executives to attempt to escape the straitjacket of public and parliamentary control whenever possible. To this end, we should expect them to resort to the politics of deception in order to finesse domestic opposition and secure reluctant domestic approval for unpopular policies. Stronger states, though, should have little need for these independence-enhancing strategies, since they already possess sufficient structural autonomy to act independently of domestic opposition. Through their practice of the politics of deception, even the most structurally constrained democratic regimes, such as the French Fourth Republic, should be able to display more policy independence than traditional realists and liberals assume. My overall expectations, then, are that all democracies will display at least a modicum of policy independence from domestic opposition, but the stronger democratic executives will act with considerable independence.

Building upon Putnam's suggestion that autonomy should undermine a state's bargaining position,[34] hypothesis A2 rests on the logic that domestic constraint projection by an autonomous democracy will not be credible and, hence, will be ineffective. Provided that their allies sufficiently value their participation in signing and implementing the final agreement, however, weaker executives should be able to win concessions at the international bargaining table by highlighting domestic difficulties, since they are clearly more susceptible to policy disruption.[35] As a corollary, autonomous democratic leaders should attempt this tactic less frequently than leaders of constrained democracies, since the former cannot be optimistic about their prospects for success. Thus, I expect to find that the leaders of all three democracies in 1919 and France after World War II attempted constraint projection both more frequently and more successfully than American and British leaders after World War II.

Table 1 summarizes the expectations of the three models. To make credible judgments, I do not merely check for congruence between each model's expectations and actual outcomes; I also employ the "process tracing" method to investigate: (1) multiple congruence at various stages of the decision-making process, and (2) whether the causal mechanisms specified by each model brought about observed outcomes.[36]

---

34. Putnam, "Diplomacy and Domestic Politics," 449; and G. John Ikenberry, "The Irony of State Strength: Comparative Responses to the Oil Shocks in the 1970s," *International Organization* 40, no. 1 (winter 1986). For critical perspectives, see Evans, "Integrative Approach," 402–3; and Barry Eichengreen and Marc Uzan, "The 1933 World Economic Conference as an Instance of Failed Cooperation," in Evans et al., *Double-Edged Diplomacy*, 171–206.

35. See Howard P. Lehman and Jennifer L. McCoy, "The Dynamics of the Two-Level Bargaining Game: The 1988 Brazilian Debt Negotiations," *World Politics* 44, no. 4 (July 1992): 600–644.

36. Elman, "Horses for Courses," 17–18; Stephen Van Evera, *A Guide to Methodology for Students of Political Science* (Ithaca: Cornell University Press, 1997), 58–67. On process tracing, see Alexander George and Timothy J. McKeown, "Case Studies and Theories of Organizational Decision Making," *Advances in Information Processes in Organizations* 2 (1985): 21–58; Alexander George, "Knowledge for Statecraft: The Challenge for Political Science and History," *International Security* 22, no. 1 (summer 1997): 44–52.

Table I. Predictions of the three models for the postwar settlements

	Neorealist Model	Traditional Model	Autonomy Model
Domestic impact on policies	Minimal in all six democracies under examination	High in all six democracies under examination (realist)	Very high for France after WWII, high for all three democracies in 1919, low for Great Britain and the U.S. after WWII
Effectiveness of domestic constraint projection in multilateral bargaining	Irrelevant; power determines bargaining outcomes	High for all six democracies under examination (liberal)	Very high for France after WWII, high for all three democracies in 1919, low for Great Britain and the U.S. after WWII
Frequency of domestic constraint projection	Indeterminate and irrelevant	Frequent for all six democracies under examination (liberal)	Very frequent for France after WWII, frequent for all three democracies in 1919, infrequent for Great Britain and the U.S. after WWII

Two stages are necessary to test these theoretical propositions. First, I must "measure" the structural autonomy of the countries in this study. To do so, I need to make *a priori* assessments of the relative autonomy of their foreign policy executives. This can be done through a rich contextual analysis of the constitutional principles governing each regime, the institutions that participate in policy formation, the procedures that govern foreign policymaking, and the prevailing legislative attitudes concerning rights and responsibilities in the construction of foreign security policy. I must be careful not to make these judgments about relative autonomy by considering state behavior in the cases under investigation, or else I run the risk of tautology; hence, the need for an *a priori* assessment.

The second stage is to assess the impact of structural autonomy on the two dependent variables. First, I must determine its impact on observed policy independence when leader preferences conflict with domestic opinion. For this, it is necessary to discover the preferences of the relevant policymakers and to compare them with public and parliamentary opinion, since if they agree I can conclude little about the role of the domestic decision-making environment. Then, I must identify the policy choices that were ultimately selected and the degree to which they conformed to executive preferences or the demands of domestic opinion. Furthermore, I must analyze the decision-making process to determine if and how domestic opposition complicated policy selection and implementation.

In order to make judgments about the impact of structural autonomy on a state's ability to use its domestic opposition to its advantage at the bargaining table, I must first determine the initial negotiating positions of the states involved and verify that at least one state projected its domestic opposition as a reason for its inability to compromise. Then, I can compare the outcome of negotiations with the initial stances to see which states compromised most. In addition, I must examine the decision-making processes of the state that compromised most to determine whether it made these concessions because of its counterpart's domestic constraints, or for other reasons.

Since the judgments about preferences and policy required by this study require detailed knowledge of the actors involved, their preferences, and the reasons for their actions, they are best examined using the historian's tools to penetrate the black box of the state and put one's self inside the decision-making process.[37] For this reason, I employ the process tracing method to determine why specific decisions were made and how, if at all, domestic opinion affected decision making.[38] This analysis, however, must not rely solely on secondary sources, as many process tracers do. In order to reach a definitive judgment on the impact of domestic opinion and state structures on policy, researchers must determine the answers to a variety of "what" and "why" questions. What policies did the public and the legislatures prefer? What policies were chosen? Why were these policies selected? These are specific, yet complex, empirical questions that require researchers to search a variety of primary sources, including memoirs, newspapers, and government documents.

---

37. Norrin M. Ripsman and Jean-Marc F. Blanchard, "Contextual Information and the Study of Trade and Conflict: The Utility of an Interdisciplinary Approach," in Rudra Sil and Eileen M. Doherty, eds., *Beyond Boundaries? Disciplines, Paradigms, and Theoretical Integration in International Studies* (Albany: SUNY Press, 2000), 57–85.

38. See George and McKeown, "Case Studies and Theories of Organizational Decision Making"; George, "Knowledge for Statecraft"; and John Lewis Gaddis, "History, Theory, and Common Ground," *International Security* 22, no. 1 (summer 1997): 75–85.

Judgments about public opinion can be made most easily and reliably from public opinion polls. In the post–World War II period, there is ample polling data available on French and American attitudes provided by *l'Institut Français d'Opinion Publique*, Gallup, and the National Opinion Research Center. In Great Britain, however, Gallup did not conduct polls with the same regularity; hence, less relevant polling data exist. For 1918 to 1920, no systematic polling data exist upon which to reach definitive conclusions. Consequently, for the purposes of this study, I also turn to newspapers, public correspondence with the government, and the government's own indicators of the public mood. Estimating the mood of the legislature is easier, since parliamentary and congressional proceedings are well publicized and published annually.

Determining the true nature and causes of peacemaking policies and negotiation strategies during the various stages of their evolution requires careful examination of the relevant government documents, particularly notes of cabinet and key committee meetings,[39] correspondence between decision makers, orders issued to their staffs, policy papers of the relevant ministries, and diplomatic correspondence with other governments. In addition, researchers can learn much from the memoirs of those involved in the formation of policy, provided that they attempt to corroborate their information with other sources and make judgments on their plausibility in order to avoid succumbing to decision makers' attempts to rewrite or sanitize their role in history. Finally, secondary source accounts can also shed light on policymaking, provided that they, too, are corroborated with other sources, and the arguments they make are judged to be plausible.

Relying on these sources, my objective was to answer the following questions: (1) What were the policy preferences of the key foreign policy elites of each country? (2) To what degree were these consistent with public preferences and those of the legislature? (3) When domestic and executive

39. This approach presents little problem in the British and American cases because of the availability of British cabinet minutes and papers, as well as documentation on American National Security Council meetings and those of other key American decision-making bodies. It is more difficult to study French policymaking because of the absence of official cabinet minutes during these periods. From 1947 to 1954 (excluding 1950), the researcher can rely on President Vincent Auriol's detailed summaries of cabinet meetings, but must recognize that his recollections might have been somewhat colored by his opinions and interests. Vincent Auriol, *Journal de Septennat*, 7 vols. (Paris: Librarie Armand Colin, 1970). Judgments can be made on cabinet decisions in earlier periods based on the memoirs of French cabinet ministers, although the potential for distortion there is greater, and these accounts often conflict. Therefore, the researcher must at times make "educated guesses" and corroborate judgments with other French government sources as well as foreign information on particular French decisions.

preferences diverged, to what extent did decision makers perceive themselves to be constrained by domestic opinion? (4) To what extent did policy correspond to executive rather than domestic preferences? (5) To what extent did policymakers portray themselves to their foreign counterparts as unable to compromise because of domestic opposition? (6) When this occurred, were they successful?

Findings

My analysis reaches several significant conclusions. First, it demonstrates that the national security executives of the three states possessed considerably different levels of structural autonomy. The domestic decision-making environment of the French Fourth Republic, for example, was so remarkably different from that of Great Britain after World War II that lumping them together under the rubric of "democracy" would yield a category that is too heterogeneous to provide sufficient leverage for analysts of foreign security policy. The French multiparty parliamentary system, engendering fragmentary coalition governments, coupled with legislature-dominated decision-making processes and obstructionist legislative norms, gave their foreign policy executives little structural autonomy. In sharp contrast, the British experience of a well-disciplined one-party majority government, an executive-dominated foreign policy process, and procedural norms that deferred to the executive in foreign policy matters because of their importance yielded a highly autonomous British foreign policy executive.

Furthermore, the American cases indicate that the structural autonomy of foreign policymakers can vary dramatically over time even within the same democracy. Following World War I, strong congressional foreign relations committees controlled by a rival party, a constitutional division of foreign relations powers between the two branches of government, and a powerful norm of congressional activism in foreign affairs sharply constrained the President and his Secretary of State. By the time World War II drew to a close, however, the Truman administration possessed infinitely more structural autonomy over national security matters as a result of the construction of an insulated "national security state," important Supreme Court decisions expanding executive authority over foreign affairs, and the emerging norm of bipartisan support for executive foreign policy because of its importance.

Most important, these case studies match the expectations of my structural autonomy model, rather than the more conventional alternatives.

When perceived national interests conflicted with residual domestic fear and distrust of the former enemy, the more autonomous executives selected policy choices they believed were warranted without excessive time delays, forced modifications by the legislature, or humiliating defeats and reversals of policy. Thus, the Truman administration and the Attlee Government could relax the Occupation regime, take steps to stimulate the German economy, and initiate the creation of the Federal Republic of Germany as soon as they deemed it necessary. Moreover, immediately after the outbreak of the Korean War, the United States was able to press for, and Great Britain was quick to accept, the immensely unpopular measure of German rearmament. The ease with which they ignored domestic hostility to Germany belies the traditional realist expectation of democratic paralysis in the face of domestic opposition. Conversely, the other four governments, which were determined *a priori* to have less autonomous national security executives, demonstrated considerably less policy independence from domestic pressures. Thus, for example, Prime Minister Lloyd George in 1919 felt unable to present the British public and the Unionists in his coalition with a reparations settlement that appeared soft, even though he would have preferred a more moderate settlement. Most strikingly, the government of the least autonomous state in the study, the French Fourth Republic, was forced to drag its feet on a host of policy programs that it knew to be in the French interest—including German rearmament as a means of resisting a Soviet attack—because the executive was structurally weak and risked collapse if it alienated the public and the National Assembly. For these executives, domestic opposition affected policy to a far greater extent than neorealists would expect. Indeed, three successive French premiers in the early 1950s who viewed German rearmament as an essential prerequisite of French security proved unable to allow the Germans to field a military contribution. Their paralysis undermines neorealist expectations that all democratic regimes should formulate policy exclusively in accordance with the dictates of the international system.

Furthermore, the less autonomous executives were able to escape some of their domestic constraints by practicing the politics of deception. By keeping the National Assembly in the dark about the content of the peace negotiations, French Prime Minister Georges Clemenceau, for example, could agree to a settlement of World War I without a permanent occupation of the left bank of the Rhine or permanent French sovereignty over the Saar, despite domestic attitudes. Even the executive of the fragile French Fourth Republic was able to commit—albeit very slowly, tentatively, and inconsistently—to the extremely unpopular measures of a West German state and German rearmament despite persistent and vocal opposition throughout the country, in the legislature, and even within the cabinet. In fact, the only executive in this study whose plans were completely defeated at home was that of the United States after World War I. As I demonstrate in Chapter 4, the principal reason that President Woodrow Wilson failed to free himself at all from the powerful constraints of his domestic decision-making environment was that, for reasons of pride and principle, he refused to condescend to the politics of deception. Nonetheless, deception could not enable weak democratic executives to escape all, or even most, of their structural constraints, and it entailed high political costs. Clemenceau was defeated in the 1920 presidential election, Bidault was expelled from the cabinet after the London Accords of 1948, and Mendès-France was toppled from power by the National Assembly soon after ratification of the German rearmament settlement, on account of the unpopular measures they pushed through. These political costs made deception only an occasional and unreliable refuge for structurally constrained leaders.

Finally, as expected, the weaker democracies were more successful at wringing concessions from their structurally insulated counterparts in international negotiations through domestic constraint projection. By highlighting the magnitude of public and, especially, parliamentary pressure in Britain to "make the Hun pay," Lloyd George defeated Wilson's efforts to fix a definite and moderate limit on German reparations payments at the Paris Peace Conference, and deferred most of the major decisions on the reparations settlement until 1921. Since Clemenceau insisted that his government would encounter severe difficulties if it faced the French public without demonstrable security from Germany, he secured a fifteen-year occupation of the Rhineland and a guarantee against future German aggression from his reluctant English-speaking colleagues. After World War II, though the Anglo-Americans held all the political and economic cards, French foreign ministers Bidault, Schuman, and Mendès-France were all repeatedly able to delay decisions and wrangle considerable concessions from them because of the effect compromise would have had on French governmental stability. Conversely, post–World War II American appeals based on domestic opposition were seen as hollow as a result of the regularity with which the executive could ignore domestic opposition; they were, consequently, largely ineffectual.

Thus, empirical analysis confirms my hypotheses on structural autonomy and democratic foreign security policy against the neorealist, traditional realist, and liberal alternatives. In addition, I demonstrate that other alternative explanations of these results, including those focusing on institutional learning, geographical proximity, and the intensity of public opinion, also are outperformed by my emphasis on structural autonomy. I conclude, therefore, that structural autonomy is a powerful tool for the foreign security policy analyst and, indeed, is a more useful variable than merely "democracy."

Overview of the Book

I develop my argument in Chapter 1 and put it to the test in the following three chapters. Chapter 1 is the theoretical heart of the book. After demonstrating that the assumption of democratic homogeneity in foreign affairs is prevalent throughout the foreign security policy literature, it explains why the assumption is incorrect. It, therefore, unpacks the category "democracy," specifying which institutional, procedural, and normative factors contribute to or detract from a democratic executive's structural autonomy over foreign security policy. Furthermore, it presents a model of the domestic decision-making environment of democratic states that takes variations in institutional structures, decision-making procedures, and procedural norms into account. It concludes by analyzing the opportunities and the limits of independence-enhancing strategies of deception as a means by which weaker executives can escape their structural constraints.

In order to put the theoretical model developed in Chapter 1 to the test, Chapter 2 examines the domestic decision-making environments of the states in this study to reach *a priori* judgments of the relative degree of structural autonomy they afforded their executives in national security matters. To this end, it devises a series of questions about each state's foreign policy institutions, procedures, and norms that can assist in categorizing the autonomy of their executives.

The case studies are presented in Chapters 3 and 4. In Chapter 3, I examine the dynamic between domestic and executive preferences in the construction of the political/territorial and reparations settlements with Germany in 1919. Chapter 4 studies three central issue areas of the post–World War II peace with Germany: the political/territorial settlement, the economic settlement and German industry, and the question of postwar German rearmament.

Chapter 5 summarizes the conclusions reached in this study and explores avenues for further research. In addition, it discusses the theoretical and policy-relevant implications of this research. On the theoretical plane, it requires greater sophistication of theories, such as the democratic peace theory, that treat democracies as a coherent category of like states. Moreover, it specifies under what conditions a neorealist model, emphasizing systemic constraints in the construction of foreign security policy, is appropriate, and under what conditions a more traditional realist/liberal approach is more useful.

Thus, this book contributes new insights on two central theoretical controversies in international relations. It also has policy relevance for a range of contemporary problems, such as the resolution of ethnic conflicts in democratizing regions and the structure of the American national security executive after the Cold War.

Domestic Opinion and Democratic Foreign Security Policy

What effect do democratic political institutions have on foreign security policy? Does public and parliamentary input into the policy process improve or hinder foreign policymaking in democratic states? Are these effects relatively uniform across democracies, or does the domestic impact on policy vary in different democratic states? While scholars give different answers to the first two questions, the conventional wisdom is that the domestic impact on policy is similar in different democratic states. Therefore, "democracy" is treated as a powerful analytical category for foreign policy analysts. In this chapter, I will demonstrate that the conventional wisdom is wrong because it ignores the differences between democracies that can cause the domestic impact on foreign security policy to vary considerably across democratic states.

I will begin by showing that, despite their well-known

disagreements, the leading schools of international relations theorists share this problematic assumption of democratic uniformity. Traditional realists, for example, contend that democracies are decidedly inferior to their autocratic or oligarchic counterparts in the international arena because they must compromise between pursuit of the national interest and the dictates of lay public opinion and the legislature. Liberals counter that an informed electorate and its principled parliamentary representatives convey indispensable advantages, particularly in policy implementation, international bargaining, and the integrity of the policymaking process, which nondemocratic regimes do not enjoy. Meanwhile, structural realists, or neorealists, assume that democracies—indeed all states—will behave in similar ways internationally, since they are compelled either to pursue the national interest in an anarchical international system or to perish.

I will then explain why we need a more nuanced model of foreign policymaking in democratic states that takes into account the distinctive political arrangements or *domestic decision-making environments* of different democratic states. The alternative model I present contends that the degree to which the foreign policymakers of a democratic state are affected, either positively or negatively, by domestic opinion depends primarily upon the degree of *structural autonomy* the foreign policy executive receives from its institutional structures, decision-making procedures, and prevailing procedural norms. Beyond these structural differences, I will also demonstrate that the leadership strategies employed by foreign policymakers—in particular their willingness to manipulate the secrecy of international negotiations to deceive their domestic opposition—cause further variance in the impact of domestic opinion on the foreign security policies of democracies. By unpacking the conventional category of "democracy" in this manner, I correct a fundamental misconception in the security literature that has inspired poorly specified theories—such as the democratic peace theory—and generated faulty policy advice.

Before proceeding, it is necessary to clarify what the term "democracy" means for the purposes of this discussion. Conventional writings on foreign policy employ the terms "democratic," "liberal," "liberal/democratic," and sometimes "republican" almost interchangeably to denote regimes that can broadly be described as modern democracies. At the most basic level, democracy implies popular sovereignty—that is, that the ultimate source of authority resides within the people as a whole.[1] Because they are sovereign,

---

1. Daniel Deudney points out that the concept of *sovereignty* is often incorrectly conflated

the constituents of the regime have the authority to determine policy, or at least set the limits within which policy must be conducted.[2] In keeping with popular sovereignty, democracies share certain procedural norms, including: virtually universal suffrage, freely contested elections, public accountability of government officials, constitutional limitations on their power, open access to information, and public expression of preferences.[3] Nonetheless, as William J. Dixon observes, states that may be termed democratic can vary significantly in the nature and character of the institutions through which public participation is exercised and the values that permeate the popular culture.[4] This chapter probes the implications of popular sovereignty for the conduct of foreign relations.

Since, as we shall see, both liberal advocates and realist critics of democratic foreign policy address their arguments to the consequences of mass public opinion and legislative review for the making of foreign security policy, this chapter will do the same. Consequently, less attention will be devoted to the problem of particular interests and lobby groups than to the influence of the legislature and the lay electorate as a whole.[5]

---

with the *authority* that flows from it. "The Philadelphian System: Sovereignty, Arms Control, and Balance of Power in the American States–Union, Circa 1787–1861," *International Organization* 49, no. 2 (spring 1995): 191–228. Hence, while authority patterns vary across democracies, it is, at least initially, the impact of this essential common feature of popular sovereignty over foreign policy that we wish to study. Later in this chapter, we will explore the utility of differentiating between democracies on the basis of the distribution of authority.

2. See, for example, V. O. Key, *Public Opinion and American Democracy* (New York: Alfred A. Knopf, 1961), 97.

3. This conception of democracy is heavily influenced by William J. Dixon, "Democracy and the Peaceful Settlement of International Conflict," *American Political Science Review* 88, no. 1 (March 1994): 14–32, esp. 15; Robert A. Dahl, *Polyarchy: Participation and Opposition* (New Haven: Yale University Press, 1971); Robert A. Dahl, *Dilemmas of Pluralist Democracy: Autonomy vs. Control* (New Haven: Yale University Press, 1982), 5–11; and G. Bingham Powell, *Contemporary Democracies* (Cambridge: Harvard University Press, 1982).

4. Dixon, "Democracy and the Peaceful Settlement of International Conflict," 15.

5. For discussions of the impact of interest groups upon the democratic foreign policy process, see Lester W. Milbrath, "Interest Groups and Foreign Policy," in James N. Rosenau, ed., *Domestic Sources of Foreign Policy* (New York: The Free Press, 1967), 231–52; Bernard C. Cohen, "The Influence of Special-Interest Groups and the Mass Media on Security Policy in the United States," in Charles W. Kegley and Eugene R. Wittkopf, eds., *Perspectives on American Foreign Policy* (New York: St. Martin's Press, 1983), 222–41; and Charles W. Kegley and Eugene R. Wittkopf, *American Foreign Policy: Pattern and Process* (New York: St. Martin's Press, 1991), 267–77.

How Does Domestic Opinion Affect Foreign Policy?
Conventional Answers

The Traditional Realist Perspective: Domestic Opinion as an Unfortunate Constraint

In his classic *Democracy in America,* Alexis de Tocqueville concluded that while democracy was promising as an instrument of domestic prosperity and order, it lacked the ability to conduct foreign affairs on equal footing with authoritarian regimes.[6] He wrote:

> As for myself, I do not hesitate to say that it is especially in the conduct of their foreign relations that democracies appear to me decidedly inferior to other governments.... Foreign politics demand scarcely any of those qualities which are peculiar to a democracy; they require, on the contrary, the perfect use of almost all those in which it is deficient. Democracy is favorable to the increase of the internal resources of a state; it diffuses wealth and comfort, promotes public spirit, and fortifies the respect for law in all classes of society: all of these are advantages which have only an indirect influence over the relations which one people bears to another. But a democracy can only with great difficulty regulate the details of an important undertaking, persevere in a fixed design, and work out its execution in spite of serious obstacles. It cannot combine its measures with secrecy or await their consequences with patience. These are qualities which more especially belong to an individual or an aristocracy; and they are precisely the qualities by which a nation, like an individual, attains a dominant position.[7]

In his view, the imprudence and impulsiveness of mass public opinion and the institutional encumbrances of representative democracy were insurmountable obstacles for democratic states, whose consequences could be profound. Perhaps it was with these concerns in mind that classical theorists of democracy, such as Jean-Jacques Rousseau and John Locke, argued that foreign policy should not be governed by the same liberal/democratic principles that must constrain domestic policy. Rousseau contended that "what matters principally to every citizen is the observance of the laws internally,

---

6. Alexis de Tocqueville, *Democracy in America* (New York: Vintage Books, 1954), esp. vol. 1, 240–45.

7. Ibid., 243–44.

the maintenance of private property, and the security of the individual. As long as all goes well with regard to these three points, let the government negotiate and make treaties with foreign powers."[8] Locke similarly concluded that foreign affairs "must be left in great part to the prudence of those who have the power committed to them, to be managed to the best of their skill and ability."[9]

Inspired by Tocqueville's pessimism, pioneers of the "realist" school of international politics, such as Hans Morgenthau, Walter Lippmann, Reinhold Niebuhr, and George Kennan, viewed the foreign security policy process as the Achilles' heel of democracies, or "the democratic malady."[10] These traditional realists[11] concluded that public input into the policy process and cumbersome democratic procedures would necessarily undermine the national interest—the rational basis of all foreign policy. Indeed, Morgenthau charged, "a foreign policy carried out under democratic control must fall short of the rational requirements for good foreign policy; for it must satisfy emotional preferences whose satisfaction is incompatible with meeting those requirements."[12] Hence, democratic states tailor policies to public whims, rather than to international requirements, which is folly in a hostile international environment.[13] Furthermore, as Kennan maintained, the democratic form of government "goes far to rule out the privacy, the flexibility, and the promptness and incisiveness of decision and action, which have marked the great imperial powers of the past and which are considered necessary to the conduct of an effective world policy by the rulers of a great state."[14]

According to traditional realists, public opinion in democratic states is inward looking, seeking to improve the quality of domestic life rather than

8. Quoted in Miroslav Nincic, *Democracy and Foreign Policy* (New York: Columbia University Press, 1992), 3.

9. Quoted in ibid., 2–3.

10. Walter Lippmann, *Essays in the Public Philosophy* (Boston: Little, Brown and Co., 1955); Hans J. Morgenthau, *Dilemmas of Politics* (Chicago: University of Chicago Press, 1958); Reinhold Niebuhr, *The Structure of Nations and Empires* (New York: Scribner, 1959); Reinhold Niebuhr and Paul E. Sigmund, *The Democratic Experience: Past and Prospects* (New York: Frederick A. Praeger, 1969); George F. Kennan, *The Cloud of Danger* (Boston: Little, Brown and Co., 1977); and George F. Kennan, "Foreign Policy and the Professional Diplomat," in Louis J. Halle and Kenneth W. Thompson, eds., *Foreign Policy and the Democratic Process: The Geneva Papers* (Lanham: University Press of America, 1978), 14–26.

11. The term "traditional realist" is used to distinguish these founders of the realist school from the later structural realists. See page 40, this volume.

12. Morgenthau, *Dilemmas of Politics*, 326.

13. Ibid., 303.

14. Kennan, *Cloud of Danger*, 4.

focusing on international military issues. Consequently, the mass electorate and the legislature tend not to interfere with the day-to-day conduct of foreign affairs. At critical junctures, however, when a substantial change in policy is required, public opinion and powerful voices in the legislature emerge to veto a new course. When this occurs, policymakers must endure endless legislative debates and the time-consuming process of overcoming the natural inertia of "large scattered varied multitudes of persons" who comprise the electorate. As a result, democracies make the transition from peace to war and from war to peace very slowly, and they reconcile with former enemies only with great difficulty and bitterness. Thus, for traditional realists, popular European support for appeasing Hitler in the 1930s, American reluctance to enter World War II, and overwhelming Western public pressure to impose a punitive peace settlement on Germany after World War I are all symptomatic of democratic politics.[15] Contemporary realist Jean-François Revel laments: "[D]emocracy tends to ignore, even deny, threats to its existence because it loathes doing what is needed to counter them. It awakens only when the danger becomes deadly, imminent, evident. By then, either there is too little time left for it to save itself, or the price of survival has become crushingly high."[16] In a similar vein, Kennan likened democracies to dysfunctional prehistoric beasts:

> But I sometimes wonder whether in this respect a democracy is not uncomfortably similar to one of the prehistoric monsters with a body as long as this room and a brain the size of a pin: he lies there in his comfortable primeval mud and pays little attention to his environment; he is slow to wrath—in fact, you practically have to whack his tail off to make him aware that his interests are being disturbed; but, once he grasps this, he lays about him with such blind determination that he not only destroys his adversary but largely wrecks his native habitat.[17]

15. Lippmann, *Essays in the Public Philosophy,* 17–21; Niebuhr, *The Structure of Nations,* 197; Kennan, *Cloud of Danger;* Jean-François Revel, *How Democracies Perish,* William Bighorn, trans. (Garden City, N.J.: Doubleday, 1984); Michael Crozier, Samuel P. Huntington, and Joji Watanuki, *The Crisis of Democracy* (New York: New York University Press, 1975), 166–67.

16. Revel, *How Democracies Perish,* 4.

17. George F. Kennan, *American Diplomacy, 1900–1950* (Chicago: University of Chicago Press, 1951), 59.

Overall, traditional realists identified the following shortcomings of democracies in the international arena, which result from public control over policy and time-consuming democratic processes:[18]

1. They tend to under-invest in military capability, since the public favors domestic spending and lower taxes. Hence, their ability to deter potential adversaries is undermined, and they are usually unprepared for the military involvements that are thrust upon them.

2. They are war averse; consequently, they are slow to respond when force is required to prevent a hostile state from disrupting the balance of power. Furthermore, their well-known reluctance to go to war encourages revisionist states to act aggressively, without fear of reprisal.

3. They tend to place universalist ideology above interests, making democracy and human rights their priorities, rather than concrete material interests, in order to enlist public support.

4. They lack flexibility, since it takes a considerable amount of time to mobilize public and legislative opinion in support of policy changes.

5. They frequently project disunity and dissension, because of public debate over policy ends. This interferes with their ability to send clear signals to potential adversaries.

6. They are incapable of secrecy, which hinders them in critical negotiations and deprives them of the element of surprise that is essential in military operations.

7. They are averse to limited war, since public passions, when stirred up, rarely give way to moderation. This hinders reconciliation with former enemies even when the Balance of Power requires them to do so.[19]

While traditional realists were critical of democratic foreign policy, they viewed these serious shortcomings as the necessary price to pay for a form of government that is in all other respects preferable to authoritarian government. Kennan, for example, emphasized that his critique was not offered for the purpose of making the U.S. foreign policy process less democratic. Instead, he stressed the importance of being aware of these weaknesses and avoiding both commitments that are unlikely to be met and arenas in

18. For related discussions, see Jack S. Levy, "Domestic Politics and War," in *Journal of Interdisciplinary History* 18, no. 4 (spring 1988): 653–73; and Nincic, *Democracy,* 6–11.

19. On this problem of peacemaking, see Niebuhr, *The Structure of Nations,* 197; Lippmann, *Essays in the Public Philosophy,* 18–21; and Sir B. H. Liddell Hart, *Strategy* (New York: Frederick A. Praeger, 1954), 350–65. See also pages 8–10.

which democracies will be at a disadvantage.[20] Morgenthau concluded that the best way to cope with this democratic handicap is through skillful leadership, which can generate public support for rational policies by resorting to clever deception and emotional appeals.[21] In his study of American foreign policy, Alexander George is less cynical than Morgenthau, suggesting that the president can overcome domestic constraints on a rational and coherent foreign policy by generating "policy legitimacy." He can do this by providing both a normative justification (which demonstrates the desirability of the policy) and a cognitive plan (to persuade the public of the feasibility of his plan).[22] Perhaps for these reasons, recent empirical examinations of many traditional realist claims regarding the foreign policy behavior of democratic polities have concluded that public opinion acts more reasonably than traditional realists assume.[23]

Clearly, the traditional realist conclusion was that, by their very nature, democratic political institutions handcuffed the foreign policy process. They did not consider whether different types of domestic institutions or democratic systems were more susceptible than others to the problems they identified, since they assumed that the only way for democratic leaders to overcome them, if at all, was through leadership strategies.

20. Kennan, *Cloud of Danger,* 7–9.

21. Morgenthau, *Dilemmas of Politics,* 326–27.

22. Alexander L. George, "Domestic Constraints on Regime Change in U.S. Foreign Policy: The Need for Policy Legitimation," in Ole Holsti, Randolph M. Siverson, and Alexander L. George, eds., *Change in the International System* (Boulder, Colo.: Westview Press, 1980), 233–62.

23. Bruce Russett, for example, reports that American public attitudes toward defense and security issues are remarkably stable and that the public responds rationally to new information and circumstances. Bruce Russett, *Controlling the Sword* (Cambridge: Harvard University Press, 1990), esp. chap. 4. Ole Holsti similarly finds that American public attitudes toward the Soviet Union during the Cold War were "neither random nor systematically out of touch with international realities." Despite realist expectations, public opinion is remarkably reasonable. Ole Holsti, *Public Opinion and American Foreign Policy* (Ann Arbor: University of Michigan Press, 1996), 39–79. Bruce Jentleson has demonstrated that American public attitudes toward U.S. military interventions have been both rational and purposive. Bruce W. Jentleson, "The Pretty Prudent Public: Post Post-Vietnam American Opinion on the Use of Military Force," *International Studies Quarterly* 36, no. 1 (March 1992): 49–74. Finally, James Burk concludes that the U.S. public is not as fickle as realists assume it is and, therefore, it does not withdraw support for military intervention merely because the United States incurs casualties. James Burk, "Support for Peacekeeping in Lebanon and Somalia," *Political Science Quarterly* 114, no. 1 (spring 1999): 53–78. See also Jeffrey W. Knopf, "How Rational is 'The Rational Public'?" *Journal of Conflict Resolution* 42, no. 5 (October 1998): 544–71.

The Liberal Perspective: Domestic Opinion
as an Enabler and a Necessary Check on Power

Like traditional realists, liberal international relations scholars also conclude that public opinion and democratic processes necessarily constrain
foreign policymakers. Nevertheless, they view democratic constraints as
functional since they prevent leaders from subverting the foreign policy
process for their own interests, thereby allowing policy to reflect true
national interests. In addition, judicious democratic constraints convey distinct advantages in policy implementation and international bargaining that
put democracies on a better footing internationally than their nondemocratic counterparts.

Classical liberals have long argued that democratic control over foreign
affairs will prevent the pursuit of policies that might be in the parochial
interests of leaders, or are consistent with their ideological visions, but
that are inimical to the true national interest. Immanuel Kant and Baron
de Montesquieu, for example, contended that in authoritarian regimes leaders abuse the foreign policy apparatus to further their own interests, rather
than the national interest. In republican regimes, however, public input
serves as a constraint on the ambitions of state leaders.[24] Kant writes:

> If, as must be so under this constitution, the consent of the subjects
> is required to determine whether there shall be war or not, nothing is
> more natural than that they should weigh the matter well, before
> undertaking such a bad business. For in decreeing war, they would of
> necessity be resolving to bring down the miseries of war upon their
> country. This implies: they must fight themselves; they must hand
> over the costs of war out of their own property; they must do their
> poor best to make good the devastation which it leaves behind; and
> finally, as a crowning ill, they have to accept a burden of debt which
> will embitter even peace itself, and which they can never pay off on
> account of the new wars which are always impending. On the other
> hand, in a government where the subject is not a citizen holding a
> vote ... the plunging into war is the least serious thing in the world.
> For the ruler is not a citizen, but the owner of the state, and does not

24. Immanuel Kant, *Perpetual Peace: A Philosophical Essay,* M. Campbell Smith, trans.
(New York: Garland, 1972); Baron de Montesquieu, *The Political Theory of Montesquieu,*
Melvin Richter, ed. (Cambridge: Cambridge University Press, 1977).

lose a whit by the war, while he goes on enjoying the delights of his table or sport, or of his pleasure palaces and gala days. He can therefore decide on war for the most trifling reasons as if it were a kind of pleasure party.[25]

Consequently, according to Montesquieu, democracies tend in general terms to be more peaceful since the people are less inclined to sanction a war for which they will bear the costs. Echoing the eighteenth-century liberals, former United States Secretary of State Elihu Root asserted: "When foreign offices were ruled by autocracies or oligarchies the danger of war was in sinister purpose. When foreign affairs are ruled by democracies the danger of war will be in mistaken beliefs. The world will be gainer by the change, for while there is no human way to prevent a king from having a bad heart, there is a human way to prevent a people from having an erroneous opinion."[26]

Recent empirical studies, however, have failed to confirm that democracies are more peaceful than nondemocratic states.[27] This may be the case because nationalism and other hostile public sentiments can actually motivate democratic leaders to choose war.[28] Alternatively, democratic leaders may inspire hatred and hostility among the electorate in order to facilitate military action.[29] Nonetheless, it has frequently been observed that because of democratic constraints, democratic states rarely, if ever, go to war with one another.[30] There are three reasons for this phenomenon, which Jack

25. Kant, *Perpetual Peace*, 122–23.

26. Elihu Root, "A Requisite for the Success of Popular Diplomacy," *Foreign Affairs* 1 (September 1922): 5.

27. Zeev Maoz and Nasrin Abdolai, "Regime Types and International Conflict," *Journal of Conflict Resolution* 33, no. 1 (1989): 3–35, and Stuart A. Bremer, "Democracy and Militarized Interstate Conflict, 1816–1965," *International Interactions* 18, no. 3 (1993): 231–50, both indicate that democracies are as war-prone as other states. Conversely, John R. Oneal and Bruce M. Russett contend that democracies are, indeed, less conflict-prone in aggregate than other states. "The Classical Liberals Were Right: Democracy, Interdependence, and Conflict, 1950–1985," *International Studies Quarterly* 41, no. 2 (June 1997): 267–94.

28. See, for example, Russett, *Controlling the Sword*, chap. 2.

29. Nehemia Geva, Karl DeRouen, and Alex Mintz, "The Political Incentive Explanation of the 'Democratic Peace' Phenomenon: Evidence from Experimental Research," *International Interactions* 18, no. 3 (1993): 215–29; Alex Mintz and Nehemia Geva, "Why Don't Democracies Fight Each Other? An Experimental Assessment of the 'Political Assessment' Explanation," *Journal of Conflict Resolution* 37, no. 3 (1993): 484–503.

30. See Michael Doyle, "Kant, Liberal Legacies, and Foreign Affairs, Part 1," in *Philosophy and Public Affairs* 12, no. 3 (1983): 205–35; "Kant, Liberal Legacies, and Foreign Affairs, Part 2," *Philosophy and Public Affairs* 12, no. 4 (1983): 323–53; "Liberalism and World Politics,"

Levy considers "as close as anything we have to an empirical law in international relations."[31] First, because they are governed by the people, these states share certain normative dispositions, which embrace the right of all people to self-government and reject coercion as a legitimate means of securing consent. Consequently, they prefer to resolve disputes—both internal and external—without resorting to the use of force.[32] Since all democracies are expected to share these norms, they do not feel threatened by other democracies and are in turn not compelled to threaten or behave aggressively. To borrow from the realist lexicon, the security dilemma between democratic states is almost nonexistent. The security dilemma between democratic and nondemocratic regimes, however, is intense, since the latter are based on coercion and not consent, both in domestic and international politics.

Second, democratic political institutions and procedures that require leaders to secure public and legislative support for policy changes slow down the process of mobilization for war considerably. Whereas traditional realists view these procedural delays as a handicap, for liberals they are a judicious constraint, since they create time for the peaceful resolution of conflicts. Other democracies are apt to seize upon this time to attempt to resolve disputes without violence, while nondemocratic states are likely to exploit this democratic weakness. Thus, democratic regimes are prone to remain at peace with each other, but in conflict with nondemocratic states.[33]

Third, since the public is primarily concerned with wealth and prosperity, liberal theorists note that democratic states are often free traders and

---

American Political Science Review 80, no. 4 (1986): 1151–61; Bruce M. Russett, Grasping the Democratic Peace (Princeton: Princeton University Press, 1993); and John M. Owen, "How Liberalism Produces the Democratic Peace," International Security 19, no. 2 (fall 1994): 87–125. Critics of the democratic peace theory include Christopher Layne, "Kant or Cant: The Myth of the Democratic Peace," International Security 19, no. 2 (fall 1994): 5–49; Raymond Cohen, "Pacific Unions: A Reappraisal of the Theory that 'Democracies Do Not Go to War with Each Other,'" Review of International Studies 20 (1994): 207–23; Joanne Gowa, "Democratic States and International Disputes," International Organization 49, no. 3 (1995): 511–22.

31. Levy, "Domestic Politics," 662.

32. Dixon refers to this as "the norm of bounded competition." See "Democracy and the Peaceful Settlement of International Conflict," 15–16. See also Joe D. Hagan, "Domestic Political Systems and War Proneness," Mershon International Studies Review 38 (October 1994): 186.

33. Margaret G. Hermann and Charles W. Kegley, Jr., "Rethinking Democracy and International Peace: Perspectives from Political Psychology," International Studies Quarterly 39, no. 4 (December 1995): 514; Russett, Grasping the Democratic Peace, 38–40.

are hospitable to foreign commerce. Therefore, a "spirit of commerce" develops between democracies, which increases the incentives to maintain peace in order to continue reaping the benefits of economic interaction.[34] This "commercial liberal" argument implies that the economic ties that bind liberal states provide them with heavy opportunity costs—in terms of trade—of using force to resolve disputes, as well as an economic means of extracting resources from territory that is more efficient than military force.[35]

Thus, according to liberals, the constraints imposed on foreign policy-makers by public participation and democratic political institutions actually improve foreign policy by preventing leader abuse and, consequently, by creating a zone of peace among democratic states. Furthermore, these constraints also convey uniquely democratic advantages in international bargaining and policy implementation.

Contemporary liberals argue that democratic leaders' lack of flexibility due to the fear of popular opposition can paradoxically empower them in the two-level game of international negotiations.[36] Since democratic leaders face higher audience costs than nondemocratic states, they are frequently unable to make compromises at the international bargaining table. If they make their negotiating partners aware of the magnitude of public or legislative opposition, they can induce others to make concessions that they otherwise would not in order to reach agreement.[37] Consequently, leaders

---

34. Doyle, "Kant, Liberal Legacies, and Foreign Affairs, Part 2," 350–51.

35. Robert O. Keohane, "International Liberalism Reconsidered," in John Dunn, ed., *The Economic Limits to Modern Politics* (Cambridge: Cambridge University Press, 1990), 177–79; John R. Oneal and Bruce N. Russett, "The Kantian Peace: The Pacific Benefits of Democracy, Interdependence, and International Organizations, 1885–1992," *World Politics* 52, no. 1 (October 1999): 1–37; and Jean-Marc F. Blanchard, Edward D. Mansfield, and Norrin M. Ripsman, "The Political Economy of National Security: Economic Statecraft, Interdependence, and International Conflict," in Jean-Marc F. Blanchard, Edward D. Mansfield, and Norrin M. Ripsman, eds., *Power and the Purse: Economic Statecraft, Interdependence, and International Conflict* (London: Frank Cass, 2000), 7–11. For recent empirical critiques of the commercial liberal argument, see Katherine Barbieri, "Economic Interdependence: A Path Toward Peace or a Source of Interstate Conflict?" *Journal of Peace Research* 33, no. 1 (1996), 29–49; Norrin M. Ripsman and Jean-Marc F. Blanchard, "Commercial Liberalism Under Fire: Evidence from 1914 and 1936," *Security Studies* 6, no. 2 (winter 1996/97): 4–50.

36. On the interaction between domestic and international politics in international negotiations, see Robert D. Putnam, "Diplomacy and Domestic Politics: The Logic of Two-Level Games," *International Organization* 42, no. 3 (summer 1988): 427–60.

37. James D. Fearon, "Domestic Political Audiences and the Escalation of International Disputes," *American Political Science Review* 88, no. 3 (September 1994): 577–92. Because the distinctive political institutions and preferences of democratic leaders enhance their ability

of democratic states have much to gain by exaggerating domestic hostility to compromise, maintaining that domestic opinion would either fail to ratify the agreement or topple the government.[38] German leader Konrad Adenauer employed this tactic of *domestic constraint projection* successfully in bargaining for the independence of the Federal Republic of Germany from the Western powers in the decade following World War II.[39] Similarly, Israeli Prime Minister Menachem Begin projected his domestic constraints effectively in negotiating peace with Egypt in 1977.[40]

Finally, and perhaps most significantly, by involving the public in the policymaking process, democracies enjoy a legitimacy of outcomes that nondemocratic regimes lack. As a result, they meet with comparatively little resistance when they seek to raise resources and revenues to pursue policy. Montesquieu, for example, observed: "Because its liberty is real, no other nation loves its liberty more than this one [a free one]. To defend it, the nation stands ready to sacrifice its wealth, its comfort, its interests; it will support the burden of taxes so onerous that even the most absolute prince would never dare impose their like on his subjects."[41] Furthermore, as David Lake argues, liberal states tend to be wealthier than autocratic regimes since they are not rent seekers and, therefore, are not as likely as nondemocratic, rent-seeking states to create economic distortions. Since national wealth is high, more absolute wealth will be devoted to defense

---

to send clear and credible signals to their adversaries and bargaining counterparts alike, their efforts are likely to be persuasive. Kurt Taylor Gaubatz, "Democratic States and Commitment in International Relations," *International Organization* 50, no.1 (winter 1996): 109–39.

38. Thomas Risse-Kappen, *Cooperation Among Democracies* (Princeton: Princeton University Press, 1995). Indeed, Robert D. Putnam observes that although ratification is not a uniquely democratic phenomenon, it is far more meaningful in a democratic context. "Diplomacy and Domestic Politics." For similar observations, see pages 11–12.

39. Adenauer portrayed himself as sympathetic to the Western desire to restrain German power, but emphasized growing domestic impatience and cautioned that if the German people felt short-changed by the final settlement, they would elect the less accommodating Social Democratic Party to power. See, for example, Dwight D. Eisenhower, *Mandate for Change, 1953–1956* (Garden City, N.J.: Doubleday, 1963), 402–5; and Thomas Alan Schwartz, *America's Germany: John J. McCloy and the Federal Republic of Germany* (Cambridge: Harvard University Press, 1991), 78–79.

40. Begin consistently stressed that he could not compromise without the full support of Israeli public opinion, especially where settlements in the Sinai were concerned, in order to limit future concessions and exaggerate their value. Shibley Telhami, *Power and Leadership in International Bargaining* (New York: Columbia University Press, 1990), esp. 172–73.

41. Montesquieu, *The Political Theory of Montesquieu*, 285.

than in nonliberal societies. Consequently, democratic states tend to be more successful in war than nondemocratic states.[42]

The liberal conclusion, then, is that democratic institutions, which grant the public and the legislature a role in foreign policy formation, assist democratic states in the international arena and improve the foreign security policies they select. In this regard, liberals and traditional realists share an important assumption. They both agree that democracies are, of necessity, structurally constrained states, in which foreign policy is subject to the control of various social forces, cumbersome legislative review procedures, or the mass electorate as a whole. I will subsequently refer to this assumption of democratic constraint as the traditional view, or the traditional realist/liberal consensus. Their disagreement is over the consequences of democratic constraints. Traditional realists conclude that this lack of policy autonomy puts democracies at a disadvantage vis-à-vis other regimes; liberals believe it puts them in a better position.

The Structural Realist Perspective:
Democratic Institutions Have Little Effect

Unlike traditional realists and liberals, neorealists contend that public participation and democratic institutions have no marked effect on the foreign security policy choices of democracies. Responding to traditional realists, Kenneth Waltz, the founder of the structural realist school, concluded that both the deficiencies of democracies and the strengths of authoritarian regimes have been greatly exaggerated.[43] Indeed, Waltz viewed the success of American policy during the Cold War as proof that democracies could behave consistently with the dictates of the international system. In his opinion, international anarchy socializes all states, regardless of their regime type or individual characteristics, to safeguard their security in accordance with the dictates of the international system. Those that fail to act rationally in defense of their interests are eliminated in wars by states that do. Therefore, he argues, foreign security policy should be explained far better by systemic variables than by domestic variables, such as regime type.[44]

42. David A. Lake, "Powerful Pacifists: Democratic States and War," *American Political Science Review* 86, no. 1 (March 1992): 24–37, esp. 30–31; Aaron Friedberg, "Why Didn't the United States Become a Garrison State?" *International Security* 16, no. 4 (spring 1992): 109–42.

43. Kenneth N. Waltz, *Foreign Policy and Democratic Politics: The American and British Experience* (Boston: Little, Brown & Co., 1967), esp. 306–11.

44. Kenneth N. Waltz, *Theory of International Politics* (New York: McGraw Hill, 1979).

Defensive structural realists, such as Jack Snyder, attribute more explanatory power to domestic politics, but they too conclude that democracies behave no differently from most other types of states. While they argue that domestic political explanations are required to elucidate irrational national security policy decisions inconsistent with systemic incentives, they typically identify regimes driven by imperialistic cartels and militaristic general staffs, rather than democratic governments, as the most likely to engender pathological behavior.[45] Democracies, they conclude, behave no differently from most other states in the international arena.

The Conventional Conclusion: Democratic Uniformity

The conventional picture of democratic states is of a rather homogenous group of states whose foreign policies are affected in similar ways by public opinion and democratic processes. Although they differ in their evaluation of the consequences, traditional realists and liberals agree that democratic foreign policy executives are necessarily weak and constrained by domestic politics. In other words, the traditional view is that all democratic states, by virtue of the principle of popular sovereignty, lack decision-making autonomy over foreign security policy. This conclusion is remarkably unsophisticated and ignores a central insight of the comparative political economy literature: namely, that even democratic states can be autonomous if their domestic political structures shield them from public opinion and interest groups.[46] Neorealists, in contrast, conclude that all democracies

45. Jack Snyder, *Myths of Empire* (Ithaca: Cornell University Press, 1991); Jack Snyder, *Ideology of the Offensive* (Ithaca: Cornell University Press, 1984); Stephen Van Evera, "The Cult of the Offensive and the Origins of the First World War," *International Security* 9, no. 1 (summer 1984): 58–108; Stephen M. Walt, *The Origins of Alliances* (Ithaca: Cornell University Press, 1987). For a critical review of defensive structural realism, see Fareed Zakaria, "Realism and Domestic Politics: a Review Essay," *International Security* 17, no. 1 (summer 1992): 177–98.

46. Eric A. Nordlinger, *On the Autonomy of the Democratic State* (Cambridge: Harvard University Press, 1981); Hugh Heclo, *Modern Social Politics in Britain and Sweden* (New Haven: Yale University Press, 1974). My argument parallels those in the comparative political economy field who argue that state autonomy, rather than democracy, correlates highly with the effective implementation of development strategies. See Stephan Haggard, *Pathways from the Periphery* (Ithaca: Cornell University Press, 1990); Peter A. Hall, *Governing the Economy* (New York: Oxford University Press, 1986), esp. 15–20; and Margaret Weir and Theda Skocpol, "State Structures and the Possibilities for 'Keynesian' Responses to the Great Depression in Sweden, Britain and the United States," in Peter B. Evans, Dietrich Rueschemeyer, and Theda Skocpol, eds., *Bringing the State Back In* (Cambridge: Cambridge University Press, 1985), 107–63.

are sufficiently autonomous to react to their international environment as necessary, regardless of domestic preferences. Their explanations are even less satisfying, since they fail to distinguish democratic states not only from each other, but also from other regimes. The balance of this chapter will present an alternative model of foreign security policy formation in democratic states that takes democratic differences into account.

Differentiating Between Democracies

The conventional wisdom on democratic foreign policy is flawed because it fails to take into account the distinctive political arrangements or *domestic decision-making environments* of different democratic states. It seems implausible, for example, that the executive of a parliamentary democracy like Great Britain or Canada, whose cabinets necessarily command a majority of support from the legislature, should be constrained to the same extent as a presidential executive that faces a legislature dominated by a rival party, like the Clinton administration in the U.S. after the 1994 congressional elections. Similarly, it is unreasonable to assume that a Westminster-style parliamentary democracy, such as Great Britain, with strong, well-disciplined, single-party majorities should face the same obstacles in foreign affairs as a multiparty parliamentary system with undisciplined parties and fragile multiparty coalitions, like Fourth Republic France or Israel. Furthermore, differences in national attitudes toward foreign policy and the proper roles for the public and the legislature in its formation should also affect the conduct of foreign relations across states.

Consequently, I argue that the degree to which the leadership of a democratic state is affected, either positively or negatively, by parliamentary oversight and mass public input into the foreign policy process depends upon the degree of *structural autonomy* accorded to the foreign policy executive by the domestic decision-making environment of that state.[47] I explain

47. For the sake of simplicity, I adopt an implicit assumption of the traditional literature in this study. Both realists and liberals conflate public and legislative opinion under the rubric of domestic opinion or domestic opposition. Their assumption is that, by and large, parliamentary opinion is a reflection of public opinion, since representatives will not maintain their seats if they oppose the wishes of their constituents. They appear not to consider that public and legislative preferences may at times diverge, nor that these two domestic constraints may have different and separate effects on the making of policy. The theoretical and empirical critique that follows will, likewise, concentrate on the policy effects of these combined domestic constraints, leaving for future work the disaggregation of separate domestic pressures.

which institutional structures, prevailing norms, and decision-making procedures contribute to or detract from structural autonomy in the realm of foreign security policy and construct a model to illustrate their operation. Finally, I consider how the leadership strategies that democratic leaders choose to pursue cause further variance in the domestic impact on foreign policy within a given domestic decision-making environment.

Foreign Policy Autonomy: The Domestic Decision-Making Environment

In her landmark study of state-society relations, Theda Skocpol defined state autonomy as the ability of a state to formulate preferences independently of social forces. Her definition is unsatisfying in that it does not include what she labels state capacity—the ability of states to act on their preferences in the face of societal opposition.[48] Without such a capacity, the ability to formulate preferences is politically insignificant. A more meaningful definition of autonomy would be *the ability of an entity to act upon its own preferences.* States are structurally autonomous to the extent that their domestic political structures should allow them, *ceteris paribus,* to construct and pursue policies independently of societal forces and public opinion.[49] Foreign policy autonomy refers to the structural capacity of the foreign policy executive to pursue policies when faced with public or legislative opposition.[50] Structural autonomy, though, must be distinguished from observed policy independence if autonomy is to be used meaningfully as an independent or intervening variable in a study that examines its effects on policy independence. Actual policy independence may be affected not only by structural autonomy, but also by individual leadership styles and other variables. By the *foreign policy executive,* I mean the group of executive policymakers and officials that have primary responsibility within the government over the determination of foreign policy.[51] This will vary from

48. Theda Skocpol, "Bringing the State Back In: Strategies of Analysis in Current Research," in Evans, et al., eds., *Bringing the State Back In,* 9–20.

49. This definition is similar to Eric A. Nordlinger's in *On the Autonomy of the Democratic State,* 8.

50. Certainly, as Nordlinger suggests, a state can act autonomously even when its actions are consistent with public preferences. Ibid., 20. Nonetheless, the essence of decision-making autonomy is the ability to act upon preferences even when opposed.

51. This definition is close to Margaret G. Hermann et al.'s "ultimate decision unit," which they describe as "a set of authorities with the ability to commit the resources of the society and, with respect to a particular problem, with the authority to make a decision that cannot be readily reversed." See Margaret G. Hermann, Charles F. Hermann, and Joe D. Hagan, "How Decision Units Shape Foreign Policy Behavior," in Charles F. Hermann, Charles W. Kegley Jr.,

government to government and from country to country, but it will typically comprise the prime minister or president, and the foreign minister, as well as the cabinet officials and political appointees charged with foreign policy decision making.

Traditional realists and liberals might object that democratic states cannot possibly make decisions autonomously, because they are by definition responsible to the electorate. In a small, direct democracy—such as that of ancient Athens—in which the public participated in and scrutinized all governmental decisions, this objection would be valid. In modern representative democracies, however, the public is removed from decision making by layers of representation and bureaucracy. Hence, governments can frequently make decisions without the public's awareness. Furthermore, the public retains the power to turn out a government that makes objectionable policy choices only during infrequent elections. Depending on the structure of political institutions within the polity as well as the procedures and norms that regulate political interaction and govern relations between the executive and the people's representatives in the legislature, democratic governments can often make decisions that the majority of the public oppose, without fear of electoral reprisal or governmental defeat. To the extent that their domestic decision-making environment makes such behavior possible, they are structurally autonomous from domestic opposition.

In Figure 1, I identify the three principal determinants of structural autonomy: the *institutional structures* that set the boundaries of the domestic decision-making environment; the *decision-making procedures* that govern the conduct of actors within these institutions; and the *procedural norms* that inform these procedures.

Institutional structures include constitutional provisions, which delimit procedures and responsibilities, and patterns of institutional growth over time.[52] We can identify two broad categories of structures that can affect foreign policymaking. First, there are structural features that determine the way in which democracy is practiced in a particular state. These include, *inter alia*, the nature of democratic governance (presidential, parliamentary,

---

and James N. Rosenau, eds., *New Directions in the Study of Foreign Policy* (Boston: Allen & Unwin, 1987), 309–36.

52. An excellent study that explains U.S. policy adaptation to the oil shocks of the 1970s in terms of the structure and growth of the American state is G. John Ikenberry, *Reasons of State: Oil Politics and the Capacities of American Government* (Ithaca: Cornell University Press, 1988).

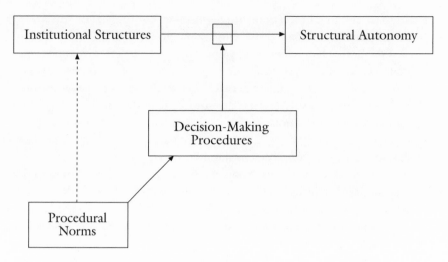

Fig. 1   The sources of structural autonomy

or mixed), the extent of concentration or separation of executive power, the electoral procedure (e.g., single-member constituencies, proportional representation, etc.), the number of political parties that participate meaningfully in the electoral and policy processes, and the frequency of elections.[53] Second, there are structural features that pertain exclusively to the foreign policy apparatus, including the number of institutions and actors that contribute meaningfully to policy determination, the extent and frequency to which these institutions and actors must report to a democratic body, and the body responsible for appointing the foreign minister and other key officials. All things being equal:

- the more concentrated executive power is, the more autonomous the state is;
- two-party systems yield greater decision-making autonomy then multi-party systems, since in the former the executive usually commands the support of the majority party;

53. For a discussion of how democratic governments in twenty-one countries vary along these dimensions, see Arend Lijphart, *Democracies: Patterns of Majoritarian and Consensus Government in Twenty-One Countries* (New Haven: Yale University Press, 1984). See also Matthew Soberg Shugart and John M. Carey, *Presidents and Assemblies* (Cambridge: Cambridge University Press, 1992). For similar observations, see Helen V. Milner, *Interests, Institutions, and Information* (Princeton: Princeton University Press, 1997), chap. 4.

- electoral systems based upon single-member constituencies will afford greater autonomy than those employing proportional representation, since the latter favor a multiplicity of parties and less stable, coalition governments. Coalition governments require the executive to consult more parties and avoid unpopular policies that might split the government;[54]
- the longer the interval between elections—the main instrument of direct popular policy evaluation—the greater the government's insulation;
- at any given point in time, the further away an election is, the more freedom to maneuver a government should possess;
- presidential executives that cannot be dissolved by the legislature under normal circumstances enjoy an advantage over parliamentary cabinets supported by a coalition of parties or even one governing party with a small majority of seats. Small majorities can whittle away due to defections and bi-elections;
- the degree to which the constitution favors the executive over the legislative branch in matters of defense and foreign affairs directly affects the government's autonomy;
- to the extent that foreign policy is conducted by appointed rather than elected officials, the domestic impact on foreign affairs will be minimized;
- if appointed diplomatic and military officials are responsible to the executive rather than the legislature, autonomy is enhanced.

Decision-making procedures refer to routinized patterns of behavior and informal rules that govern actors' conduct, but do not necessarily stem from the structure of the institutions within which they act. When procedures are routinely adhered to, they can constrain or enable policymakers just like formal institutional structures. More precisely, they modify the scope of action that institutional structures allow leaders. Some, such as the tradition of party discipline in Great Britain (requiring the majority party to support cabinet policy) enable decision makers to surpass the boundaries imposed upon them by formal structures. Others, such as the recent American practice of executive consultation with Congress before dispatching troops, can constrain leaders and prevent them from exercising

---

54. See, for example, Anthony Downs, *An Economic Theory of Democracy* (New York: Harper & Row, 1957), chap. 8. Ronald Rogowski correctly argues that proportional representation makes legislators more autonomous from their constituencies. "Trade and the Variety of Democratic Institutions," *International Organization* 41, no. 2 (spring 1987): 203–23. Nonetheless, our concern here is with *executive* autonomy, rather than *legislative* autonomy.

the full degree of their institutional authority. Many of these procedures are based merely on custom or deference to tradition, and political actors adhere to them only because they simplify political interaction. Consequently, political actors may alter them if they are willing to accept the costs of change.[55]

Many procedures, however, are inspired by prevailing *procedural norms* — widely accepted standards that provide a broad consensus on the way politics ought to be conducted in terms of the rights and obligations of political actors and institutions.[56] Such conventions are likely to remain more or less constant until the underlying norms change or lose force. For our purposes, the most important procedural norms are *legislative norms* that affect the legislature's usage of whatever structural rights it has to scrutinize the foreign policy process.[57] Nonpartisanship and congressional restraint in the conduct of American foreign relations, practices that endured for some time after World War II, for example, were inspired by a norm that required both parties to curtail bickering over the direction of foreign policy. Based on a belief that "politics stops at the water's edge" due to the importance of foreign policy in a hostile international environment and the need to present clear signals to foreign governments,[58] this norm compelled the executive to consult privately with senior members of both parties in the construction of policy. In return, both parties were obliged to refrain from open criticism of governmental policy. Since nonpartisanship and congressional restraint elevated foreign policy decision making above politicking and removed much policy debate from public purview, they granted the executive considerable autonomy, despite the constitutional division of authority over

55. See, for example, Nordlinger, *On the Autonomy,* 92–94, 131–32.

56. Robin M. Williams, Jr., "The Concept of Norms," in David L. Sills, ed., *International Encyclopedia of the Social Sciences,* vol. 11 (New York: Macmillan & Co. Ltd., 1968), 204–8; Edna Ullmann-Margolit, *The Emergence of Norms* (Oxford: Clarendon, 1977), 12; Stephen D. Krasner, "Structural Causes and Regime Consequences: Regimes as Intervening Variables," in Stephen D. Krasner, ed., *International Regimes* (Ithaca: Cornell University Press, 1983), 2; Friedrich V. Kratochwil, *Rules, Norms and Decisions* (Cambridge: Cambridge University Press, 1989), chaps. 2 and 3.

57. In her study of how legislative norms affect the character and operation of the United States Senate, Barbara Sinclair explains that "norms condition the use of institutional resources, often by limiting their use." *The Transformation of the U.S. Senate* (Baltimore: Johns Hopkins University Press, 1989), 14. See also Donald R. Matthews, *U.S. Senators and Their World* (New York: Vintage Books, 1960), 92–117. I thank Marissa Martino-Golden for drawing this literature to my attention.

58. Ellen C. Collier, ed., *Bipartisanship and the Making of Foreign Policy* (Boulder, Colo.: Westview Press, 1991), 50–51.

foreign affairs between the president and the Congress. Thus, legislative norms—and the procedures they inspire—can free an executive that is institutionally constrained or, conversely, can reign in an executive with a wide scope of institutional authority.

In addition to inspiring such procedures, norms—when they are powerful enough—can occasionally shape the way in which institutions are interpreted and operate. Constitutional provisions that define and delimit institutional structures, for example, are subject to judicial interpretation. Such interpretations vary over time and usually reflect prevailing political norms, although they typically do not alter existing institutional structures meaningfully unless prevailing norms are powerful and are sharply discordant with them. As we shall see, important American Supreme Court rulings on the division of foreign relations powers just prior to World War II reflected a sea change in American attitudes regarding the importance of foreign affairs and, hence, construed the president's authority over international affairs quite broadly. Consequently, they greatly enhanced the autonomy of the American national security executive. Finally, general political norms can influence the public's willingness and ability to voice opposition to the government's national security policies.[59]

In general:

- conventions, such as party discipline, which routinize support for the government, grant it greater autonomy;
- decision-making procedures that require the executive to consult the legislature prior to implementing policy curtail state strength;
- legislative norms that view the conduct of foreign relations as of utmost importance and that, therefore, stifle public dissent on matters of foreign affairs, grant the executive a freer hand;
- legislative norms that require representatives to scrutinize decisions closely in order to prevent excesses serve to constrain leaders;
- political norms that inspire interpretations of existing foreign policy institutions that are favorable to the executive enhance autonomy; those that inspire interpretations favorable to the legislature detract from it.

Three potential objections to my definition of autonomy need to be addressed. To begin with, some would object to including norms in such an

59. Tamar Hermann, "Grassroots Activism as a Factor in Foreign Policy-Making," in David Skidmore and Valerie M. Hudson, eds., *The Limits of State Autonomy* (Boulder, Colo.: Westview Press, 1993), 127–47.

analysis, since, if norms do have causal power, it is most likely by embedding themselves in political institutions. Therefore, they would contend that the role of norms can be subsumed within institutions, thereby yielding a more parsimonious theory.[60] As Paul Kowert and Jeffrey Legro point out, however, "international relations theory cannot afford to ignore norms" because they can elucidate "analytical blind spots and gaps" in existing theories built exclusively upon rational choice mechanisms such as formal institutional structures.[61] As we will see in Chapter 2, the post–World War II American case in this study provides an empirical example of such a blind spot because the existing institutional structure would lead us to classify the American foreign security executive incorrectly as nonautonomous. Therefore, the inclusion of procedural norms in a theory of structural autonomy and its impact on policy adds significantly to existing theories of domestic structure.

Furthermore, while my inclusion of procedural norms represents an innovation and an improvement on the definitions of autonomy offered by comparative politics researchers, the inclusion of societal factors—such as these norms—is both consistent with the broader comparative politics literature and essential to capture the true nature of executive autonomy. After all, autonomy is dynamic and determined as the result of a struggle between state and society—the state usually struggling to engineer autonomy, society usually struggling to reign in the state. Thus, both state and societal variables that condition this struggle affect state autonomy.[62] Ignoring relevant

60. Judith Goldstein, *Ideas, Interests and American Trade Policy* (Ithaca: Cornell University Press, 1993); Susan Peterson, *Crisis Bargaining and the State* (Ann Arbor: University of Michigan Press, 1996), 28–29. Judith Goldstein and Robert O. Keohane agree that norms have a powerful impact on outcomes when they become embedded in political institutions, but acknowledge that there are other ways in which norms can affect policy. "Ideas and Foreign Policy: An Analytical Framework," in Judith Goldstein and Robert O. Keohane, eds., *Ideas and Foreign Policy: Beliefs, Institutions, and Political Change* (Ithaca: Cornell University Press, 1993), 3–30. On the virtues of parsimony in theory building, see Gary King, Robert O. Keohane, and Sidney Verba, *Designing Social Inquiry: Scientific Inference in Qualitative Research* (Princeton: Princeton University Press, 1994).

61. "Norms, Identity, and Their Limits: A Theoretical Reprise," in Peter J. Katzenstein, ed., *The Culture of National Security: Norms and Identity in World Politics* (New York: Columbia University Press, 1996), 453–54. See also Albert S. Yee, "The Causal Effects of Ideas on Politics," *International Organization* 50, no. 1 (winter 1996): 69–108; and Peter A. Hall and Rosemary C. R. Taylor, "Political Science and the Three New Institutionalisms," *Political Studies* 44, no.5, (December 1996): 955–57.

62. See, for example, Joel S. Migdal, *Strong States and Weak Societies: State-Society Relations and State Capabilities in the Third World* (Princeton: Princeton University Press, 1988); Peter B. Evans, Dietrich Rueschemeyer, and Theda Skocpol, "On the Road to a More Adequate

societal variables, such as procedural norms, would sacrifice far too much explanatory power at the altar of parsimony.

Others might prefer to include more societal influences, particularly the organized business and social interests that comprise the governing coalition.[63] I decline to do so, however, for two reasons. First, while the governing coalition helps to shape the government's basic direction, it is unlikely to determine—or even to be consulted on—specific policy initiatives. Indeed, those who highlight the influence of the governing constellation of interests on American foreign policy focus on "programmatic change" and address the ability of these interests to swing the broad orientation of the government between the poles of imperialism and anti-imperialism or economic nationalism and internationalism, rather than the content of specific policies.[64] This must necessarily be the case, I argue, since these coalitions are comprised of large numbers of actors with overlapping, but not identical, interests.[65] In order to secure agreement and maintain the coalition,

Understanding of the State," in Evans, et al., *Bringing the State Back In,* 355–56; Alfred Stepan, "State Power and the Strength of Civil Society in the Southern Cone of Latin America," in Evans et al., *Bringing the State Back In,* 317–43; Thomas M. Callaghy, "Political Passions and Economic Interests: Economic Reform and Political Structure in Africa," in Thomas M. Callaghy and John Ravenhill, eds., *Hemmed In: Responses to Africa's Economic Decline* (New York: Columbia University Press, 1993), 463–511; Michael Mann, "The Autonomous Power of States: Its Origins, Mechanisms, and Results," in John A. Hall, ed., *States in History* (London: Basil Blackwell, 1986), 109–36; and Nordlinger, *On the Autonomy of the Democratic State.* Gabriel A. Almond goes so far as to argue that this image of a struggle between state and society for the control of policy is common not only to the "neostatist paradigm" of the late 1970s and 1980s, but also to the earlier pluralist writings that dominated the field of comparative politics. "The Return to the State," *American Political Science Review* 82, no. 3 (September 1988): 853–74.

63. Thomas Ferguson, "From Normalcy to New Deal: Industrial Structure, Party Competition and American Public Policy in the Great Depression," *International Organization* 38, no. 1 (winter 1984): 41–94; Peter Alexis Gourevitch, "Breaking with Orthodoxy: The Politics of Economic Policy Responses to the Depression of the 1930s," *International Organization* 38, no. 1 (winter 1984): 95–129; Jeffry Frieden, "Sectoral Conflict and U.S. Foreign Economic Policy, 1914–1940," *International Organization* 42, no. 1 (winter 1988): 59–90; and Peter Trubowitz, *Defining National Interests: Conflict and Change in American Foreign Policy* (Chicago: University of Chicago Press, 1998).

64. Trubowitz, *Defining National Interests,* esp. 8–9. See also Frieden, "Sectoral Conflict and U.S. Foreign Economic Policy," esp. 67; and Benjamin O. Fordham, *Building the Cold War Consensus: The Political Economy of U.S. National Security Policy* (Ann Arbor: University of Michigan Press, 1998), esp. 3–4.

65. This is especially the case in first-past-the-post electoral systems—such the United States and Great Britain. These systems encourage the formation of "catch-all" parties that need to form broad-based political coalitions in order to win elections. Anthony Downs, *An Economic Theory of Democracy* (New York: Harper & Row, 1957). On the phenomenon of

the content of that agreement must be broad and rather vague, leaving the state to determine the specifics of policy.[66] Second, we should expect interest group influence to be especially limited in the foreign security policy issue area, where many of the organized socioeconomic interests that tend to comprise governing coalitions have few direct economic interests at stake.[67] While so-called "iron triangle" groups, such as weapons manufacturers, might have a direct stake in general security issues, such as defense spending, they are not likely to be significantly affected by decisions on German sovereignty or whether Western defense is carried out with or without German military units.[68] Thus, the interest of the governing coalition of business and societal forces in, and their influence over, the specific postwar settlement policies a government pursues should be quite limited. As a result, we do not sacrifice explanatory power by leaving them out of the model.

Finally, some might object to the exclusion of international factors in the determination of state autonomy. Neorealists, for example, might expect that both domestic political institutions and societal attitudes are merely reflections of the degree of international threat that the state faces. States in a high threat environment might tailor their political institutions to enhance executive autonomy, which is essential to meeting those threats. In addition, domestic attitudes in these states might also grant the executive greater leeway in matters of foreign affairs because of their importance. Conversely, states facing stable international threat environments might build institutions and shape domestic attitudes that constrain the executive.[69]

As we shall see in the next chapter, however, international factors do not have a uniform or predictable effect, particularly where autonomy is concerned. Instead, state and societal actors interpret these pressures through the prism of existing institutions, political culture, and history, yielding a unique response. Thus, while a threatening international environment

---

catch-all parties, see Otto Kircheimer, "The Transformation of Western European Party Systems," in Joseph LaPalombara and Myron Weiner, eds., *Political Parties and Political Development* (Princeton: Princeton University Press, 1966), 177–200.

66. In a similar vein, Peter Swenson argues that the governing party has wide latitude to determine the specifics of policy and uses its coalition of likeminded interests to provide it with *post facto* support. "Arranged Alliance: Business Interests in the New Deal," *Politics and Society* 25, no. 1 (March 1997): 66–116.

67. See, for example, Milbrath, "Interest Groups and Foreign Policy"; and Cohen, "The Influence of Special-Interest Groups."

68. Gordon Adams, *The Politics of Defense Contracting: The Iron Triangle* (New Brunswick, N.J.: Transaction Books, 1982).

69. I thank Benny Miller and an anonymous reviewer for suggesting this argument, which I return to in Chapter 4.

inspired norms of public and legislative restraint in Great Britain and the United States after World War II due to the importance of foreign security policy (i.e., it was too important to tie the executive's hands internationally), in France it inspired exactly the reverse norms of legislative interference in foreign security policy because of their importance (i.e., it was too important to leave to the executive). Consequently, my model excludes international pressures, instead concentrating on the societal preferences they help to shape.

Taken together, institutional structures, decision-making procedures, and procedural norms determine the level of structural autonomy a foreign policy executive possesses. We can represent the difference between my structural autonomy model and other models of democratic foreign security policy graphically. Figure 2 represents the neorealist conception of foreign security policy in democratic states. As in all other states, executive preferences—which are themselves dictated by the international balance of power—determine policy. Figure 3 represents the traditional view of the domestic decision-making environment in democratic states. Both traditional realists and liberals agree that domestic preferences intervene between executive preferences and policy choices. Realists believe that domestic opinion disrupts the nexus between national interests and policy selection. Liberals believe that the governed can simultaneously filter out the influence of unwholesome, particularistic leader interests and enable true state

Fig. 2   Neorealist model of policymaking in democratic states

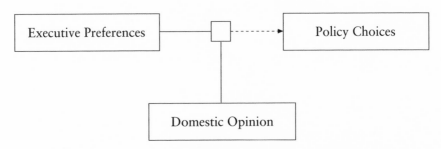

Fig. 3   Traditional model of policymaking in democratic states

interests to shape policy. It is important to note that since the traditional model seeks to explain only the impact of domestic opinion on policy, it does not specify the source of state preferences.

Figure 4 illustrates the richer picture generated when the role of structural autonomy is considered. When executive and domestic preferences diverge, the two groups may try to convert each other to overcome the disagreement. Decision makers can attempt to convert public and legislative attitudes with public opinion campaigns designed to persuade influential opinion of the merits of the government's position. Similarly, segments of the public and the legislature might try to convince the foreign policy executive of the correctness of their preferred policy. If either party is converted, then confrontation is avoided and the independence of the executive is not tested. Conversely, when conversion is either not attempted or is unsuccessful, the degree of structural autonomy the executive possesses determines who will prevail. Autonomy enables decision makers to filter out domestic pressures, thereby allowing them to formulate policy consistent with their own preferences. While policymaking in less autonomous states more closely approximates the traditional model, in highly autonomous states the public and legislative impact is severely curtailed. Once again, the sources of state preferences are exogenous, since it is only the effect of domestic politics on policy, rather than preference generation itself, that the model seeks to explain.

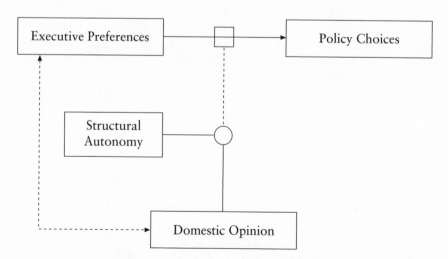

Fig. 4   Improved model of policymaking in democratic states

My model of the domestic decision-making environments of democratic states represents an improvement over not only the traditional and neorealist alternatives, but also three recent attempts by international relations scholars to differentiate between democracies. In their studies of democratic differences, Thomas Risse-Kappen and Susan Peterson each consider two sources of these differences. Risse-Kappen concentrates on "domestic structure" and "coalition-building processes," which roughly correspond to institutional structures and decision-making procedures. Beyond equating the former with the degree of centralization of political institutions, though, he does not specify how particular types of institutional arrangements should affect policymaking. Nor does he specify how domestic structures interact with coalition-building processes to affect state autonomy over matters of foreign affairs.[70] Peterson contends that the nature of the foreign policy processes in democratic states derives from "the degree of executive autonomy from the legislature" and "the structure of the foreign policy executive." She does not explain what determines the former, and she asserts that the latter is determined merely by "the number of offices of the state that have responsibility for making foreign policy during a crisis."[71] This lack of specificity causes her to err in her categorization of the two states in her study. She incorrectly asserts that the French executive in 1898 was more autonomous in matters of foreign affairs than its British counterpart. Such a conclusion ignores the utter dependence of the fragile Third Republic French coalition government—which needed to secure the approval of both parliamentary chambers for declarations of war and most international treaties—upon the support of a majority of deputies in a legislature comprised of a multiplicity of undisciplined parties. Similarly, it ignores the fact that the British single-party majority cabinet necessarily commanded a majority of support in the legislature because of the practice of party discipline, as well as long-standing procedural norms granting the cabinet special leeway in matters of foreign affairs.[72] Neither author considers the important role of procedural norms.

Perhaps the most sophisticated attempt to determine the impact of domestic political institutions on foreign policy outcomes is Helen V.

70. Thomas Risse-Kappen, "Public Opinion, Domestic Structure, and Foreign Policy in Liberal Democracies," *World Politics* 43, no. 4 (July 1991): 484–86.

71. Susan Peterson, "How Democracies Differ: Public Opinion, State Structure, and the Lessons of the Fashoda Crisis," *Security Studies* 5, no. 1 (autumn 1995): 16–18; Peterson, *Crisis Bargaining and the State*, 24–30.

72. See Chapter 2.

Milner's study of the domestic politics of international cooperation.[73] While not studying autonomy directly, Milner considers the balance of executive versus legislative control over key foreign policy powers as essential for determining the impact of the legislature on the outcome of international negotiations. She does not, however, consider the important impact of procedural norms, nor does she examine the executive's autonomy from public opinion.

Since procedures and norms affect state autonomy, three important implications follow. First, a state's level of autonomy varies over time, as decision-making procedures and the norms that inspire them change. Thus the practice of nonpartisan foreign policy eroded after the Vietnam War and, consequently, so did the power of the president over foreign affairs.[74] Second, autonomy does not lend itself to quantitative measurement. Much can be learned about policy outcomes, though, by estimating the *relative* autonomy of two or more states, or the same state at different times.[75] Third, autonomy is issue specific. A state can simultaneously be circumscribed in its ability to redistribute wealth and independent in its ability to negotiate international treaties, since different institutions, procedures, and norms affect each issue area.

Indeed, as we shall see in the next chapter, the postwar French executive, which has been characterized as highly autonomous in economic policy, was actually fragmented and weak in the conduct of foreign affairs. Similarly, the American executive, constrained in the economic arena, enjoyed considerable foreign security policy autonomy in the first two decades of the Cold War. Institutional, procedural, and normative factors can also cause structural autonomy to differ *within* the foreign policy issue area. For example, the constitution of the French Third Republic (1871–1940) granted the cabinet primacy in ordinary matters of foreign affairs (low politics) but required it to secure the approval of both the National Assembly and the Senate for declarations of war, peace treaties, and other major international treaties (high politics). Conversely, the British and American executives

73. Milner, *Interests, Institutions, and Information*, chap. 4.

74. I. M. Destler, Leslie H. Gelb, and Anthony Lake, *Our Own Worst Enemy: The Unmaking of American Foreign Policy* (New York: Simon & Schuster, 1984), 61; and Collier, *Bipartisanship*, 28–30.

75. This is the approach taken by Peter J. Katzenstein, "Conclusion: Domestic Structures and Strategies of Foreign Economic Policy," in Peter J. Katzenstein, ed., *Between Power and Plenty: Foreign Economic Policies in Advanced Industrial States* (Madison: University of Wisconsin Press, 1978), 295–336. See also Robert A. Dahl, *Dilemmas of Pluralist Democracy: Autonomy vs. Control* (New Haven: Yale University Press, 1982), 21–22, 26.

after World War II, as we shall see, were more autonomous in matters of high politics than in other areas of foreign affairs because of prevailing norms that security matters were far too important to allow legislative interference.

It is particularly plausible that, all things being equal, states should command more structural autonomy in the conduct of national security policy than they do in other issue areas, such as that of allocational politics. As Thomas Callaghy argues, states can enhance their structural autonomy by delegating decision-making authority to a bureaucracy or a cabinet committee and insulating this apparatus, by both formal and informal means, from the public and the legislature.[76] The engineering of autonomy—or the process of statebuilding—therefore, is undertaken by the state itself as an autonomy-seeking entity, but it is unlikely to succeed if it meets powerful popular opposition.[77] Once autonomy has been generated, however, to the extent that it has been insulated, the executive can act even when opposed. In the realm of allocational politics (e.g., questions of taxation, income redistribution, and industrial planning), which directly affects a broad range of public interests that have a clear stake in the policy process, we can expect that resistance to autonomy engineering should be high.[78] This expectation is compounded by the fact that allocational politics are not perceived as critically important for the survival of the state, so societal actors are less likely to fear that opposing state policy could bring about the state's demise. National security policy, however, does not affect public interests as directly and not all perceive a personal stake in policy outcomes.[79]

76. Callaghy calls this process "engineering." If states are unable to insulate themselves completely from social forces, however, they must engage in "buffering," which amounts to bargaining and compromising policy for the sake of consensus. Callaghy, "Political Passions and Economic Interests."

77. It is for this reason that many argue that states can act decisively and build their power in moments of crisis, such as after a war or during economic disarray, when opposition is weakest. See, for example, Fred Block, "The Ruling Class Does Not Rule," in Thomas Ferguson and Joel Rogers, eds., *The Political Economy* (Armonk, N.Y.: M. E. Sharpe, 1984), 32–46; Theda Skocpol, "Political Response to Capitalist Crisis: Neo-Marxist Theories of the State and the Case of the New Deal," *Politics and Society* 10, no. 2 (1980): 155–201; and Michael N. Barnett, *Confronting the Costs of War* (Princeton: Princeton University Press, 1992).

78. Theodore J. Lowi, for example, links the scope of societal actors that particular policy issues affect to the manner in which they are resolved. See "American Business, Public Policy, Case Studies, and Political Theory," *World Politics* 16, no. 4 (July 1964): 676–716; and "Four Systems of Policy, Politics, and Choice," *Public Administration Review* 32, no. 4 (July/August 1972): 298–310.

79. For similar perspectives, see Milbrath, "Interest Groups and Foreign Policy"; and Cohen, "The Influence of Special-Interest Groups."

Moreover, due to the great importance attributed to security policy for the survival of the state and the need for the thoughtful construction of policy by experts, we would expect less opposition to the insulation of the national security apparatus. The individual costs of military service or higher taxes to support defense spending pale in comparison to the prospect of foreign domination. Finally, in an anarchic international environment where the security of the state may depend on rational policy formation, the state itself has a heightened interest in seeking foreign policy autonomy.[80] To the extent that it can be insulated, the national security apparatus will subsequently be able to resist public opposition.

Since the national security executives of democratic states vary in the level of structural autonomy they enjoy, it is unwise for traditional theorists to assume that all democratic foreign policy executives are similarly constrained. It is likewise implausible that foreign policy executives with such a wide array of different domestic structures should behave in a uniform manner when faced with international imperatives, as neorealists assume. Instead, we can predict more about a democracy's foreign security policy choices by studying its domestic decision-making environment and its relative autonomy. These structural features, though, are not the only source of variations in the domestic impact on policy across democracies. As we shall see in the next section, leaders of weak democratic states can escape some of their structural constraints by pursuing independence-enhancing leadership strategies.

Foreign Policy Independence:
Leadership Strategies and the Politics of Deception

While domestic structures account for most of the variance in the domestic impact on foreign security policy across democratic states, it stands to reason that the strategies that actors pursue within those structures can also influence policy independence. In particular, the unique dynamics of international negotiations provide opportunities for leaders of weak democratic states to escape their domestic structural constraints with independence-enhancing leadership strategies.

---

80. It is for these reasons that early liberals such as Rousseau and Locke felt that foreign policy should be entrusted to public officials. See pages 30–31. In this regard, it is telling that the drafters of the American constitution did not place foreign affairs fully under the purview of the legislature, despite their fear of the abuse of executive power. See the discussions in Alexander Hamilton, James Madison, and John Jay, *The Federalist Papers,* Clinton Rossiter, ed. (New York: Mentor Books, 1961), esp. nos. 22–26, 64, and 75.

Robert Putnam has observed that international negotiations are complex two-level games in which national leaders seek to satisfy both domestic and international political imperatives. Progress on the two game boards is interdependent, since concessions made to domestic opinion may impede a leader's ability to compromise with other states, while international concessions can ignite domestic opposition, thereby damaging the prospects for ratification. In the meantime, the demands of both groups might be inimical to the objectives that national leaders themselves wish to pursue.[81] This dilemma is most acute for leaders of weak democratic states, who possess little structural autonomy to pursue policies independently of domestic pressures. Because of the interdependence of the two boards, however, a skillful democratic politician can manipulate and even exaggerate constraints on one board in order to free herself from constraints on the other. Moreover, due to the secret nature of many international negotiations—particularly those pertaining to security matters—even relatively constrained foreign policy executives can circumvent public and parliamentary opposition with three complementary strategies: *hiding, misleading,* and *blaming.*[82]

Hiding refers to taking advantage of the secrecy of particular negotiations to keep the public and parliament in the dark about the true aims the government actually pursues. Since there is no independent source of information for *in camera* proceedings, domestic groups must rely on the reports of national leaders in order to hold them accountable.[83] In fact, the opportunity to hide from domestic scrutiny may entice less autonomous executives to request secret meetings from their bargaining partners and to delay the publication of agreements in order to give themselves maximum flexibility when conducting diplomacy. Secrecy also allows the foreign policy executive to mislead the public and parliament about: (1) the objectives it pursues, in order to grant it more negotiating freedom, and (2) the nature

81. Putnam, "Diplomacy and Domestic Politics"; Andrew Moravcsik, "Introduction: Integrating International and Domestic Theories of International Bargaining," in Peter B. Evans, Harold K. Jacobson, and Robert D. Putnam, eds., *Double-Edged Diplomacy* (Berkeley and Los Angeles: University of California Press, 1993), 3–42.

82. Helen V. Milner similarly concludes that leaders can manipulate asymmetric information to improve the prospects for ratifying an unpopular agreement. *Interests, Institutions, and Information,* 22. See also Andrew Moravcsik, "Why the European Community Strengthens the State: International Cooperation and Domestic Politics," Center for European Studies Working Paper Series, no. 52 (Cambridge: Harvard University, 1994).

83. It would be difficult to hold the government accountable based on reports from other governments, since these reports could always be denied in the absence of a definitive record of the proceedings.

of the agreements it reaches, in order to secure domestic approval after the fact. Finally, secret negotiations of this type afford democratic leaders the opportunity to blame their negotiating partners for outcomes that diverge from national aspirations. Blaming other governments can help secure ratification of unpopular agreements by presenting the outcome as "the best deal we could get," even if it truly was not. With these tactics — which I will refer to collectively as *the politics of deception* — national leaders can follow their own goals, yet claim: "we tried to do what the public and Parliament wanted us to do, but were forced to concede because the other states involved would not accept our proposals."[84]

Since democratic leaders may suffer political costs when they employ deceptive strategies, and since deception may be repugnant to some leaders, not all leaders will take advantage of these tactics to enhance their policy independence.[85] Those who do are unlikely to do so all the time. Nevertheless, leaders of structurally constrained democratic states who are willing to resort to the politics of deception will be able to act with greater policy independence from domestic opinion than their domestic decision-making environments would ordinarily lead us to expect. Leadership strategies are, therefore, an additional source of variance in the domestic impact on foreign security policy across democratic states and within the same state at different times.

Conclusion: Structural Autonomy and Foreign Security Policy Analysis

In this chapter, I demonstrated that the conventional wisdom that democratic foreign policymakers are all comparably constrained by domestic opinion is flawed. It incorrectly assumes that differences between democracies will have little effect on policymaking. In fact, different domestic political contexts can have profound effects on the autonomy foreign policymakers

---

84. This logic underlies the argument that a democratic deficit exists within the European Union because national leaders are freed from domestic constraints when they reach decisions in closed-door European summit sessions. See James A. Caporaso, *The European Union: Dilemmas of Regional Integration* (Boulder, Colo.: Westview Press, 2000), 48–58; Brigitte Boyce, "The Democratic Deficit of the European Community," *Parliamentary Affairs* 46 (October 1993): 458–77; and J. H. H. Weiler, Ulrich R. Haltern, and Franz C. Mayer, "European Democracy and Its Critique," *West European Politics* 18 (July 1995): 4–39.

85. For a discussion of the political costs of deception, see Norrin M. Ripsman, "The Politics of Deception: Weak Democratic Governments, Domestic Opposition, and Foreign Security Policy" (Unpublished ms: Concordia University, 2002).

have from the public and the legislature. To correct this error, I have advanced a model of the domestic decision-making environments of democratic states that explains variations in the impact of domestic opinion across democracies and within the same democracy over time. I argue that this variation is caused by the different levels of structural autonomy afforded by the institutional structures, decision-making procedures, and procedural norms of each state. Moreover, I identify which institutions, procedures, and norms are more likely to affect structural autonomy and how they do so. I argue that this model yields a richer understanding of the foreign security policy processes of democratic states than either the traditional realist/liberal consensus that democracies are all comparably constrained by domestic opinion or the neorealist assumption that all democratic national security executives are fundamentally autonomous.

In essence, I argue that structural autonomy is a better indicator of foreign security policy independence from domestic opinion than is regime type. Furthermore, I argue that we should expect further variance in the policy independence of structurally constrained, nonautonomous democracies, depending on the willingness of the foreign policy leadership to engage in the politics of deception. Leaders that are willing to manipulate the shroud of secrecy that cloaks international negotiations will be able to escape some of their domestic constraints and, therefore, achieve more independence than we would expect from a structurally constrained democracy.

The concept of autonomy, of course, is not new. Peter Katzenstein and others have employed it as a conceptual tool in explaining the foreign economic policies of advanced economies.[86] Stephen Krasner and others have examined the impact of state autonomy on national strategic raw materials policies.[87] Surprisingly, though, state autonomy has been almost completely ignored in studies of high politics. In the 1990s, analysis of institutional structures began to creep into the broader foreign security policy literature, as scholars began to realize that state structures affect the policy process.[88]

---

86. See, for example, the contributions to Katzenstein, *Power and Plenty.*

87. Stephen Krasner, *Defending the National Interest* (Princeton: Princeton University Press, 1978); Ikenberry, *Reasons of State.*

88. Risse-Kappen, "Public Opinion, Domestic Structure, and Foreign Policy in Liberal Democracies"; Friedberg, "Garrison State"; Matthew Evangelista, "The Paradox of State Strength: Transnational Relations, Domestic Structures, and Security Policy in Russia and The Soviet Union," *International Organization* 49, no.1 (winter 1995): 1–38; Barnett, *Confronting the Costs of War;* Barry Buzan, "Peoples, States, and Fear: The National Security Problem in the Third World," in E. Azar and C. Moon eds., *National Security in the Third World* (Hants: Edward Elger, 1988), 14–43; Benjamin Miller, *When Opponents Cooperate* (Ann Arbor: University of Michigan Press, 1995), chap. 4.

Very recently, some theorists have even criticized the democratic peace theory for failing to distinguish between presidential and parliamentary democracies.[89] Nonetheless, researchers have neglected to account systematically for the normative and procedural bases of autonomy and to address its other important institutional determinants. Consequently, these recent studies have oversimplified the domestic decision-making environment at the expense of accuracy.

To test the model presented in this chapter against the traditional and neorealist alternatives, the balance of this book will analyze empirically how structural autonomy and leadership strategies can explain differences in the nature and content of the peacemaking policies that the British, French, and American governments pursued toward Germany after both world wars. I shall test whether the more autonomous democracies actually demonstrate greater policy independence from domestic pressures and whether the less autonomous states more easily translate domestic constraints into international gains. Furthermore, I will investigate whether the willingness of their executives to engage in the politics of deception accounts for differences in the policy independence of structurally constrained democratic states. Before conducting the decision-making case studies, though, we shall need *a priori* judgments of the structural autonomy of the democracies under investigation. Therefore, the next chapter will build upon the discussion in this chapter to operationalize the independent variable of structural autonomy and assess the relative autonomy of foreign policymakers in the United States, Great Britain, and France following each of the two world wars.

---

89. Peterson, "How Democracies Differ"; Peterson, *Crisis Bargaining and the State;* Miriam Fendius Elman, "Testing the Democratic Peace Theory," in Miriam Fendius Elman, ed., *Paths to Peace* (Boston: CSIA, 1997), 473–506; Miriam Fendius Elman, "Unpacking Democracy: Presidentialism, Parliamentarism, and Theories of Democratic Peace," *Security Studies* 9, no. 4 (summer 2000): 91–126.

2

The Domestic Decision-Making Environments of Great Britain, France, and the United States After Two World Wars

In order to test the hypothesis advanced in Chapter 1 that the impact of domestic opinion on democratic foreign policy depends on the level of structural autonomy granted by the domestic decision-making environments of particular states, the balance of this book studies the policy processes of Great Britain, France, and the United States as they negotiated peace with Germany after both world wars. Before we can study the impact of executive autonomy on policy, however, we must make *a priori* assessments of the relative structural autonomy of the states under investigation. The purpose of this chapter, therefore, is to determine the degree of autonomy afforded by the domestic decision-making environments of the three democracies at both time periods under investigation.

In each case, I evaluate the formal division of powers

between the executive and legislative branches of government, particularly as they relate to foreign affairs, as well as the informal procedures and norms that impact on executive authority, in order to answer a uniformly applied set of guiding questions. Based on the discussion in Chapter 1, I have selected the following questions to enable me to build a composite picture of the various determinants of autonomy in each state's domestic decision-making environment.[1] Does the constitution favor the executive or the legislative branch in foreign affairs? Do prevailing executive practices in foreign affairs facilitate executive independence? Do prevailing legislative practices in foreign affairs facilitate executive independence? Do prevailing legislative norms in foreign affairs facilitate executive independence? In addition, when considering parliamentary systems, I address two supplemental questions. Is the government a one-party majority government? Does the government command a strong majority of support in the legislature? Finally, for presidential systems, I consider whether the same party controls both the executive and the legislature. The answers to these questions are presented in table form after the richer contextual analyses of the three states' domestic decision-making environments during both periods.

Great Britain

1918–1919

In the absence of a formal constitution, the British political system is governed by various parliamentary laws and constitutional conventions. The frequency of parliamentary elections, the legislative power of the House of Lords, civil liberties, and various other matters are all regulated by written laws. Nonetheless, these laws may be altered or repealed by Parliament

1. These questions are guiding questions, intended to ensure that we have examined all aspects of the state's domestic decision-making environment that are relevant to the conduct of foreign security policy. I have deliberately resisted the temptation to impose an artificial aggregation scheme to classify executives on the basis of these questions, since that could corrupt the qualitative and contextual judgments that follow. Significantly, as we shall see, in the case of Great Britain in 1919, I judge the executive to be weak because of Lloyd George's precarious position as a junior partner within his governing coalition, despite institutional and procedural arrangements that would otherwise have augured well for executive autonomy. Similarly, I have judged the post–World War II American executive to be highly autonomous primarily because of prevailing procedural norms in that period. Thus, it would be unwise to specify *a priori* which specific contextual factors will count most in determining any particular executive's degree of autonomy, as would be necessary for an aggregation scheme.

at any time. Many other central aspects of British politics, such as the functions and operation of the cabinet and the diminished power of the monarch, are not provided for or regulated by law. Instead, they are governed by long-standing conventions of the constitution, which have the force of law.[2]

Technically, British sovereignty resides in the Crown. The king opened and dissolved Parliament, commanded the armed forces, declared war, concluded peace, and possessed a veto power over all bills. Tradition, however, has transferred monarchical power to the cabinet, which is responsible to Parliament. Ostensibly acting as advisors to the Crown, cabinet ministers actually make the decisions and issue orders in the name of the monarch. The diminished capacity of the Crown is so firmly entrenched that it would be regarded as unconstitutional for the monarch to wield the political powers technically at her disposal. With monarchical authority existing in name only, true political power resides in the Parliament, a bicameral legislature consisting of the popularly elected House of Commons and the House of Lords, whose members either inherit their titles or are appointed by the monarch on the advice of the cabinet. In the twentieth century, the House of Lords became largely devoid of power, leaving the Commons as the predominant parliamentary body. Executive power is exercised by the prime minister—typically the leader of the party with the most seats in the House of Commons—and the ministers he appoints to the cabinet. Since convention dictates that the cabinet must resign if it does not command the confidence of the Commons, ministers are usually chosen from the majority party, except in rare instances when no party controls a majority of seats or when political crises require a coalition government in order to preserve national unity.[3] The cabinet, referred to as His/Her Majesty's Government (HMG), takes the initiative in proposing legislation for the Commons to debate and approve.

By long-standing convention, the conduct of foreign affairs is a royal prerogative, exercised by the monarch and his or her ministers of the cabinet.[4]

2. See, for example, John Dearlove and Peter Saunders, *Introduction to British Politics: Analysing a Capitalist Democracy,* 2nd ed. (Cambridge: Polity Press, 1991), chap. 1; Bill Jones and Dennis Kavanagh, *British Politics Today,* 6th ed. (Manchester: Manchester University Press, 1998), 56–64.

3. Winston Churchill, for example, invited prominent Labour leaders into his war cabinet during World War II, despite the fact that his Conservative party possessed a majority of seats in the House of Commons.

4. In fact, the cabinet was initially known as "the committee for foreign affairs." Charles

As a result, the British foreign policy process, more than any other policy area, has traditionally been dominated by the executive. The prime minister and foreign secretary play the leading roles in policy formation and direction of the Foreign Office (FO) administration. The prime minister lays out general programmatic guidelines for all ministers and, at least potentially, has final say on all policy matters. Moreover, he must have a sufficient command of British foreign policy to guide him through the international conferences, ambassadorial meetings, and meetings with heads of state that he must attend.[5] The specific degree of control he has over the direction of foreign policy within the cabinet depends primarily on his personality and his relationship with his foreign secretary. Since prime ministers have the sole authority to appoint and dismiss cabinet ministers, if they wish to retain an active hand in foreign affairs they can appoint foreign secretaries who either agree with them on general policy guidelines or who will, due to their personality, defer to the prime minister in matters of importance. Conversely, prime ministers who choose to be less directly involved in foreign policy may select senior parliamentarians experienced in foreign affairs and allow them considerable independence in policy construction.[6]

The foreign secretary enjoys one of the most prestigious portfolios in the cabinet, second only to the Chancellor of the Exchequer in importance. The position itself commands respect, and the individuals who have been selected to fill it—be they Sir Edward Grey, Lord Balfour, Anthony Eden, or Ernest Bevin—were typically held in high esteem due to their own experience and accomplishments. As a result of this prestige, foreign secretaries who were granted a free hand by the prime minister were typically also given substantial leeway by their cabinet colleagues, Parliament, and the nation. The foreign secretary's power was enhanced by his placement at the helm of the Foreign Office bureaucracy and diplomatic corps. The Foreign Office reported to the cabinet through the foreign secretary, placing him in a uniquely advantageous position. His monopoly on expert knowledge insulated him further from his cabinet colleagues, if not the prime minister, on foreign policy matters. Certainly, other cabinet ministers, most notably

---

Carstairs and Richard Ware, "Introduction," in Charles Carstairs and Richard Ware, eds., *Parliament and International Relations* (Buckingham, England: Open University Press, 1991), 3.

5. David Vital, *The Making of British Foreign Policy* (London: George Allen & Unwin, 1968), 54.

6. Michael Clarke, "The Policy-Making Process," in Michael Smith, Steve Smith, and Brian White, eds., *British Foreign Policy: Tradition, Change and Transformation* (London: Unwin Hyman, 1988), 73–76.

the chancellor, the minister of defence, and the colonial secretary, were frequently involved in the foreign policy process, but they did not normally approach the foreign secretary's influence.

While the cabinet is central to the conduct of international affairs, Parliament plays a comparatively minor role. To be sure, the House of Commons does involve itself in foreign affairs in several ways. First, at least one parliamentary debate per parliamentary session is devoted to foreign policy. Other debates may follow statements by the foreign or defence secretaries. Second, question time in the House of Commons addresses matters of foreign policy on the third Wednesday of each month. Third, members can pass motions that indicate the state of opinion in Parliament. Fourth, parliamentary committees in the Houses of Commons and Lords deliberate on foreign affairs. Finally, Parliament retains the power of the purse and can refuse to fund overseas activities of which it disapproves.

Nevertheless, three important considerations—two structural and one normative—prevent Parliament from using these mechanisms to achieve a major role in foreign policymaking. First, since the British system is adversarial in nature, Parliament is rigidly divided into Government and Opposition. The role of the Government, which of necessity commands a majority of seats, is to support the policies of the prime minister and the cabinet; the role of the loyal Opposition is to oppose. These roles are amplified by the tradition of party discipline, enforced by the party Whips, which ensures that the first duty of M.P.s is to their party rather than to their constituents or themselves. Consequently, debates tend to be routine and ritualistic, reflecting the current state of Government-Opposition relations, rather than earnest expressions of popular concerns; question time is frequently used by the Opposition as an opportunity to embarrass the Government; and parliamentary committees, with a majority of members from the Government side of the bench, are unwilling or unable to generate serious criticism of Government policy.

The second structural impediment to a strong parliamentary voice in foreign affairs is the cabinet's ability to keep vital information confidential. Since the cabinet and the various cabinet committees meet privately and since the Whitehall administrative staffs are responsible to the cabinet, rather than to the legislature, Parliament is dependent on the cabinet for most of the information on foreign policy it receives. As a result, parliamentary input lacks power at the stage of policy formation, since it is frequently unaware of both the minutiae of the political and military matters that occupy the Government's attention, as well as the options under consideration by the cabinet. Often matters are not brought before Parliament's and the public's attention at the early stages of policy construction except by way of Government leaks and the foreign press. Thus, Parliament is more commonly relegated to the less important position of criticizing policymakers after the fact, or debating the implementation of policies already chosen.

The role of Parliament in foreign affairs is further constricted by the prevailing norm that foreign policy ought to be left to the cabinet. As one observer has commented, "(m)ore than any other policy area, foreign policy is identified as that which must be conducted by the executive; it is concerned with the exercise of sovereignty in relations with the outside world."[7] Although M.P.s still try to involve themselves in foreign relations, and although they can still censure the Government for foreign policies they oppose on moral or political grounds, they typically allow the prime minister and the cabinet substantially more leeway than in domestic matters.

Despite these enduring institutional features that should have augured well for executive independence over foreign security policy, there were particular circumstances in the aftermath of World War I that considerably reduced the executive's scope of autonomy. Most important, Prime Minister David Lloyd George's Government was a coalition comprised of his faction of the divided Liberal party together with the Conservatives and a small Labour faction. Coalition governments are typically weaker than one-party cabinets, and they tend to be more dependent upon the legislature. Significantly, the prime minister and his loyal Liberal party supporters were by far the weaker partner in the coalition, with only 133 seats out of the parliamentary total of 707. His Unionist allies, led by Andrew Bonar Law, held 335 seats and together with the noncoalition Conservatives, in fact, could command a majority on their own without Lloyd George if his policies were to diverge sharply from their own.[8] Indeed, Bonar Law did precisely that in October 1922, abandoning Lloyd George and forming a Government on his own.

In addition, the popular mood in Britain—as in the rest of the democratic world—viewed diplomats with considerable distaste. It was popularly believed that the secret diplomacy of the past was responsible for war in 1914 and could be avoided only if elected political leaders conducted

---

7. Ibid., 72.
8. British election results for this chapter were obtained from David Butler and Jennie Freeman, *British Political Facts* (London: MacMillan & Co. Ltd., 1969).

international negotiations in full view of the public.[9] This atmosphere meshed well with Lloyd George's own inclination to exert personal control over diplomacy. Consequently, in his Government, the Foreign Office and, indeed, the foreign secretary were increasingly isolated from the centers of power. During the war and negotiations to conclude it, the prime minister concentrated foreign security policy decision making in a war cabinet. Lord Balfour, the foreign secretary, was not granted membership in this body, although he was allowed to attend whenever he wished. From 1916 through 1919, the secretariat of this war cabinet, under the direction of Sir Maurice Hankey, allowed the prime minister to "conduct foreign policy without the inconvenience of Foreign Office intervention."[10] At the Paris Peace Conference, Lloyd George preferred to settle matters himself in private discussions with foreign leaders and allowed his own private aides to usurp the role of professional diplomats.

It would overstate the point to assert that Foreign Office isolation kept policy in the hands of democratically elected officials rather than a bureaucracy that was insulated from public and legislative scrutiny. In fact, by involving the war office, the Admiralty, the war cabinet secretariat, and his own private aides in policymaking and negotiations, Lloyd George, to some extent, supplanted one group of insulated officials with another. Nonetheless, keeping foreign security policy in the hands of a weak parliamentary leader such as Lloyd George—who was only too aware of his dependence on the support of the Unionist back bench—did ensure Parliament an almost unprecedented influence over foreign affairs.

Based on the above information, we can distill the picture of the British domestic decision-making environment summarized in the following list of determinant questions and answers. Clearly, the constitution favors the executive in foreign affairs, as did prevailing legislative norms and procedures.

9. Gordon A. Craig, "The British Foreign Office from Grey to Austen Chamberlain," in Gordon A. Craig and Felix Gilbert, *The Diplomats, 1919–1939* (Princeton: Princeton University Press, 1965), 22–25; Zara Steiner, *The Foreign Office and Foreign Policy, 1898–1914* (Cambridge: Cambridge University Press, 1969), 164–71. Even before the war, professional diplomats and secret diplomacy were seen as a cause of war. An editorial in *The Times*, November 26, 1912, seeking to determine who makes war, charged, "The answer is to be found in the Chancelleries of Europe, among the men who have too long played with human lives as pawns in a game of chess, who have become so enmeshed in formulas and the jargon of diplomacy that they have ceased to be conscious of the poignant realities with which they trifle. And thus will war continue to be made, until the great masses who are the sport of professional schemers and dreamers say the word." Quoted in Paul Gordon Lauren, *Bureaucrats and Diplomats* (Stanford: Hoover Institution Press, 1976), 47.

10. Craig, "The British Foreign Office," 18.

By virtue of his weak position within the coalition Government, though, Lloyd George's cabinet was poorly positioned to take advantage of these institutional and procedural blessings. Hence, numbers 5 and 6 indicate that the coalition commanded a considerable majority in the legislature, but that the prime minister himself could not count on that support if he did not tow the Unionist line.

The Determinants of Executive Autonomy in Great Britain After World War I

1. Does constitution favor executive or legislature in foreign affairs?

    Executive

2. Do prevailing executive practices in foreign affairs facilitate executive independence?   Yes

3. Do prevailing legislative practices in foreign affairs facilitate executive independence?   Yes

4. Do prevailing legislative norms in foreign affairs facilitate executive independence?   Yes

5. Is the government a one-party majority government?   No

6. Does the government command a strong majority of support in the legislature?   Qualified Yes

1945–1954

The institutional structure of the British Government underwent only limited change between the two wars. Under pressure from democratic forces, particularly in the Labour and Liberal parties, cabinet practices were altered so as to require greater consultation with Parliament in foreign affairs. This movement culminated in the Ponsonby rule of 1924, formalizing Parliament's right to review treaties at least twenty-one days prior to ratification.[11] The effect of the new rule was to make Parliament and the public more aware of the Government's foreign policy; it did not, however, pose a significant challenge to executive supremacy in external affairs, since the executive still negotiated treaties independently and typically commanded the support of the majority party in the Commons.

What did have a marked effect on the conduct of foreign relations during this period, though, was the Government's composition. Unlike in 1919,

11. Peter G. Richards, *Parliament and Foreign Affairs* (London: George Allen & Unwin, 1967), 29; and Richard Ware, "Parliament and Treaties," in Carstairs and Ware, *Parliament and International Relations* (Buckingham, England: Open University Press, 1991), 38–39.

from 1945 to 1954 one-party majority governments were formed. They consequently enjoyed considerably more autonomy than Lloyd George's unstable coalition of 1919. There were, however, two phases of majority government following the postwar elections of July 1945 that replaced Winston Churchill's coalition war cabinet: the phase of substantial majority Government and the phase of bare majority Government. The Labour Government, which held power from July 1945 to the February 1950 election, was a strong majority Government. Out of 640 possible seats, the Labour party won a commanding 392 to the Conservatives' 210. It therefore possessed a clear and powerful mandate to govern and could make controversial policy choices without the fear of losing a vote of confidence in the Commons.

The two Governments that succeeded it, however, were more vulnerable. In February 1950, Clement Attlee was reelected prime minister by the barest of majorities; his Labour party won 319 out of 633 seats, yielding an overall majority of only five seats. This placed him in an extremely unenviable position. Unless his political agenda satisfied the leadership of the Opposition, he could not be assured of the necessary parliamentary support to pass it. If any of his aged and ill cabinet members were to become indisposed, if any of his M.P.s were not able to report for votes, or if any Labour members defected, his Government's policies could be defeated in the Commons. Worse still, the Government itself could fall in a vote of confidence if it could not consistently muster a nearly perfect voting turnout. Indeed, the difficulty of governing with such a small majority forced Attlee to call a new election only eighteen months into his mandate.[12] The Conservative Government elected in October 1951 was only marginally stronger, controlling an overall majority of seventeen seats. Prime Minister Churchill did possess a larger margin for error and, consequently, greater freedom of action. Nonetheless, with a slim majority, some accommodation of Labour concerns would have been the surest way to ensure success in Parliament.

The disadvantage of small majority Government may have been somewhat offset by the fact that the leading members of both parties had served together in the wartime coalition. Coalition and common struggle had, in particular, forged a bond between Anthony Eden and Ernest Bevin, the two men who would serve as foreign secretaries for their respective parties

---

12. This decision was taken in light of the government's defeat on several minor votes in the Commons and the loss of three prominent cabinet ministers to death and defection, whittling his majority further. See David E. Butler, *The British General Election of 1951* (London: Macmillan & Co. Ltd., 1952), 12–21.

during the period under study.[13] Because of their mutual respect, Bevin was occasionally able to call upon Eden to forestall Conservative opposition to his foreign policy.[14] Nevertheless, we cannot assume that this relationship significantly mitigated the consequences of reduced majorities. Consequently, we must conclude that the post-1950 British Governments were noticeably—though not tremendously—more constrained than their predecessor.

The list of determinants below summarizes the British domestic decision-making environment after World War II. The only changes from the earlier list are the answers to numbers 5 and 6. From 1945 to 1954, all governments were formed by a single party, although the size of the majority varied. The executive, therefore, possessed greater autonomy to conduct foreign security policy than it did in 1919.

The Determinants of Executive Autonomy in Great Britain After WWII

1. Does constitution favor executive or legislature in foreign affairs?
   Executive
2. Do prevailing executive practices in foreign affairs facilitate executive independence?   Yes
3. Do prevailing legislative practices in foreign affairs facilitate executive independence?   Yes
4. Do prevailing legislative norms in foreign affairs facilitate executive independence?   Yes
5. Is the government a one-party majority government?   Yes
6. Does the government command a strong majority of support in the legislature?   45–50 Yes 50–54 No

France

1918–1919

The Third French Republic was institutionalized and governed by the Constitutional Laws of 1875. These laws provided for a legislature, the National

---

13. Eden wrote in his memoirs of his respect for Bevin, concluding: "The period 1945–50 in British foreign policy was dominated by his personality, and it was fortunate for our country and for Europe that this was so." *Full Circle: The Memoirs of Sir Anthony Eden* (London: Cassell, 1960), 5.

14. Allan Bullock, *Ernest Bevin: Foreign Secretary, 1945–1951* (London: Heinemann, 1983), 98.

Assembly, comprised of an upper house (the Senate) and a lower house (the Chamber of Deputies). Although the two houses were theoretically equal, the Chamber was in fact considerably more powerful, since the executive was directly responsible to it. The constitution formally granted formidable executive powers to the president, who was elected by both houses at a special sitting. In practice, however, his power was largely artificial, as he was required to secure ministerial countersignatures on all his acts.[15] Consequently, all executive power resided in the ministry, a body made up of cabinet ministers nominally appointed by the president and headed by a premier. The ministry was drawn primarily from the Deputies, was responsible to the Chamber and could govern only if it enjoyed the confidence of that house. If it was defeated in a vote of confidence in the Chamber, it was obliged to resign collectively. Frederick Schuman observed, therefore, "Parliament is thus the maker and breaker of ministries, the source of all executive authority, and the axis about which the whole governmental machinery of the Third Republic revolves."[16]

Within the legislature, politics were chaotic and unstable, due to the multiplicity of bitterly divided, poorly organized, and virtually undisciplined political parties, spanning the political spectrum from ultra-conservative Royalists to Communist Internationalists.[17] Since no political party or grouping of parties possessed anywhere close to a majority of seats, fragile multiparty coalition governments were the rule. The instability of these governments was compounded by the astounding lack of unity—and frequently leadership—within parties, the large number of contentious political issues that divided French society, and the absence of a strong president to unite a fractious ministry. As a result, ministries lasted, on average, no more than about ten months.

In the realm of foreign relations, the constitution gave the president sole power over treaty negotiation and ratification, provided that he informed both houses as soon as the security of the Republic permitted. For peace treaties and all treaties affecting trade, finance, territory, or the rights of French nationals abroad, however, the consent of both houses was required.[18] The constitution also empowered the president to dispose of the French armed forces and to receive the diplomatic representatives of other

15. Frederick L. Schuman, *War and Diplomacy in the French Republic* (New York: AMS Press, 1970), 12.
16. Ibid., 14.
17. Raymond L. Buell, *Contemporary French Politics* (New York: Appleton, 1920), 48–78.
18. Loi Constitutionelle du 16 juillet 1875 sur les rapports des pouvoirs publics, Article 8.

states, but he could not declare war without the assent of both Chambers.[19] Although these provisions theoretically made the president the dominant actor in foreign affairs, his influence was actually marginal and, with few notable exceptions, decreased steadily since 1877.[20] The real initiative in French foreign policy came from the ministry. Decisions in coalition ministries were taken by consensus and were presented to the National Assembly with an effort to preserve the appearance of unanimity whenever possible. Typically, the foreign minister—who frequently retained his position in multiple coalitions—was given wide latitude by his colleagues except "when his policies demand[ed] the immediate expenditure of large sums of money or [led] to a diplomatic 'crisis'."[21]

The parliamentary role in foreign affairs was, thus, extremely limited, at least initially. Short of defeating the Government on a measure of confidence—which was far more common over domestic matters—deputies had several ways to involve themselves in the process, but each was of only limited utility.[22] The first was the interpellation, a device that allowed deputies to put questions before ministers and initiate a general debate on the replies before a vote of confidence was held.[23] Since the parties that formed the ministry determined which questions were to be answered and since the foreign minister could refuse to answer "dans l'intérêt du pays," this device was not a very effective instrument for parliamentary review of foreign policy. Nor were the ordinary oral and written questions more successful at getting around the Government's right to keep the Chamber in the dark on matters affecting national security.[24] The Chamber, which controlled spending, could also review the administration of the Quai d'Orsay in its review of the annual budget, but that rarely allowed it to get involved in the formulation of policy rather than merely debating its implementation.

19. Ibid., Article 9; and Loi Constitutionelle du 25 février 1875 relative à l'organization des pouvoirs publics, Article 3.

20. Mark B. Hayne, "The Quai D'Orsay and the Formation of French Foreign Policy in Historical Context," in Robert Aldrich and John Connell, eds., *France in World Politics* (London: Routledge, 1989), 194–95; and Henry Leyret, *Le Président de la République* (Paris: A. Cohn, 1973), 31–42, 109–22.

21. Schuman, *War and Diplomacy*, 20–21.

22. See John Eldred Howard, *Parliament and Foreign Policy in France* (London: Cresset, 1948), 61–68.

23. Pierre de Saint-Mart, *Etude historique et critique sur les interpellations en France* (Paris: Societé de Recueil Sirey, 1912).

24. Schuman, *War and Diplomacy*, 24–25.

As the Third Republic matured, though, the National Assembly developed an important institution to assist its review of the Government's international agenda. The permanent parliamentary committee on foreign affairs (*Commission des Affaires Extérieures, des Protectorats et des Colonies*), established in the Chamber in June 1914 and in the Senate in February 1915, was endowed with the authority to prepare reports on treaties, establish permanent contact with the diplomatic corps at the Quai d'Orsay, submit questionnaires to the foreign minister and his staff, and require their presence for interrogations.[25] Its efforts were frequently stymied by tight-lipped ministers and bureaucrats, but it did represent the beginning of a shift in foreign relations power from the cabinet to Parliament, and its influence increased steadily throughout the Third Republic and into the Fourth.[26]

For our purposes, it is important to note that the authority of the committee—and, indeed, of the Chamber itself—was significantly broader over matters relating to treaties of peace. The bulk of the committee's work was devoted to the scrutiny of international treaties.[27] And, as already mentioned, the constitutional laws required the president to secure the approval of both houses of the National Assembly for peace treaties. In effect, this provision made it necessary for the ministry to be more forthcoming to the legislature and its committees regarding treaty negotiations and provisions, and to accommodate legislator concerns. Consequently, we can conclude that the structural autonomy of French foreign policymakers varied across policy areas; they were considerably autonomous in most areas, but were constrained in the making of peace treaties.

The Determinants of Executive Autonomy in France After WWI

1. Does constitution favor executive or legislature in foreign affairs?

   Executive

2. Do prevailing executive practices in foreign affairs facilitate executive independence?   Yes

3. Do prevailing legislative practices in foreign affairs facilitate executive independence?   No

4. Do prevailing legislative norms in foreign affairs facilitate executive independence?   No

5. Is the government a one-party majority government?   No

25. Ibid., 25.

26. Edgar S. Furniss, Jr., *Weaknesses in French Foreign Policy-Making* (Princeton: Center for International Studies, Princeton University, 1954), 18.

27. Schuman, *War and Diplomacy*, 384.

6. Does the government command a strong majority of support in the
   legislature?   Qualified Yes

This list of determinants characterizes the executive's restricted power
over peace treaties (as opposed to foreign affairs in general where it was
more autonomous). Although the president (read the ministry) was empowered by the constitution to negotiate and conclude such treaties,
the requirement that the executive win the Assembly's support ultimately
weakened the ministry's authority in this area. And although the Government, by virtue of the parties included in the coalition, was comprised of a
significant majority of the electorate, the fragility of these large coalitions as
well as the lack of party coherence and unity frequently served to undermine
this support. Consequently, answer 6 is designated "qualified yes."

1945–1954

The French constitution of October 1946, which established the Fourth
Republic, fundamentally altered the French government's structure.[28] It further curtailed the president's power—reducing him to a figurehead—and
expanded the role of the lower parliamentary house at the expense of the
cabinet. These changes had the disastrous consequences of undermining
what little governmental efficacy and stability the French Republic possessed. They also eliminated the small measure of foreign security policy
autonomy the executive had possessed under the Third Republic.

Like the 1875 laws, the new constitution provided for a bicameral legislature, consisting of an upper house, the Council of the Republic, and a
lower house, the National Assembly. The bulk of legislative power was
clearly vested in the Assembly, which the premier and his cabinet presided
over. The Council possessed little real power, except that it could veto decisions of the Assembly. Once again, the two houses jointly elected the president, whose main political function was to appoint the premier, subject to
confirmation by the Assembly and his ability to form a government.[29]

---

28. On the constitutional changes and their effect on the stability of the French political
system, see Dorothy Pickles, *French Politics: The First Years of the Fourth Republic* (London:
RIIA, 1953), 43–46.

29. The ability to form a government after confirmation by the Assembly was not a fore-
gone conclusion. In 1949, for example, Jules Moch and René Mayer were consecutively
appointed by the president and confirmed by bare majorities in the Assembly, yet were unable
to secure the participation of enough political parties to command a majority of support in the
Assembly.

The premier, who together with his cabinet comprised the executive of the Fourth Republic, was considerably constrained in the exercise of his power in several ways. To begin with, he was not allowed to appoint cabinet ministers until he secured Assembly approval of his political program, and he was required by a procedure of double investiture to secure the votes of an absolute majority of Assembly delegates both before and after naming his ministers. Thus, he frequently had to make significant domestic and foreign policy compromises to the legislature in order to proceed with the task of government. Furthermore, the multiplicity of political parties in France required the premier to form a coalition with several other parties and invite prominent members of these parties into his cabinet. Consequently, policymaking was frequently a partisan struggle not only in the Assembly, but also within the cabinet.

By far the most powerful political institution in the Fourth Republic was the Assembly. Labeled "omnipotent, divided, and irresponsible" by one contemporary observer, the Assembly could frustrate any cabinet endeavor in both domestic and foreign affairs.[30] The Assembly set its own agenda and, although the legislature was required to listen to the cabinet's request for a particular schedule of priorities, the cabinet lacked the power to impose these priorities. Furthermore, powerful parliamentary committees could reject the government's program, in whole or in part, or delay it in endless polemical debates.

Overcoming the parliamentary committees was, perhaps, the most serious hurdle for the executive.[31] No policy or program could be discussed by the Assembly as a whole until it had been considered by the appropriate committees, which had the authority to reject it outright or make revisions. Membership in these committees, which proportionally represented the distribution of parties in the Assembly, was frequently used either to curry favor with the leaders of one's own party, or to garner national attention. The easiest way to get noticed, of course, was to obstruct. This problem was compounded by the fragility of the government, which meant that legislative obstruction could bring down the government and enhance the power of prominent committee members in the next government. Criticizing and derailing the premier's program was thus the preferred way for politicians to achieve national recognition, to rise in their party organizations, and to bring about governments in which they could play a greater part.

---

30. Furniss, *Weaknesses in French Foreign Policy-Making*, 4.
31. Edgar S. Furniss, Jr., *France, Troubled Ally* (New York: Harper & Row, 1960), 242.

This chaotic institutional environment was further complicated by the norm of legislative interference in matters of foreign affairs. Inspired by the belief that foreign security policy was far too important to leave to the cabinet or to the Quai d'Orsay—which had both failed France with disastrous consequences before the war—deputies to the Assembly used their foreign policy powers to the fullest.[32] Hence, the Assembly granted the premier little leeway.

While the premier's power was constrained and his tenure brief, cabinet ministers enjoyed greater staying power, since successive coalitions typically included the same political parties and, consequently, the same senior politicians. This was especially true of the foreign minister. From 1945 through 1954, despite some twenty government changes, there were only four different foreign ministers: Georges Bidault, Léon Blum, Robert Schuman, and Pierre Mendés-France. This contributed some degree of stability to interactions with foreign nations and also allowed the foreign minister to build up his personal influence in the Quai d'Orsay through the strategic distribution of appointments and recruitment after the postwar bureaucratic purges. Moreover, since Bidault and Schuman, both of the Mouvement Républicain Populaire (MRP), together held the office for over nine years, with only a two-month interregnum, their party consistently exerted more influence over foreign policy than any other party. Nonetheless, the foreign minister still had to win the approval of a bitterly divided cabinet and push his program through the Assembly. As a consequence, policy compromise and strategic retreat were frequently the only options available to the foreign minister in an always fragmented and often hostile domestic decision-making environment. For Bidault and Schuman, this became increasingly the case in the early 1950s as the centrist MRP became progressively marginalized within right-wing governing coalitions.[33] Although Mendés-France had the advantage of serving simultaneously as foreign minister and premier, his tenure was brief and his freedom of action was limited by intense public

32. Pickles, *French Politics*; Alfred Grosser, *Affaires Extérieures: La Politique de la France, 1944–1984* (Paris: Flammarion, 1984), 12–14. Significantly, this postwar French norm was exactly the reverse of American and British norms during this period. In both Anglo-Saxon countries, foreign security policy was deemed far too important to allow legislative interference with executive authority. Therefore, the level of autonomy is not merely an indicator of the degree of international threat. Structural, cultural, and normative factors determine how international situations affect executive autonomy in each state, if at all.

33. See Russell B. Capelle, *The MRP and French Foreign Policy* (New York: Frederick A. Praeger, 1963).

and parliamentary scrutiny coupled with a divided cabinet that included both radical Gaullists and moderate MRP ministers.

Despite the relative security of the foreign minister's position within the cabinet, then, he possessed little real autonomy in the construction of foreign policy. The premier, himself, was dependent on both his coalition partners and the Assembly, and the cabinet was typically too divided to overcome the obstruction of the lower house. Hence, at least in the field of foreign affairs, the Fourth Republic's executive was extremely constrained.

We can distill from this analysis the picture of foreign policy authority presented in the following list. Unlike in the Third Republic, the legislature was the dominant actor in foreign affairs. And although the executive (particularly the foreign minister) tried to preserve some autonomy, legislative norms and procedures coupled with fragmentary coalitions shackled the cabinet.

The Determinants of Executive Autonomy in France After WWII

1. Does constitution favor executive or legislature in foreign affairs?
Executive
2. Do prevailing executive practices in foreign affairs facilitate executive independence? Yes
3. Do prevailing legislative practices in foreign affairs facilitate executive independence? No
4. Do prevailing legislative norms in foreign affairs facilitate executive independence? No
5. Is the government a one-party majority government?   No
6. Does the government command a strong majority of support in the legislature? Qualified Yes

United States

1918–1919

In the United States, there is simultaneously the potential for extensive executive autonomy in foreign affairs as well as strong prospects for effective popular and legislative control of foreign policy. On the one hand, the president is granted a four-year mandate to govern and cannot under normal circumstances be impeached or dismissed by the legislature. Unlike in parliamentary democracies, his administration officials—most notably, for our purposes, the secretaries of state and war (after 1947, the secretary of defense)—are not themselves elected politicians; they are appointed by the president and, after initial confirmation by the Senate, cannot personally be removed either by direct election or by the Congress. Nonetheless, several factors combined to restrain presidential authority over foreign affairs. Notwithstanding the facade of the Electoral College, it is fair to say that the president is directly elected by the American people, and he must satisfy them if he wishes to be reelected. Moreover, the split ticket ballot implies that the president and his administration do not necessarily reflect the composition of the Congress and, therefore, cannot be assured of majority support in the legislature. Congress and the White House are frequently controlled by rival parties, a situation which can be problematic, given the constitutional allocation of authority over foreign relations.

Whereas in England the executive is clearly granted a preponderance of institutional control over foreign policy, and in the French Fourth Republic the legislature was the privileged foreign policy institution, the United States constitution explicitly divided power over foreign relations between the president and the Congress. The president is empowered to negotiate treaties with foreign nations with the advice and consent of the Senate, provided that two-thirds of the Senate approves; the president may appoint ambassadors and consular staff, provided a majority of senators concur; the president is commander-in-chief of the armed forces, but Congress has the power to declare war; the president has the power to receive ambassadors, and as a corollary, to recognize foreign governments; Congress has the power of the purse, which affects all troop deployments and foreign programs. This constitutional stalemate amounts to what one prominent commentator has labeled "an invitation to struggle for the privilege of directing American foreign policy."[34] The struggle is ongoing and dynamic. Over time, the balance of foreign policy power between Congress and the president has fluctuated due to a variety of factors, most notably: Supreme Court rulings, procedural norms in the Congress, and the personal style of the president. It would be fruitful to consider each of these factors in turn.

While the national and state legislatures together can change the constitution, the Supreme Court is its ultimate interpreter. The Court has frequently declined to rule on the distribution of foreign relations power between the executive and legislative branches, arguing that it was not its role to settle political questions.[35] Nevertheless, in several landmark cases it

34. Edward S. Corwin, *The President: Office and Powers, 1787–1957* (New York: University Press, 1957), 171.
35. Louis Henkin, *Foreign Affairs and the Constitution* (New York: Norton, 1975), 210–16.

has made a considerable impact on the way foreign policy is conducted in the United States. In *The Prize Cases* (1863), for example, the Court expanded the commander-in-chief power to allow the president to respond to an attack without waiting for a congressional declaration of war, and to determine the degree of force that is necessary.[36] The post–World War I period under study, though, predated several important high court rulings, most notably *United States v. Curtiss-Wright Export Corporation* (1936), which dramatically supported the president's leadership in matters of international concern. At this point, the Court's *juris prudence* did not materially favor one branch over the other.

During this period, procedural norms in Congress relating to foreign policy were tied up with the long-standing American tradition of isolationism. Since the United States achieved its independence from the British Crown, the federal government had consistently and consciously rejected the idea of permanent alliances or overseas commitments.[37] Believing that internationalism would constitute a "betrayal of the Republic and a sacrifice of its institutions,"[38] a substantial portion of the American public and, more significantly, a powerful group of senators believed that it was the duty of Congress to use whatever powers it had at its disposal to keep the president from permanently entangling the United States in politics overseas. The president was thus faced with an activist Congress in matters of international import and confronted with an influential Senate Foreign Relations Committee with a history of flexing its muscles.[39]

Despite congressional activism during this period, Woodrow Wilson— president from 1912 through 1920—sought to retain as much personal control over the direction of foreign policy as he could. He preferred neither to delegate authority to appointed officials nor to involve congressional leaders in international negotiations. Indeed, during the armistice negotiations of 1918, Wilson opted to use the services of his devoted personal representative, Colonel Edward House, rather than those of Secretary of State Robert Lansing, in order to retain personal control. At the Paris Peace Conference, the president insisted upon attending himself as the chief American

36. *The Prize Cases*, 2 Bl. (67 U.S.) 635 (1863).

37. For a brief discussion of the intellectual and historical foundations of isolationism, see Ronald E. Powaski, *Toward an Entangling Alliance: American Isolationism, Internationalism, and Europe, 1901–1950* (New York: Greenwood, 1991), Introduction.

38. Senator Hiram Johnson, quoted in Thomas N. Guinsburg, *The Pursuit of Isolationism in the United States Senate from Versailles to Pearl Harbor* (New York: Garland, 1982), 19.

39. David Lloyd George, *Memoirs of the Peace Conference*, 2 vols. (New York: Howard Fertig, 1972), 92.

representative. Moreover, he declined to appoint any of the influential Republican senators to the U.S. delegation, despite the fact that all treaties required the support of two-thirds of the Senate and that, since the November 1918 congressional elections, the Republicans controlled both the House of Representatives and the Senate. Wilson's efforts to retain firm control over the direction of U.S. foreign policy were, nonetheless, in conflict with the prevailing American juridical and congressional norms during this period. Indeed, the Senate ultimately rejected the treaty that Wilson negotiated in Paris, confirming the president's limited authority over foreign affairs. We must conclude, therefore, that the American executive possessed little structural autonomy in the construction of foreign policy in the period following World War I.

The following list illustrates the American president's lack of structural autonomy. The constitution clearly does not favor either branch in the construction of foreign policy and, while Wilson's own actions could have served to enhance his authority, legislative norms and procedures greatly constrained his power.

The Determinants of Executive Autonomy in the United States After WWI

1. Does constitution favor executive or legislature in foreign affairs?
   Neither
2. Do prevailing executive practices in foreign affairs facilitate executive independence?   Yes
3. Do prevailing legislative practices in foreign affairs facilitate executive independence?   No
4. Do prevailing legislative norms in foreign affairs facilitate executive independence?   No
5. Is the legislature controlled by the same party that controls the executive?
   No

1945–1954

In the time between the Versailles Conference of 1919 and the conclusion of World War II, the American state had undergone a startling transformation in both domestic and foreign affairs. In the domestic sphere, the New Deal—Franklin D. Roosevelt's response to the economic upheaval of the Great Depression—carved out impressive federal powers to regulate the economy and provide for the welfare of its citizens.[40] Due to a variety of normative, juridical, and institutional changes, the executive's authority over foreign relations underwent a transformation that was no less remarkable.

Prior to World War II, reflecting growing public awareness of the importance of foreign policy following the Great Depression, the Supreme Court issued a ruling that dramatically altered the balance of foreign policy power in the president's favor. In *United States v. Curtiss-Wright Export Corporation* (1936), the Court was called upon to decide on the constitutionality of a congressional joint resolution authorizing the president to prohibit the sale of arms to Bolivia and Paraguay, then embroiled in war. Justice Sutherland, writing for the majority, argued that the joint resolution was not even necessary, since the president possessed the authority to act in this manner irrespective of Congress, due to the foreign relations power that passed directly from the British Crown to the United States executive even before the constitution distributed power between the branches. He ruled:

> Not only ... is the federal power over external affairs in origin and essential character different from that over internal affairs, but participation in the exercise of the power is significantly limited. In this vast external realm, with its important, complicated, delicate and manifold problems, the President alone has the power to speak or listen as a representative of the nation.... As Marshall said in his great argument of March 7, 1800, in the House of Representatives, "The President is the sole organ of the nation in its external relations, and its sole representative with foreign nations."[41]

The Court concluded, therefore, that in order to avoid serious embarrassment of the United States internationally, the Congress should grant the president much wider latitude in external relations than in internal matters. Furthermore, it maintained that secrecy on the part of the president and his information-gathering agents was acceptable in foreign affairs and should

---

40. William E. Leuchtenburg, *Franklin D. Roosevelt and the New Deal, 1932–1940* (New York: Harper Colophon, 1963); Theda Skocpol, "Political Response to Capitalist Crisis: Neo-Marxist Theories of the State and the Case of the New Deal," *Politics and Society* 10, no. 2 (1980): 155–201; Kenneth Finegold and Theda Skocpol, *State and Party in America's New Deal* (Madison: University of Wisconsin Press, 1995).

41. *United States v. Curtiss-Wright Export Corporation* (1936), 299 U.S. 304 (1936).

be tolerated by the legislature due to the harmful international consequences that could result if information were to be disclosed prematurely.[42] The normative sea of change reflected in the *Curtiss-Wright* decision helped pave the way for a dramatic postwar expansion of executive authority over national security policy.

Following the war, a change in threat perception by Americans also facilitated the expansion of executive control over external affairs. Throughout the history of the Republic, the security provided by two large oceans separating them from the rest of the Great Powers instilled in Americans a pronounced aloofness or disinterest in international relations. Despite being moved reluctantly to participate in the Great War, a large segment of the population reverted to isolationism once the war was over and the danger met.[43] After World War II, however, changes in the nature of military technology and shifts in the international balance of power irrevocably altered the American worldview. The Japanese attack on Pearl Harbor in December 1941 painfully ushered in a new era for Americans. No longer were they invulnerable from foreign invasion. The advent of aircraft carriers and long-range aircraft significantly downgraded the defensive buffer provided by the two oceans and allowed potential enemies to carry out offensive operations against U.S. soil.[44] Advances in long-distance rocketry—while still not able to traverse the oceans—represented a graver impending threat in the near future, especially if other states were to develop nuclear weapons. The potential damage that a future adversary could wreak upon the United States compelled American decision makers and, indeed, the American public to abandon the cavalier detachment with which they viewed international affairs.[45]

American fears were accentuated by the international balance of power that emerged from World War II. To begin with, aside from the United States, the greatest international power was the Soviet Union. Wedded as it was to Marxist-Leninism, Soviet power represented both an ideological and military challenge to the American leadership. The ideological threat was strong enough, with the growth in popularity of Moscow-directed Communist parties throughout the war-ravaged countries of Europe; the

42. Ibid. The president's right to keep secret information pertaining to external affairs was upheld in *Chicago and Southern Airlines v. Waterman Corp.* 333 U.S. 103 (1948).

43. H. Schuyler Foster, *Activism Replaces Isolationism* (Washington: Foxhall Press, 1983), 19; Guinsburg, *The Pursuit of Isolationism.*

44. Foster, *Activism Replaces Isolationism,* 19–20.

45. See, for example, Bernard Brodie, *Strategy in the Missile Age* (Princeton: Princeton University Press, 1959), esp. 390–409.

military challenge was staggering. Not only did the Soviet Union boast the world's largest army, but it also possessed its own share of captured German scientists and engineers who had participated in Hitler's nuclear program. It would only be a matter of time before the Russian leadership would possess the capability to inflict immense devastation upon the American homeland. The changed American threat perception that resulted required a more active American role in international affairs. After all, with Europe in tatters, the United States could not count on the Europeans to hold Russia in check. The only problem was that if the United States was to act decisively in foreign affairs, the executive needed unfettered authority over foreign security policy. Consequently, the Truman administration with the help of Congress proceeded to construct the foreign policy institutions that comprise what some have termed the "national security state."[46]

The passing of the National Security Act of 1947 marked the institutional turning point in executive authority over foreign affairs, accomplishing three important objectives. First, it created the Central Intelligence Agency (CIA), an organization designed to gather information on the adversary and other nations, which would report directly to the president with only limited congressional oversight.[47] Second, the three independent armed services (the Army, the Navy, and the Air Force) were reorganized within a Joint Chiefs of Staff system and placed under the authority of the secretary of defense. Finally, the Act established the National Security Council (NSC), a foreign policy cabinet to provide policy-relevant information to the president and facilitate coordinated action among the various foreign security policy institutions. On the grounds of national security, NSC deliberations were classified, thereby shielding the executive from congressional and public scrutiny.[48]

46. See Daniel Yergin, *Shattered Peace* (Boston: Houghton Mifflin, 1977); and Marcus G. Raskin, *Essays of a Citizen: From National Security State to Democracy* (Armonk, N.Y.: Sharpe, 1991).

47. The Bureau of the Budget was directed not to report to Congress on CIA activities or expenditures. The director of the Central Intelligence Agency did make periodic reports to the congressional committees and subcommittees on armed services and appropriations, but these were presented in secret executive sessions and not divulged to the rest of Congress. Moreover, the director and his staff supplied the committees with what they deemed to be "adequate information" and frequently withheld extremely sensitive information. Harry Howe Ransom, *Central Intelligence and National Security* (Cambridge: Harvard University Press, 1965), 81, 144–46; and Rhodri Jeffreys-Jones, *The CIA and American Democracy* (New Haven: Yale University Press, 1989), 42.

48. United States National Security Council, *Organizational History of the National Security Council During the Truman and Eisenhower Administrations* (Washington: National Security Council, 1988).

In the new postwar international threat situation, congressional leaders also recognized the executive's need to take decisive and resolute action when necessary. Since domestic political bickering could undermine resolution, they recognized that, within reason, politics must stop "at the water's edge." The resultant norm of nonpartisanship allowed the president a free hand to react internationally as he saw fit, provided he could justify his policies to the leaders of both parties in terms of the Cold War as attempts to contain communism.[49] Under these conditions, even an embattled President Truman and his advisers were able to direct American foreign policy despite facing a Republican Congress in 1947–1948. Although Republicans staged the occasional revolt against Secretary of State Dean Acheson, they were unable to alter the course of the administration's policy.[50] President Eisenhower had the added advantages of national respect for his military leadership and the Republican Congress that was elected with him in 1953. Due to prevailing norms, both men enjoyed a degree of foreign policy autonomy that was unprecedented in American history and that would undoubtedly have been coveted by nondemocratic leaders, despite an institutional structure that granted the president only a minimal scope of authority.

The following list summarizes the conclusions suggested by the above analysis. As indicated in answer 1, the constitution still favored neither branch of government in the realm of foreign relations; nonetheless, judicial interpretation of that document provided for a wide range of executive authority. Moreover, unlike in 1919, legislative norms and practices served to enhance the president's autonomy over foreign policy.

The Determinants of Executive Autonomy in the United States After WWII

1. Does constitution favor executive or legislature in foreign affairs?

    Neither/Executive

2. Do prevailing executive practices in foreign affairs facilitate executive independence?   Yes

3. Do prevailing legislative practices in foreign affairs facilitate executive independence?   Yes

49. See, for example, Thomas G. Paterson, "Presidential Foreign Policy, Public Opinion, and Congress: The Truman Years," *Diplomatic History* 3, no. 1 (1979): 14–17.

50. Acheson smugly observed that "congressional approval is pleasant but largely irrelevant to the outcome of international enterprises, unless they call in one way or another for congressional votes." Dean Acheson, *Present at the Creation* (New York: Norton, 1969), 442.

4. Do prevailing legislative norms in foreign affairs facilitate executive independence?   Yes
5. Is the legislature controlled by the same party that controls the executive?
46–48, 50–54 Yes 48–50 No

Conclusions: The Relative Autonomy of the Six States in the Study

As expected, the democracies in this study conduct foreign relations in strikingly different manners with different levels of structural autonomy for their foreign policy executives. In addition, the degree of structural autonomy afforded to leaders within the same state can vary considerably over time. Thus, for example, the French executive, which was somewhat autonomous over most foreign policy matters (excluding peacemaking) during the Third Republic, became almost impotent in all aspects of foreign policymaking under the Fourth Republic. At the same time, without undergoing constitutional changes, the United States insulated its executive between the periods under study to such an extent that Presidents Truman and Eisenhower possessed a degree of authority over foreign affairs that was unimaginable in President Wilson's time.

Table 2 groups the executives in this study into three broad categories: highly autonomous executives that had few structural impediments to the conduct of foreign affairs and, specifically, postwar peacemaking; somewhat autonomous executives that had considerable structural impediments; and not autonomous executives with impediments so severe that they had no meaningful structural authority to conduct foreign security policy independently of the legislature. As Table 2 indicates, the United States and Great Britain had highly autonomous foreign security executives after World War II. The American president dominated the foreign policy process during this period because of prevailing norms that the executive ought to have unfettered authority over foreign affairs, the powerful security institutions created in the 1940s, and the considerable leeway that Congress

Table 2   The relative autonomy of the three states after both World Wars

Highly Autonomous	Somewhat Autonomous	Not Autonomous
United States, 1945–54	Great Britain, 1918–20	France, 1945–54
Great Britain, 1945–54	France, 1918–20	
	United States, 1918–20	

granted to the president because of the Soviet threat. The Royal prerogative over foreign affairs granted by the British constitution, the prevailing
tradition of party discipline in a two-party system, and the norm that
Parliament should not embarrass the cabinet in matters of foreign policy
combined to grant the British Governments of the 1945–1954 period a
comparable level of autonomy. British executives may have been marginally
more constrained by the movement for greater parliamentary involvement
in external affairs that culminated in the Ponsonby rule and the period
of small majorities from 1950 to 1954; nonetheless, they were still highly
autonomous.

The three democracies after World War I were only somewhat autonomous. Lloyd George's Government of 1919 was constrained in the conduct of foreign affairs, despite its institutional and procedural advantages,
because of the prime minister's desperately weak position within his ruling
coalition. The executive of the French Third Republic was reasonably autonomous over most foreign policy matters, since its constitution concentrated
control over most aspects of foreign affairs in the ministry. The ministry's
control over peacemaking policy, however, was considerably weaker, due to
the constitutional provision requiring National Assembly consent for peace
treaties. Furthermore, the ministry's cohesiveness was frequently undermined by the fragile multiparty coalitions of which it was composed. The
U.S. president was similarly constrained in the making of American
foreign policy in the period following World War I, due to the unresolved
constitutional division of powers and a strong isolationist movement in an
activist Senate.

Finally, the executive of the French Fourth Republic had by far the least
structural power over foreign policy of all the governments under investigation thanks to a constitution that enshrined parliamentary authority and
favored extremely unstable multiparty coalitions. Under these conditions,
legislative norms that encouraged interference and obstruction made autonomous action by the cabinet exceedingly difficult.

These findings are noteworthy for several reasons. First, comparative
studies of the domestic and foreign economic policies of Western democracies have concluded that the postwar American state is significantly less
autonomous than the French state.[51] Our analysis of structural autonomy

51. Peter J. Katzenstein, "Conclusion: Domestic Structures and Strategies of Foreign Economic Policy," in Peter J. Katzenstein, ed., *Between Power and Plenty: Foreign Economic Policies in Advanced Industrial States* (Madison: University of Wisconsin Press, 1978), 306–23. On
the strength of the Fourth and Fifth Republic French states in international economic policy,

in the realm of foreign security policy reveals that the relationship is completely inverted for this issue. Consequently, the relative autonomy of states in one area is not a good indicator of state power over other types of policy. Moreover, as the experience of the French Third Republic indicates, executive autonomy can vary even within issues. Its executive was relatively autonomous on most aspects of foreign policy, but constrained when negotiating treaties of peace. Second, since the autonomy of each of these democratic executives over foreign security policy underwent profound changes between the two peace settlements, these findings support my assumption that autonomy varies not only across states, but also within states over time.

Finally, these findings demonstrate the significant and independent effect of procedural norms in amplifying or diminishing the scope of action that a given institutional structure grants its foreign policy executive. If we were to ignore such norms in conceptualizing and operationalizing the domestic decision-making environment and focus solely on institutional and procedural factors—as Thomas Risse-Kappen and Susan Peterson do—we would incorrectly classify the United States in the immediate post–World War II era as structurally constrained.[52]

Having estimated the relative foreign security policy autonomy of the executives in this study, we shall now turn our attention to the peacemaking strategies pursued by these states to determine the impact of structural autonomy on policy choices and international bargaining outcomes. To this end, the next chapter will focus on the post–World War I settlement.

---

see John Zysman, "The French State in the International Economy," in Katzenstein, ed., *Between Power and Plenty*, 255–93. For discussions of American weakness in this policy area, see Stephen D. Krasner, "United States Commercial and Monetary Policy: Unraveling the Paradox of External Strength and Internal Weakness," in Katzenstein, ed., *Between Power and Plenty*, 51–87; and G. John Ikenberry, *Reasons of State: Oil Politics and the Capacities of American Government* (Ithaca: Cornell University Press, 1988).

52. See Introduction. Interestingly, Peterson similarly concludes that the American executive from 1958 to 1961 was autonomous. She does so precisely because she brings norms in through the back door in her brief treatment of the American case, even though she claims that state structure can be deduced solely with reference to state institutions. She states that despite the constitutional division of foreign relations power, "Congress largely abdicated its foreign policy-making powers in pre-Vietnam era conflicts" because of the consensus in favor of containment of the Soviet Union. See *Crisis Bargaining and the State* (Ann Arbor: University of Michigan Press, 1996), 27–30. This, however, is an illustration of norms operating to defeat institutional structures, rather than an objective consequence of existing institutional arrangements as she claims.

3

The Post–World War I
Settlement, 1919

The infamous Treaty of Versailles concluded the most destructive international conflict the world had ever known. It was the first important postwar settlement negotiated almost exclusively by mass democracies, and the first effort by democratic states to construct a stable world order. History has judged this effort to be an unremitting failure and the principal cause of World War II. A widely accepted interpretation is that the treaty failed because it treated the Germans too strictly, imposing economic and territorial restrictions so onerous that the Germans could not possibly believe that their interests corresponded with preserving the post-Versailles *status quo*.[1] Many have placed the blame for

1. This interpretation is so widely accepted by both historians and political scientists that it would be impossible to provide an exhaustive list of those who subscribe to it. For an influential historian who argues in this vein, see A. J. Taylor, *The Origins of the Second World*

this overly punitive peace settlement squarely on the shoulders of Allied public opinion, which handcuffed their leaders and precluded any generosity to the defeated foe.[2]

Traditional realists have used the experience of the 1919 settlement to justify their assertion that public hostility prevents democracies from concluding conciliatory peace settlements with former enemies, even when their leaders are inclined to bury the hatchet.[3] If a careful analysis of this important case confirms that the democratic leaders of Great Britain, France, and the United States were indeed constrained by domestic opinion in the making of such an important postwar settlement, that would cast doubt upon the neorealist model of democratic foreign security policy. A case study of peacemaking in 1919 will, therefore, enable us to test the explanatory power of neorealist hypotheses N1 and N2, on the one hand, against the traditional and structural autonomy alternatives, on the other.

Since we have determined *a priori* in the preceding chapter that the three Western democracies all possessed comparably weak executives in 1919, the expectations of the traditional model of democratic foreign security policy and my structural autonomy model will be similar (Table 3). Thus we will be unable to test the relative power of these two models based on this case alone. Nonetheless, we *can* assess whether these structurally constrained democratic executives were able to act with greater independence than traditional realists would expect by employing independence-enhancing strategies of deception. Furthermore, in conjunction with the case studies presented in Chapter 4, this analysis will help us to choose between the traditional model and my structural autonomy model, since it will enable us to compare the behavior of democratic states at the middle-to-low-end of the structural autonomy scale (all three states in 1919) with that of considerably more insulated executives (the United States and Great Britain after World War II) and one substantially more constrained executive (France after World War II). If the three great democracies in 1919 were forced by domestic pressure to treat the defeated foe more harshly than the Anglo-Saxons after World War II—but less so than the French

---

War (New York: Atheneum, 1961), esp. 18–40. Hans J. Morgenthau and Kenneth W. Thompson are prominent political scientists who also accept it. *Politics Among Nations,* 6th ed. (New York: McGraw-Hill, 1985), 79–83, 111.

2. This tragic, bottom-up view of peacemaking in 1919 is best expressed in Harold Nicolson, *Peacemaking 1919* (New York: Grosset & Dunlop, 1974).

3. Walter Lippmann, *Essays in the Public Philosophy* (Boston: Little, Brown and Co., 1955), 18–21; and Reinhold Niebuhr, *The Structure of Nations and Empires* (New York: Scribner, 1959), 197.

Fourth Republic—that would support my autonomy model, rather than the traditional realist conceptualization. Similarly, if the democracies in 1919 employed domestic constraint projection in international negotiations more successfully than Great Britain and the United States from 1945 to 1954, but less so than France in that period, that would support the structural autonomy explanation of democratic foreign security policy against the traditional liberal model.

Background: The armistice of November 1918 halted active hostilities between Germany and the Allied and Associated Powers, and provided for a peace conference to negotiate a settlement based on American President Woodrow Wilson's Fourteen Points for peace, with two Allied reservations on the freedom of the seas and the need for reparations to restore the devastated regions of France and Belgium. At the Paris Peace Conference, Allied leaders dealt with a staggering complexity of problems that arose out of the war, including the creation of many new states, the dissolution of the Ottoman and Austro-Hungarian Empires, the establishment of an international league to promote peace, and, of course, the conclusion of the war with Germany. In this chapter, we will consider the two most important aspects of the settlement between the three democracies and Germany: the territorial settlement, including the drawing of postwar German borders, and the irksome reparations question.

Table 3   Predictions of the three models for the post–World War I settlement

	Neorealist Model	Traditional Model	Autonomy Model
Domestic impact on postwar settlement policies	Minimal in all three democracies	High for all three democracies (realist)	Relatively high for all three democracies
Effectiveness of domestic constraint projection in multilateral bargaining	Irrelevant; power determines bargaining outcomes	High for all three democracies (liberal)	Relatively high for all three democracies
Frequency of domestic constraint projection	Indeterminate and irrelevant	Frequent for all three democracies (liberal)	Relatively frequent for all three democracies

Initial Attitudes: Executive, Legislative, and Public

Domestic Opinion in the Three Countries

After a bitter and destructive war, public opinion in the West was uniformly hostile to the Germans. In all three countries, the Germans were regarded as militaristic villains who dragged the world into the apocalypse to satisfy their own petty ambitions. Particularly within Great Britain and France, who had suffered unprecedented casualty levels and physical destruction, the public was envenomed and desired to avenge themselves with monstrously punitive peace terms.[4] Public hostility was reflected in—and amplified by—the mainstream press in both countries, which almost universally denounced "the Hun" as an imperialistic warmonger who could not be trusted to behave responsibly. British Prime Minister David Lloyd George writes of the difficulty of conducting negotiations amidst the great public clamor for vengeance, fanned by a hostile press that demanded to bring the "Hun to justice":[5]

> It is worthy of note that all vocal criticism of the peace delegation in France, as well as in England, came from powerful political groups who were anxious to make the terms harsher and more stern than those which the Peace Council ultimately presented to Germany. During the progress of the Peace Conference there was not a voice raised in favour of moderation except from the men who were conducting the negotiations, and who for that reason were assailed

4. For the state of British public opinion, see U.S. Chargé in Great Britain, Irwin B. Laughlin, to the Acting Secretary of State, December 4, 1918, United States Department of State, *Foreign Relations of the United States (FRUS)*, Paris Peace Conference (PPC) 1919, I, 409–12; Nicolson, *Peacemaking 1919*, 58–63. The best single source on French public opinion in 1919 is Pierre Miquel, *La paix de Versailles et l'opinion publique Française* (Paris: Flammarion, 1972), which documents public and parliamentary attitudes toward the postwar settlement as it was being constructed. Arno J. Mayer, *Politics and Diplomacy of Peacemaking: Containment and Counterrevolution at Versailles, 1918–1919* (New York: Alfred A. Knopf, 1967) discusses the interplay between public opinion and each of the victors' policies.

5. The Northcliffe Press was particularly anti-German. On November 13, 1918, the *Daily Mail* front page headline ridiculed widespread starvation in defeated Germany, calling it "Hun Food snivel." On December 15, the paper declared, "Germany can pay, if there is any ginger in the Allied Governments." Starting in late December, moreover, the *Daily Mail* included the epigraph "The Junkers will cheat you yet" on the front page of each issue. Most other newspapers endorsed the demand for an indemnity that reimbursed the Allies for the cost of the war and many favored capital punishment for the kaiser and the expulsion of German aliens in England. See Nicolson, *Peacemaking 1919*, 57–63; Mayer, *Politics and Diplomacy*, 150–56.

with suspicion, misrepresentation and abuse. I cannot recall a word uttered in the French Assembly or a sentence printed in the French Press pleading for clemency to the vanquished. In Britain even, when I had to face hundreds of my own supporters in Parliament who were disaffected by Press reports about the leniency of my attitude toward Germany, not a voice was heard from any section of the Parliamentary Opposition which expressed any sympathy with the fight I was putting up against redoubtable critics for moderation on reparations, frontiers or disarmament, nor did I receive any tender of support in my struggle on any of these vital issues.[6]

In Britain, public sentiments manifested themselves clearly in the December 1918 coupon election. Despite efforts by the parliamentary leaders to focus the electorate on matters of domestic politics, by election day the peace issue "overshadowed all others."[7] Leading organs of the press, notably *The Morning Post, The Daily Mail,* and *The Times,* called for the coalition to declare its intention to enforce a tough peace on not only the kaiser, but on the entire German people. In fact, there was unanimity within the center and right-wing press that the Allies should force Germany to pay the entire cost of the war.[8] Moreover, the public made itself heard directly. Lloyd George's campaign speeches frequently degenerated into calls from his audience to punish Germany and expel German nationals from the British Isles. In addition, throughout the campaign, Downing Street was flooded with letters from the public beseeching the prime minister to commit himself to a punitive postwar settlement.[9]

With the gauntlet thrown down, Lloyd George committed himself to a German day of reckoning in order to return a coalition majority to the House of Commons. Promising "a just peace, a sternly just peace, a relentlessly just peace," Lloyd George assured the crowd that "[t]here is absolutely no doubt ... that Germany must pay the cost of the war up to the limit of her capacity to do so."[10] He later assured the public that while

6. David Lloyd George, *Memoirs of the Peace Conference* (New York: Howard Fertig, 1972), vol. I, 285–86.

7. Mayer, *Politics and Diplomacy,* 148.

8. A group of Conservative members of Parliament added to this media barrage on reparations with an advertisement in *The Times* stating, "Germany can pay. Germany must pay." Alan Sharp, *The Versailles Settlement: Peacemaking in Paris* (New York: St. Martin's Press, 1991), 81.

9. Peter Rowland, *Lloyd George* (London: Barrie & Jenkins, 1975), 466–68.

10. Lloyd George's November 29 speech at Newcastle-on-Tyne, reproduced in *The Times,* November 30, 1919.

the Germans would probably not be able to repay the estimated £24 billion in damages, his financial advisors believed that they should be able to tender approximately £20 billion—an extraordinary sum.[11] Lloyd George's stern peace rhetoric was immensely successful. The coalition won a combined 478 seats or almost 80 percent of all available seats. Rather than freeing the prime minister from further domestic pressure, his election victory filled the Parliament and, in particular, the Government benches with staunch partisans of a punitive peace.[12]

As reflected in the mainstream French press, the French public had little faith in the new democratic German regime and believed that the German people would always be a menace to French security. "Le boche sera toujours le boche" was a recurrent theme throughout the Peace Conference and reflected a desire for a peace of victory to shackle a German beast that would always seek glory in militarism and imperialism. Consequently, the public demanded security precautions, including separating the Rhineland from Germany and a permanent French occupation of the Rhine area. Powerful elements of the French right even called for a return to 1814 borders, which would mean the outright annexation of the Rhenish provinces. In addition, they insisted that Germany pay fully for the damage it caused to the industrial regions of Northeast France and Belgium.[13]

The American people had not suffered the same deprivations as the Europeans, nor had they suffered casualties on the same scale, having joined the

11. Lloyd George's December 11 speech at Bristol, reproduced in *The Times*, December 12, 1919. On Lloyd George's resort to anti-German campaign rhetoric, see Nicolson, *Peacemaking 1919*, 20–22; Rowland, *Lloyd George*, 468–70; Mayer, *Politics and Diplomacy*, 156–58. A. Lentin observes that the changing rhetoric also brought about a change in policy, as in the heat of the campaign Lloyd George called upon the war cabinet to study the matter of an indemnity—something that had not previously been discussed, except by the press. *Lloyd George, Woodrow Wilson and the Guilt of Germany* (Leicester: Leicester University Press, 1984), 19–20.

12. Robert E. Bunselmeyer has compiled a list of 54 Members of Parliament (M.P.s) elected in December 1918 who agitated for an excessively punitive peace. Most of them sat on the Government benches and had the support of many of their quieter colleagues. See *The Cost of the War, 1914–1919: British Economic War Aims and the Origins of Reparation* (Hamden, Conn.: Archon Books, 1975), 187–90.

13. Miquel, *la paix de Versailles*, 236–48, 425–33. The attitude that Germany should be weakened because it would necessarily remain a threat was echoed in newspapers of the center and the right and even in some of the moderate left. *L'Action Française* (January 23, 1919) declared, "For a thousand years, the German has not changed; he will not change in fifteen days." "If the spirit of the world has changed," lamented *Le Temps* (February 12, 1919), "that of Germany remains untouched. There reigns the spirit of arrogance, conquest and megalomania." Therefore, *l'Echo de Paris* (March 31, 1919) charged, "we must impose on the Huns the feeling of defeat."

war only in 1917, after it had reached a stalemate. Nevertheless, the events that brought the United States into the war—the unrestricted submarine warfare practiced by the Germans that claimed American lives and the infamous Zimmermann Telegram—together with the wartime propaganda that helped sustain the American war effort, made the American public anti-German and caused them to demand a harsh peace settlement, too.[14] Significantly, even the moderate American press—epitomized by *The New York Times*—was openly hostile not just toward German leaders, but toward the German people themselves. In October, for example, in a scathing attack on the German character, *The New York Times* rejected "the idea that we regard the German people as an aggregation of saints, who have gone wrong because they had wicked leaders. That is not at all the view we take of the people who struck off and wore medals to commemorate the sinking of the Lusitania, or of the people to whom the sacred vessels of churches were boxed up and sent home as acceptable loot."[15] The congressional mood was similarly anti-German. On August 23, for example, future Senate majority leader Henry Cabot Lodge addressed the Senate, declaring that "[n]o peace that satisfies Germany in any degree can ever satisfy us."[16] More ominously, in an October Senate debate on the peace negotiations, every single senator who spoke—Republican and Democrat—declared that the Fourteen Points were far too lenient a basis for peace with Germany.[17]

President Wilson made the peace settlement the central issue of the November 1918 congressional elections. Significantly, in October he published an appeal to the country to return Democrats to the Congress so that his authority to negotiate peace would not be undermined.[18] The president's petition signaled an end to wartime nonpartisanship, and Republicans of all stripes took the opportunity to lambaste him for his soft treatment of the Germans. Republican leaders, including Lodge and Republican National Committee (RNC) Chairman William H. Hays, spoke out within a matter of days, criticizing the president for agreeing to negotiate with the Germans on the peace terms and insisting that the Allies impose harsh peace terms

14. Thomas A. Bailey, *Woodrow Wilson and the Lost Peace* (Chicago: Encounter Paperbacks, 1963), 1–70.

15. *The New York Times,* October 23, 1918.

16. *Congressional Record,* 65th Congress, 2d session, August 23, 1919, 9393–94.

17. *Congressional Record,* 65th Congress, 2d session, October 7, 1919, 11155–63.

18. For the text of Wilson's appeal of October 19, 1918, see Arthur S. Link et al., eds., *The Papers of Woodrow Wilson (PWW)* (Princeton: Princeton University Press, 1987), vol. 51, 381–82.

on Germany without negotiations.[19] Notably, the Republicans wished to grant France the Rhine as a strategic frontier and advocated an extensive territorial commitment to Poland in order to make the new state strategically viable. The most severe attack on Wilson's liberal attitude toward the peace came from Theodore Roosevelt, whose fiery invectives indicted Wilson, his Fourteen Points, and the German people.[20] It is noteworthy that the Republicans were able to parlay their harsh peace platform into an election victory in November, gaining control of both the House of Representatives and the Senate.

Executive Attitudes

The leaders of the three countries each either eschewed an excessively harsh peace on principled or strategic grounds or realized that a sufficiently stern peace was unobtainable. Wilson was least amenable to a harsh peace. In the pre-armistice negotiations of October 1918, he had agreed to conclude a peace on the basis of his Fourteen Points, which would have restored Alsace and Lorraine to France and granted Poland some German territory to allow Polish access to the sea, but should not otherwise have been too onerous for the Germans. In particular, point 5 promised "a free, open-minded, and absolutely impartial adjustment of all colonial claims," and the principle of national self-determination should have precluded excessive territorial amputations.[21] Having given his word to the Germans that he would abide by these terms, which he felt were just, Wilson was loathe to allow the Europeans to impose excessive penalties in the final peace treaty.[22] He certainly was determined to thwart domestic advocates of a harsh peace, whom he viewed to be misguided.[23] Indeed, during the run-up to the 1918 election, he

19. Mayer, *Politics and Diplomacy,* 123–32. Indeed, Lodge was a strong advocate of a stern peace from the beginning, declaring in September 1918, "the main thing to do is to put Germany under such physical bonds ... that it does not matter who signs the peace for her or whether there is a league of nations or not...." Quoted in William C. Widenor, *Henry Cabot Lodge and the Search for an American Foreign Policy* (Berkeley and Los Angeles: University of California Press, 1980), 294.

20. On October 27, Roosevelt raged against the negotiation of a peace treaty based on the Fourteen Points, which "had been greeted with enthusiasm by Germany and all the pro-Germans on this side of the water." *The New York Times,* October 29, 1918.

21. The text of the Fourteen Points is reproduced in Bailey, *Woodrow Wilson and the Lost Peace,* 333–34.

22. See, for example, Alexander L. George and Juliette L. George, *Woodrow Wilson and Colonel House* (New York: Dover Publications, 1964), 200–203; and August Heckscher, *Woodrow Wilson* (New York: Scribner, 1991), 522–23.

23. After the November electoral defeat, he assured Democratic Senator Key Pittman that he would not let the bellicose Republicans interfere with a just peace: "America is the leader of the

lamented, "We must face such intolerant hatred of the Germans, I may have to become their advocate for justice and against American Prussianism."[24]

French Premier Georges Clemenceau clearly would have wanted a punitive settlement that dismantled the bases of German power and left an Allied presence on the Rhine. He believed that this would be the only way to ensure that Germany did not again threaten the peace of Europe by virtue of its larger population and formidable industrial base. In this respect, the premier was in step with French public and political opinion. Nonetheless, the French premier was also a realist who knew that the settlement could not endure without Anglo-American cooperation, which would in turn require French concessions and leniency.[25] In this regard, his policy diverged sharply from public and parliamentary preferences, since he was more than willing to sacrifice some French strategic and economic interests vis-à-vis Germany in order to maintain Allied unity, which would ensure that France would not alone face Germany in the future. Thus, historian David Robin Watson concludes that Clemenceau "had argued for the separation of the Rhineland from Germany only as a bargaining counter" and Robert McCrum reaches the more measured conclusion that his Rhineland policy "was far from tactical, but open to compromise."[26] It is instructive that, when he was pressed by the Assembly before the Peace Conference to divulge his plans for a harsh German settlement, he declined "because some of them I might have to compromise in a higher interest."[27]

Lloyd George was a more complex character. Overall, he preferred a moderate peace. He believed that excessively punitive peace terms would be counterproductive since they would allow the French to dominate the

---

liberal thought of the world, and nobody from any quarter should be allowed to interfere or impair that leadership without giving an account of himself, which can be made very difficult." Wilson to Pittman, November 7, 1918, *PWW,* vol. 51, 620. See also his letter to Democratic Senator Hitchcock, in which he dismissed Republican attacks on the Fourteen Points as "perversions and misrepresentations." Wilson to Hitchcock, October 22, 1918, *PWW,* vol. 51, 405.

24. Quoted in Klaus Schwabe, *Woodrow Wilson, Revolutionary Germany, and Peacemaking, 1918–1919: Missionary Diplomacy and the Realities of Power,* Rita and Robert Kimber, trans. (Chapel Hill: University of North Carolina Press, 1985), 51.

25. David Robin Watson, *Georges Clemenceau* (New York: McKay, 1974), 338–39; Marc Trachtenberg, *Reparation in World Politics* (New York: Columbia University Press, 1980), 29–31.

26. Watson, *Georges Clemenceau,* 353; Robert McCrum, "French Rhineland Policy at the Paris Peace Conference, 1919," *Historical Journal* 21, no. 3 (1978): 624.

27. *Journal Officiel de la République Française, Débats Parlementaires, Chambre des Députés (JO),* December 29, 1918, 3733. Alan Sharp also queries whether Clemenceau ever "really had much faith in the policy, except as a bargaining counter." *The Versailles Settlement,* 107.

continent and might encourage German *revanchism,* as they ultimately did. In addition, the fear of driving the Germans to bolshevism also preyed upon Lloyd George's mind and inspired moderation.[28] He thus cautioned that a stable peace could only be built "by avoiding conditions which would create a legitimate sense of wrong" and "which would excite national pride needlessly to seek opportunities to redress."[29] His dominant preference for moderation, however, was occasionally clouded by a desire to punish the German people for the destruction they had caused.[30] On balance, though, without public and parliamentary intervention, Lloyd George would have preferred to terminate the war without excessive territorial amputations, and with heavy, but manageable reparations payments.[31] Thus, the leaders of all three countries were more amenable to a moderate peace than their domestic opinion.

The Political and Territorial Settlement

The French delegation took the most severe position on the territorial settlement with Germany, advocating early "the disunion of the countries that compose" Germany and territorial adjustment of the German state to favor France, Belgium, Denmark, Luxembourg, and Poland.[32] Specifically, they required: restitution of Alsace and Lorraine, including additional portions of the Saar that were not French territory in 1870; military neutralization and Allied administration of German territories on the left bank of the Rhine; the transfer of portions of Prussia, Posen, and Upper Silesia to Poland; the return of Schleswig to Denmark; Belgian territorial gains at German expense in the Malmedy region; and an end to German colonial possessions abroad.[33]

The British did not articulate a coherent overall blueprint for the territorial settlement. They appear to have favored the return of Alsace and

28. Raymond J. Sontag, *A Broken World, 1919–1939* (New York: Harper & Row, 1971), 2–3; Fontainebleau Memorandum of March 25, 1919, reproduced in *PWW,* vol. 56, 259–70.

29. Speech by Lloyd George, *Hansard,* 5th series, 114, April 16, 1919, cols. 2936–56.

30. See, for example, Harold I. Nelson, *Land and Power: British and Allied Policy on Germany's Frontiers* (London: Routledge & Kegan Paul, 1963), 47–50.

31. See, for example, Kenneth O. Morgan, *Lloyd George* (London: Weidenfeld and Nicolson, 1983), 130–34.

32. Jusserand to Lansing, November 29, 1918, *FRUS,* PPC 1919, vol. 1, 365–68.

33. French Proposed Basis for the Preliminaries of Peace with Germany, December 1918, *FRUS,* PPC 1919, vol. 1, 372–78.

Lorraine to France, the surrender of all German colonies to the most interested Great Power, and the creation of an independent Poland on ethnic lines. They disapproved of French aims in the Rhineland and Polish claims to a secure corridor to the sea, which would require a transfer of predominately German territory.[34] Lloyd George, in particular, counseled moderation in setting the boundaries of Germany proper, and insisted that the conference apply Wilson's principle of self-determination to the Germans as well as to their victims.

Wilson's plan for the postwar territorial settlement with Germany was stated succinctly, if vaguely, in the Fourteen Points. He advocated: the restoration of Alsace and Lorraine to France, but no other frontier rectification in France's favor; the creation of an independent Poland with secure access to the sea; and an impartial adjudication of colonial claims against Germany, balancing the interests of the populations with those of the interested Great Powers. Beyond these general goals, American policy was formulated, to a great extent, at the Peace Conference itself.

We shall now consider, in turn, three contentious territorial issues decided by the three democracies: the status of the Rhineland and the Saar, the German-Polish border, and the disposition of German colonial possessions.[35]

France and the Rhineland

After the war, the French public and a large segment of the French military and political elite desired to sever the German states west of the Rhine from the rest of Germany in order to use the river as a natural strategic buffer against a future German invasion. In addition, they wished to annex the mineral-rich Saar basin and to associate the independent Rhenish states economically, politically, and militarily with France. French Commander-in-Chief Marshal Ferdinand Foch articulated this policy in two notes to Allied governments calling for a Rhine frontier, the political and military organization of the states on the left bank in order to contain Germany, and an Allied occupation of the right bank bridgeheads until the main clauses of the peace treaty were fulfilled.[36]

34. Nelson, *Land and Power,* 93–111.

35. Other territorial questions that are not considered here include the northern borders of Germany with Belgium, Holland, and Denmark and its southern borders with Czechoslovakia and Austria. These are omitted, since there was a large measure of agreement between the three democracies over these matters and since public sentiment does not appear to have been terribly concerned about their disposition. See Nelson, *Land and Power,* 282–320.

36. The text of the January 10 note is reprinted in *PWW,* vol. 55, 502–10.

The marshal's proposals were welcomed by the parliament and the public. The foreign affairs commission of the National Assembly advocated an active Rhineland policy, provided that no Rhenish populations were annexed against their will. The mainstream French press also endorsed it heartily, although influential papers on the right and center called for an outright return to the border of 1814, which would return the Rhenish states of the left bank to direct French control.[37] Indeed, the proliferation of books and pamphlets by private citizens advocating annexation is testimony to the popularity in postwar France of an expansionist Rhineland policy.[38]

Clemenceau agreed with Foch's proposals, and he too wanted France and its allies to occupy the Rhine permanently. Profoundly moved by the humiliating French defeat at German hands in 1870–71, the Tiger was staunchly committed to weakening German power as a key to French security. Hence, he brought Foch to London in December 1918 to present his case to Lloyd George and American representative Colonel Edward House. Moreover, after hearing their objections to the plan, he directed Foch and André Tardieu to draft a memorandum that would answer Anglo-Saxon reservations and serve as the basis for French Rhineland policy at the Peace Conference.[39] In February and March, Clemenceau pursued this line relentlessly, much to Wilson's and Lloyd George's consternation.

For Clemenceau, however, Foch's bottom line and the Tardieu memorandum merely constituted "an excellent basis for negotiation" rather than a firm goal from which he would not budge.[40] Consequently, his policy differed significantly from what public and parliamentary leaders demanded. The essential difference was that Clemenceau believed that Allied support in a future war with Germany would be far more valuable than possessing the Rhine as a strategic frontier. If France were to stand alone in a conflict with a revived Germany, the Rhine frontier would not be an effective counterweight to German numerical and industrial superiority. Therefore, Government policy was to persuade Wilson and Lloyd George to accept as much of a Rhenish occupation as possible, but to surrender its permanence and Rhenish separatism to the cause of Allied unity.[41]

37. Miquel, *La paix de Versailles*, 292–327.

38. Jere Clemens King, *Foch Versus Clemenceau: France and German Dismemberment, 1918–1919* (Cambridge: Harvard University Press, 1960), 3–11.

39. André Tardieu, *The Truth About the Treaty* (Indianapolis: Bobbs-Merrill, 1921), 174. The resulting Tardieu memorandum is reproduced there on 147–70.

40. Miquel, *La paix de Versailles*, 292.

41. Georges Clemenceau, *Grandeur and Misery of Victory* (New York: Harcourt, Brace, 1930), 232–46; King, *Foch Versus Clemenceau*, 63; Walter A. McDougall, *France's Rhineland*

Clemenceau's task was complicated immeasurably by British and American attitudes. The very idea of Rhineland separation and a French presence on the Rhine alarmed Lloyd George, who saw in the suggestion the twin nightmares of Bolshevik revolution in Germany and French domination of the continent. He also feared that transferring German populations to French rule would create a "new Alsace-Lorraine" which could inspire, rather than prevent, a future war.[42] Lloyd George was on reasonably safe ground domestically on this point. While there was considerable sympathy for French strategic concerns both in the press and the Parliament, the prevailing opinion was that separating the Rhineland from Germany would be unfair to the local population, which was, after all, German. There was more sympathy for a French occupation on the Rhine, but as *The Times* concluded, that would be unnecessary if the Rhineland were to be demilitarized.[43]

The American delegation—or, more accurately, Wilson—also opposed Rhenish separation under French domination because it would violate the principle of self-determination, the centerpiece of the Fourteen Points. Wilson was equally adamant that the Saar should remain part of Germany, since "we violate the principle of self-determination as much by giving one people an independence it does not request as by making them pass under the sovereignty of another."[44] During his absence from the conference in late February (he returned to the United States to sell his League of Nations idea to a hostile American public), when House, his personal representative and confidant, became converted to a temporary separation of the Rhineland, the president quickly intervened. He cabled House sharply, "I hope you will not even provisionally consent to the separation of the Rhenish Provinces from Germany under any arrangement."[45] Clearly, the French designs were intolerable for him.

Diplomacy, 1914–1924 (Princeton: Princeton University Press, 1978), 60–61; Pierre Miquel, *Clemenceau: la guerre et la paix* (Paris: Tallandier, 1996), 322–34.

42. Anthony Adamthwaite, *Grandeur and Misery: France's Bid for Power in Europe, 1914–1940* (London: Arnold, 1995), 47; McDougall, *France's Rhineland Diplomacy,* 59–60; Keith L. Nelson, *Victors Divided: America and the Allies in Germany, 1918–1923* (Berkeley and Los Angeles: University of California Press, 1975), 79–80. On the prime minister's fear of bolshevism, see the Fontainebleau Memorandum of March 25, 1919, *PWW,* vol. 56, 259–70.

43. See articles and commentary in *The Times,* March 25 and 26, 1919.

44. Minutes of a Meeting of the Council of Four, March 26, 1919, Arthur S. Link, ed., *The Deliberations of the Council of Four (DCF)* (Princeton: Princeton University Press, 1992), vol. I, 67.

45. Charles Seymour, ed., *The Intimate Papers of Colonel House* (New York: Houghton Mifflin, 1928), vol. IV, 358n.

In this regard, Wilson was out of step with public and legislative opinion in the United States. Traditional skittishness about foreign entanglements made the French demand for a permanent inter-Allied force on the Rhine unpopular,[46] but there was considerable support for a French occupation and territorial amputation on Germany's western frontier. Significantly, as Lodge informed French journalists, the Republican majority in the Senate "heartily endorsed setting Germany's western boundary at the Rhine."[47] He confirmed this position in his February 28, 1919, critique of the League of Nations covenant from the Senate floor: "[I]t is also in our immediate and selfish interest as a nation that France should be made as strong as possible. Alsace and Lorraine she must have without question and without reduction, *and other barriers if necessary to make her impregnable to German assault.*"[48] As usual, however, the president ignored popular sentiment in favor of the lofty ideals that he knew to be just.

Bargaining over the Rhineland began in earnest in March. On March 11, in a secret committee on the western boundaries of Germany, French representative Tardieu and British representative Philip Kerr reached a deadlock. Kerr rejected the Tardieu memorandum on the grounds that British public opinion and the Dominions would accept neither a continued British presence on the Rhine nor a solution that forced peoples to separate from Germany against their will. Tardieu countered that not only were these measures essential to assure French security, but "French public opinion demands the protection of the Rhine barrier, and the French government cannot recede."[49] Lloyd George and Wilson attempted to break the stalemate by offering the French a joint guarantee against unprovoked German aggression in order to obviate the need for the French security measures on the Rhine. In addition, they were willing to grant a short French occupation in order to guarantee that the Germans made their initial reparations payments. Clemenceau welcomed these concessions on four conditions: France

---

46. However, Senate Majority Leader Lodge was prepared to keep American forces in Germany until the Germans paid their indemnity. See page 122.

47. McDougall, *France's Rhineland Diplomacy,* 411n; Louis A. R. Yates, *United States and French Security* (New York: Twayne, 1957), 31. In fact, the French attempted to mobilize Republican opposition to their advantage during the Rhineland and reparations negotiations, keeping them informed of Council of Four negotiations behind Wilson's back. Grayson diary, March 28, 1919, *PWW,* vol. 56, 347–49.

48. *The New York Times,* March 1, 1919, italics added. After the treaty was signed, some Republican senators chastised the president "for having made the French 'back down'" from their demand for a secure Rhine frontier. Yates, *United States and French Security,* 129–30.

49. Sydney Mezes to Wilson, March 11, 1919, *PWW,* vol. 55, 475–77.

must retain the right to occupy the Rhineland and bridgeheads on the right bank of the river for a sufficient time; the entire Rhineland from a line drawn fifty kilometers east of the river had to be demilitarized and all German fortifications dismantled; France would retain the right to reoccupy the region if Germany were to violate the terms of peace; and the French were entitled to territorial compensation in the Saar basin. Significantly, though, he dropped the requirement of an autonomous Rhineland.[50]

On grounds of principle and practical policy, the British and American delegations rejected French annexations in the Saar region. For domestic political reasons, moreover, they could not commit their troops to a prolonged occupation. They did, however, accept the French proposal for the demilitarization of the German Rhineland, which Wilson thought would make any territorial annexations unnecessary.[51] For strategic reasons, though, the French demanded something more than a guarantee from two geographically removed allies. Consequently, negotiations almost broke down over the Saar basin, as Wilson refused to accept the French historical and economic claim to the Saarland, an area populated almost exclusively by Germans. In a heated March 28 exchange in the Council of Four, Clemenceau accused the president of being "the friend of Germany" and making a pro-German peace. The premier further warned that he would be forced to resign if he could not bring the Assembly a treaty that at least returned the Saar to French control. Wilson, in turn, threatened to return home to conclude a separate peace with Germany.[52]

After two more weeks of bitter haggling, Wilson presented his final offer to Clemenceau by way of Tardieu. He offered essentially what he had offered previously and stated flatly that he could go no further to meet French concerns or "there will be no possible hope of my obtaining the proposed treaty" from the Senate.[53] Clemenceau informed House on April 14 that he appreciated the president's offer and accepted it, even though "[i]t was not what he wanted." Nonetheless, he would face stiff domestic

50. Clemenceau to Wilson, March 17, 1919, *PWW*, vol. 56, 10–14.

51. See, for example, Minutes of a Meeting of the Council of Four, March 27, 1919, *DCF*, vol. 1, 40.

52. This exchange is curiously absent from the official minutes of the meeting in *DCF*, vol. 1, 55–58. It is, however, reported in the memos and diary entries of House, Lansing, Vance McCormick, and Ray Stannard Baker, March 28, 1919, *PWW*, vol. 56, 349–54. The exchange prompted Wilson to ask House to convince Tardieu to restrain his premier. Tardieu agreed to try, but highlighted Clemenceau's domestic difficulties. House diary, April 3, 1919, *PWW*, vol. 56, 558–60.

53. Wilson to House, April 12, 1919, *PWW*, vol. 57, 295.

opposition unless the Americans would agree to let him occupy three zones of the Rhineland for periods of five, ten, and fifteen years, with the participation of token American and British forces. "If the President would consent to it he, Clemenceau, could beat his Marshals in the Chamber of Deputies and Senate."[54] Grudgingly, the beleaguered president capitulated.[55] Lloyd George held out for another week, protesting that the British people and the Dominions would not accept a military commitment on the continent. On April 22, however, his resistance was also overcome, but not without his bitter complaints that it would be difficult to tell the English—who wanted to terminate compulsory military service—that they would have to remain on the Rhine for fifteen years. Clemenceau appealed, however, for at least "one battalion a flag," imploring the Welshman, "[i]f I don't have your flag beside mine on the left bank of the Rhine, I won't be able to go before our Parliament." Lloyd George swallowed his objections and muttered, "All right; I accept."[56]

After reaching this compromise, Clemenceau complained that French security was still in jeopardy—particularly since the American Senate might not ratify the treaty of guarantee and British adherence depended upon American ratification—and, consequently, he would have great difficulty selling the settlement to the public and the Assembly.[57] To rectify this problem, he demanded that Germany be precluded from fortifying or stationing troops on either bank of the Rhine. In addition, he proposed articles 429 and 430 of the treaty, allowing France to extend its occupation of the Rhine beyond fifteen years if the Allies were to deem that the guarantees against German aggression were insufficient, and permitting France to reoccupy the Rhineland "if the Inter-Allied Commission on Reparations recognise that Germany refuse [sic] to execute the whole or part of the ... present treaty." With great reluctance, the Allies consented.[58]

The Saar issue was also resolved by the middle of April, but not without intense discussions and numerous flare-ups. After Clemenceau's March 28 clash with Wilson, the French abandoned their efforts to annex the Saarland

---

54. House diary, April 14, 1919, *PWW*, vol. 57, 335.

55. House diary, April 15, 1919, *PWW*, vol. 57, 352–55.

56. Minutes of a Meeting of the Council of Four, April 22, 1919, *DCF*, vol. 1, 317–19.

57. Nelson, *Land and Power*, 243; Tardieu, *The Truth*, 210–12.

58. Lloyd George's final agreement on these extra provisions was obtained at an April 30 session of the Council of Four from which the interpreters and secretaries were asked to withdraw. Therefore, there is no record of what exactly transpired at the meeting, nor is there an indication of what persuaded the British prime minister to yield. Minutes of a Meeting of the Council of Four, April 30, 1919, *FRUS*, PPC 1919, vol. 5, 357.

outright, and instead proposed a fifteen-year French mandate for the region under the League of Nations, after which the League would administer a plebiscite to allow the residents to determine their own political fate.[59] Lloyd George accepted the new French line, claiming both that the plebiscite would overcome objections on the grounds of self-determination and that "part of the people of this district have retained anti-Prussian sentiments." Wilson objected strenuously that American public opinion would not tolerate the creation of an independent state, even in the interim, if the Saarois people favored continued German sovereignty. "I cannot return to the United States and say to the American people: 'After consideration, we found it convenient to go back on our word.'" Once again, Clemenceau called attention to the importance that the French public attached to the Saar region.[60] The president's objection, however, won the day, and the French delegation agreed to forgo a French administration, as well as permanent French ownership of the region's mines.[61]

The final chapter in the Rhineland negotiations came in June when Lloyd George tried to reduce the length of the occupation in order to make German compliance more likely. Lloyd George requested some movement on Clemenceau's part to help him persuade his coalition partners to support the occupation. He pleaded: "This question causes me great difficulties. I could provoke a crisis in my government and in the Labour party. Mr. Barnes, who represents the working class in our delegation, threatens to leave if no change is made. I ask you to help me."[62] Because of the intensity of French sentiment on the issue, Clemenceau was reluctant to make any significant public concessions. After speaking to Lloyd George, Bonar Law, and Barnes on July 13, however, he agreed to specify that the occupation would terminate before fifteen years if the Germans furnished adequate guarantees that they would fulfill the reparations settlement. He made this concession to ease the British leader's political difficulties, and, in return, the three coalition leaders agreed not to require a specified date when these guarantees were to be furnished.[63]

59. French Government Note on the Sarre Question, March 29, 1919, reprinted in Tardieu, *The Truth*, 266–69.

60. Minutes of a Meeting of the Council of Four, April 8–9, 1919, *DCF*, vol. 1, 181–208.

61. Minutes of a Meeting of the Council of Four, April 9, 1919, *DCF*, vol. 1, 204–8.

62. Minutes of a Meeting of the Council of Four, June 12, 1919, *DCF*, vol. 2, 401–5.

63. Conversation between Clemenceau, Lloyd George, Bonar Law, Barnes, and Loucheur, July 13, 1919, *DCF*, vol. 2, 437–41. Georges-Henri Soutou finds in Clemenceau's June behavior on the Rhineland and reparations issues a desire to draft a harsh settlement that could, nonetheless, be implemented moderately in order to improve Franco-German relations. See

The final Rhineland compromise thus required each of the Big Three to make considerable sacrifices. Clemenceau had to surrender an independent Rhineland, a permanent occupation, French control over the Saar, and permanent French ownership of the Saar mines. For their parts, Wilson and Lloyd George were forced to accept a limited international force on the Rhine for up to fifteen years and an Anglo-American guarantee to France against German aggression. In addition, Wilson had to stomach the removal of the Saar from German authority.

Many of these compromises were spawned by conjuring up the spectre of domestic opposition. Lloyd George consistently opposed an Allied occupation of the Rhineland and Rhenish autonomy on the grounds that the British public would not support him. Wilson invoked public attitudes when the principle of self-determination was being challenged. It was Clemenceau, however, who used this tactic most successfully when bargaining over the Rhineland. Throughout these troubled negotiations, the premier warned Wilson and Lloyd George of the consequences of failing to satisfy at least some of his program. His policy, he emphasized, "was to keep a perfect entente with Great Britain and the United States of America." Because of his willingness to compromise, however, "he had been strongly attacked" both publicly and in the Assembly. He warned the other leaders, therefore, that they would be wise to accommodate him, for "[if] he were obliged to retire from office, his colleagues would find themselves met by a much stronger opposition."[64] Rumors circulated throughout the duration of the conference that Clemenceau would have to step down if he could not achieve some satisfaction for France. As exasperated as Wilson became with the Tiger, he acknowledged privately that "[a] new premier would probably be no better than Clemenceau" and would merely delay the proceedings while Europe collapsed around them.[65] The success of Clemenceau's domestic constraint projection is most vividly captured in Lloyd George's frustrated admission that "This [Rhineland] occupation has no other aim than to protect the French government against the opposition."[66]

Clemenceau's victories, though, were too small for the Assembly and the French public, who were incensed by the Rhineland settlement and the

"L'Allemagne et la France en 1919," in J. Bariéty, A. Guth, and J. M. Valentin, eds., *La France et l'Allemagne entre les deux guerres mondiales* (Nancy: Presses Universitaires de Nancy, 1987), 9–20.

64. Ray Stannard Baker, *Woodrow Wilson and World Settlement*, vol. 2 (Gloucester, Mass.: Peter Smith, 1960), 13.

65. Diary of Ray Stannard Baker, April 2, 1919, *PWW*, vol. 56, 542–43.

66. Minutes of a Meeting of the Council of Four, June 12, 1919, *DCF*, vol. 2, 401–5.

treaty as a whole. Parliamentary leaders from across the political spectrum, President Poincaré, Foch, and the center-to-right press all accused him of betrayal for failing to secure France's overriding strategic interests in the Rhineland.[67] The first speaker in the two-month Assembly debate on the treaty, M. de Chappedelaine, complained that "the Treaty of Versailles had neither assured the peace of the world nor guaranteed France against fresh aggression on the part of Germany." "The occupation of the bridge-heads on the Rhine would," moreover, "cease at the moment when the hope of revenge was reviving in Germany."[68] This chord was repeatedly struck by the many speakers that followed. Henri Franklin-Bouillon, the respected chairman of the Foreign Relations Commission, chastised Clemenceau for the lackadaisical way in which he advanced French claims to the Rhine as a strategic frontier and denigrated the value of the Anglo-American treaty of guarantee. Jean-Louis Barthou charged that it was uncertain if the United States would ratify the treaty, in which case Clemenceau had traded in concrete security measures for a scrap of paper.[69] Even prominent Socialists Albert Thomas and François Fournier, who had been more favorably disposed to a soft peace, lamented that the treaty did not secure "the return to France of the Rhine, which geographically belongs to it."[70] On this point, the Chamber was united against Clemenceau. Dissatisfaction was not confined to the Assembly, but could be found at the heart of the traditionally more realistic diplomatic corps, where two seasoned diplomats, Camille Barrère and Philippe Berthelot, sighed dejectedly, "c'est la paix boche."[71]

The Tiger ultimately won his ratification vote by misleading the country about his peace aims and by blaming Lloyd George and Wilson for the domestically unpopular treaty that resulted. At every stage prior to the ratification, he kept the country in the dark about the peace terms he was pursuing. On December 29, 1918, he asked for, and received, an overwhelming vote of confidence by the Assembly, without giving the deputies even an inkling of what he would demand from Germany and the Allies.[72] When the Assembly and the Foreign Relations Committee demanded to

67. King, *Foch Versus Clemenceau,* 113–20; McDougall, *France's Rhineland Diplomacy,* 85–89; Miquel, *La paix de Versailles,* 548–63.

68. Grahame to Curzon, August 27, 1919, in Kenneth Bourne and D. Cameron Watt, eds., *British Documents on Foreign Affairs (BDFA),* Part 2, series 1, vol. 1, 56–57.

69. Grahame to Curzon, September 5, 1919, *BDFA,* Part 2, series 1, vol. 1, 62–64; Grahame to Curzon, September 25, 1919, *BDFA,* Part 2, series 1, vol. 1, 69–71.

70. Quoted in King, *Foch Versus Clemenceau,* 113.

71. McDougall, *France's Rhineland Diplomacy,* 70.

72. *JO,* December 29, 1918, 3733–36.

be kept apprised of the negotiations taking place across town, Clemenceau ignored them, taking refuge behind Article VIII of the Constitution Law, which gave the executive the sole authority to negotiate treaties and directed him to inform both chambers of these negotiations "as soon as it is compatible with the interests and safety of the State to do so."[73] In other words, he was not required to consult the Assembly until the ratification debate. Time and again in the Assembly, Foreign Minister Stéphen Pichon refused to provide details on the negotiations, urging legislators to wait until the treaty was presented to the legislature for ratification.[74]

When the treaty was signed, Clemenceau faced his critics by emphasizing that he too was dissatisfied with the end result. He had done his best to secure the Rhine as the French military frontier and had worked tirelessly to advance the cause of French separatism, but in spite of his heroic efforts, the Anglo-Saxons would not grant France any more than was provided for in the treaty. "It is not our fault," the Tiger asserted, "if when I want to go to the Rhine today I encounter German countries between the Rhine and me." "The English and the Americans did not agree with our point of view, but this was not a reason to disrupt Allied unity." Therefore, if the Assembly were to reject this treaty, France could do no better and would likely fare much worse, since it would lose the Anglo-American guarantee and would face Germany alone.[75] In this manner, Clemenceau coaxed the reluctant deputies to ratify the peace treaty. His own political stock declined in value, however, as a result of the treaty. After the American Senate declined to ratify the treaty of guarantee, Clemenceau no longer was "Père la Victoire." He was the premier who lost the Rhine. Indeed, his Rhineland compromises contributed to his defeat in the January 1920 presidential elections.[76]

Germany's Eastern Boundaries

Initially, the British Government disapproved of extensive frontier rectification in Poland's favor, despite sympathy for the Poles in the British press.[77]

---

73. Loi Constitutionelle du 16 juillet 1875 sur les rapports des pouvoir publics, Article 8.

74. Mayer, *Politics and Diplomacy*, 660–61.

75. Jean-Baptiste Duroselle, *Clemenceau* (Paris: Fayard, 1988), 772. See also Sir George Grahame's account of André Tardieu's speech to the deputies on September 4, 1919, *BDFA*, Part 2, series 1, vol. 1, 58–60; King, *Foch Versus Clemenceau*, 118–19; Grahame to Lord Curzon, September 26, 1919, *BDFA*, Part 2, series 1, vol. 1, 71–73.

76. Duroselle, *Clemenceau*, 852.

77. See, for example, *The Times*, March 6, 1919, editorial "Poland and Danzig" and commentary on March 26, 1919 advocating the return of Danzig to Poland.

The British Foreign Office and General Staff opposed granting Polish control over Danzig and the corridor to the Baltic Sea.[78] Lloyd George himself considered the Polish claims to be "by every canon of self-determination extravagant and inadmissible."[79] Conversely, the French and American delegations were well disposed to Polish leaders and their need for economically and strategically secure frontiers. Clemenceau wanted a strong and secure Poland as an eastern counterweight to German power. In addition, any territory transferred from Germany to Poland would reduce German economic and military strength, making France more secure in the process.[80] Therefore, French policy favored extensive territorial transfers, including Danzig, parts of East and West Prussia, almost all of Upper Silesia, and the province of Posen. The French public fully endorsed this "strong Poland" policy.[81]

The American government was also sympathetic to Polish aspirations. Perhaps this sympathy stemmed from Wilson's natural affinity for a people seeking to establish republican self-government. Or, more cynically, perhaps it was because of the sizeable Polish vote in the United States.[82] The American public was also favorably disposed toward Polish claims, and even *The New York Times* — a newspaper that, on balance, advocated moderate peace terms — called for the return of Danzig and parts of Posen, Upper Silesia, West Prussia, and East Prussia to Poland.[83] It was no surprise,

78. Anna M. Cienciala, "The Battle of Danzig and the Polish Corridor at the Paris Peace Conference of 1919," in Paul Latawski, ed., *The Reconstruction of Poland, 1914–23* (New York: St. Martin's Press, 1992), 72; Nelson, *Land and Power*, 150.

79. Lloyd George, *Memoirs*, vol. 2, 631. Indeed, his vigorous resistance to Polish demands throughout the peace conference led Sally Marks to accuse him of being "intensely anti-Polish in all respects" and of "having fought to keep it [Poland] as small as possible." See *The Illusion of Peace* (New York: St. Martin's Press, 1976), 10. It is possible, as Jan Karski suggests, that he was merely skeptical of the stability of small states and preferred to construct a postwar order based upon larger, more stable powers. See *The Great Powers and Poland, 1919–1945* (Lanham, Md.: University Press of America, 1985), 36. This explanation is inconsistent, however, with the prime minister's comparative willingness to assist Czechoslovakia in its pursuit of secure borders.

80. Karski, *The Great Powers and Poland*, 37–38; Edouard Briault, *La paix de la France, les traités de 1918–1921* (Paris: Librairie de Recueil Sirey, 1937), 33ff.

81. Miquel, *La paix de Versailles*, 149–53.

82. Seth P. Tillman, *Anglo-American Relations at the Paris Peace Conference of 1919* (Princeton: Princeton University Press, 1961), 203–8.

83. In an October 15, 1918 editorial, the newspaper declared that these restorations "would be an act of justice to the Polish people, and incidentally a valuable safeguard against Prussia in the future." On March 28, 1919, in an editorial entitled "Stand by Poland," the editors repeated their support for Polish control over Danzig, so as not to create "a 'free' Poland with a rope around her neck."

therefore, that Wilson's thirteenth point called for an independent Poland with free and secure access to the sea. This implied his support for a corridor to the sea and, most likely, Polish control over the port city of Danzig. Wilson believed it was unnecessary, however, to transfer to the Poles any other territory that was inhabited primarily by Germans, since the League of Nations would assure Polish independence.[84]

On March 19, the Council of Ten considered the Commission on Polish Affairs report on Polish-German borders. The commission recommended a border drawn principally on ethnographic lines, with exceptions to satisfy Polish economic and strategic interests. Most importantly, it recommended: the transfer of Danzig to Polish sovereignty, despite its predominately German population, to provide Poland a commercial port; Polish control over a corridor connecting Danzig and Northern Poland to assure Polish access to the sea; Polish control over sections of West Prussia to secure the Danzig-Warsaw railway from German interference; the demilitarization of all of East Prussia to prevent an attack on Poland from the northeast; and a plebiscite to determine sovereignty over the southern regions of East Prussia.[85]

Lloyd George objected strenuously to the commission's recommendations because they assigned too many Germans to Polish control. He was particularly vexed by the award of Danzig and the West Prussian town of Marienwerder to the Poles, which was a complete violation of the principle of self-determination and, he believed, would inspire German *revanchism*. In his opinion, it was irresponsible, unjust, and dangerous to present the Germans a settlement that was so prejudicial to their interests and a blatant violation of the Fourteen Points—the agreed basis of the peace treaty. Surprisingly, Wilson defended this violation of the principle of self-determination both on strategic grounds and on the basis of fair play. The president accepted that the extension of Polish authority over German populations was "justified by reciprocity" since "[m]any Poles in areas historically Polish were to be left within Germany." The French maintained that departure from ethnographic principles was necessary to ensure the requisite economic and strategic frontiers to establish "a Polish state with some prospect of

84. Karski, *The Great Powers and Poland*, 38; Kay Lundgreen-Nielsen, "Aspects of American Policy towards Poland at the Paris Peace Conference and the Role of Isaiah Bowman," in Latawski, *The Reconstruction of Poland*, 95–97; Kay Lundgreen-Nielsen, *The Polish Problem at the Paris Peace Conference* (Odense: Odense University Press, 1979), 84.

85. The text of the report is reproduced in David Hunter Miller, *My Diary at the Conference of Paris*, with documents [microform] (New York: Printed for the author by the Appeal printing company, 1924), vol. 6, 350–66.

continued life."[86] The British prime minister remained intractable, though, fearing that the Weimar German Republic would be overthrown if it accepted such onerous terms. Consequently, he reserved the right to reconsider the Polish border question at a later date.[87]

In his Fontainebleau Memorandum of March 25, Lloyd George declared his opposition to an excessively punitive settlement that would transfer large numbers of ethnic Germans to neighboring states. This would undoubtedly lead to legitimate German dissatisfaction with the treaty and, ultimately, a future war or a Bolshevik revolution in Germany. He specifically targeted "[t]he proposal of the Polish Commission that we should place 2,100,000 Germans, under the control of a people which is of a different religion and which has never proved its capacity for self-government throughout history." In his opinion, this proposal, if implemented, "must ... lead sooner or later to a new war in the East of Europe." His recommendation, therefore, was to grant Poland a corridor to Danzig "to be drawn irrespective of strategic or transportation considerations so as to embrace the smallest possible number of Germans."[88] In other words, Danzig itself and Marienwerder were to remain German.

Clemenceau responded vigorously in the Council of Four on March 27, highlighting the Allies' duty to give Poland "the means to live." If the Council were to accept the prime minister's proposal to draw Polish borders on ethnic lines only, he prophesied, "we would leave a sad legacy to our successors." Above all, he warned that by concerning themselves excessively with the threat of bolshevism in Germany, they would be ignoring the more important peril of revolutionary dissatisfaction in France and England if they failed to impose a peace of victory. Lloyd George countered disingenuously that in Great Britain, although the more powerful upper classes manifested "an unlimited hatred of the German," the working classes wanted a more moderate peace. Furthermore, if war were to erupt as a result of the Polish Commission's recommendations, American and British public opinion would certainly oppose intervention because of the justice of the German position.[89] This heated exchange set the stage for an eight-day offensive by Lloyd George that succeeded in revising the Polish frontier significantly in Germany's favor.

86. Notes of a Meeting of the Council of Ten, March 19, 1919, *FRUS,* PPC 1919, vol. 4, 404–22.
87. Notes of a Meeting of the Council of Ten, March 22, 1919, *PWW,* vol. 56, 165–67.
88. *PWW,* vol. 56, 259–70.
89. Minutes of a Meeting of the Council of Four, March 27, 1919, *DCF,* vol. 1, 31–38.

In the April 1 Council of Four meeting, Wilson agreed to back Lloyd George in a plan to grant Danzig and the surrounding area to the League of Nations, rather than to Poland. The League would administer the city as an international port city that would be tied to Poland in an economic union. Marienwerder would hold a plebiscite to determine its disposition — which, because of its considerable German majority, would inevitably be a return to Germany. Poland would be granted control of the railways to Danzig, even when they passed through German territory. Clemenceau was taken aback by this plan and tried to postpone a final decision until the Poles could present their case to the Council, but he caved in to Anglo-American pressure and reluctantly accepted the British plan on April 3.[90] Together with the Commission on Polish Affairs, military and political experts within all three delegations, and the Poles themselves, Clemenceau tried to reopen the issue in the ensuing weeks, but Lloyd George was immovable.[91] The only revision that was subsequently made worked against the Poles. In June, at Lloyd George's insistence, the Council of Four agreed to hold a plebiscite in Upper Silesia rather than to grant the region to Poland.[92]

German Colonies

Compared to other postwar territorial questions, the disposition of former German colonies caused only minor conflict at the conference. Notwithstanding point 5 of his Fourteen Points—which held open the possibility that Germany would retain some of its colonial possessions—even Wilson proved willing to strip the defeated foe of all of its overseas territories on strategic grounds and because "[i]n many cases, the Germans had treated the native populations very badly."[93] The main source of controversy was whether these territories should be annexed by the other great powers as the French, the British, and the British Dominions required, or whether, as

90. Minutes of a Meeting of the Council of Four, April 1, 1919, *DCF*, vol. 1, 106–9; Minutes of a Meeting of the Council of Four, April 3, 1919, *DCF*, vol. 1, 123–29.

91. Nelson, *Land and Power*, 186–97.

92. See, in particular, Minutes of a Meeting of the Council of Four, June 3, 1919, *DCF*, vol. 2, 278–86; Minutes of a Meeting of the Council of Four, April 1, 1919, *DCF*, vol. 1, 386–95.

93. Point 5 promised "A free, open-minded, and absolutely impartial adjustment of all colonial claims, based upon a strict observance of the principle that in determining all such questions of sovereignty the interests of the populations concerned must have equal weight with the equitable claims of the government whose title is to be determined." On the unanimous agreement in the Council of Ten to confiscate German territories, see Notes of a Meeting of the Council of Ten, January 24, 1919, *PWW*, vol. 54, 249.

Wilson insisted, they should be placed under a League of Nations protectorate administered by a neutral power until these territories were capable of self-government and independence.[94] In his appeal for a mandatory administration, the president invoked both world opinion and American public opinion, which "would feel that their sacrifice in coming into the war had been in vain."[95] In order to overcome Wilson's opposition, Clemenceau and Lloyd George conceded mandatory League administrations, provided that they were granted to the states most directly interested in the particular colonies. The main objection to this compromise came from Australia and New Zealand, who wanted to annex New Guinea and Samoa, respectively, but they too were forced to concede in the face of Allied unity on the question.[96]

The Reparations Settlement

The postwar reparations settlement caused more anguish and recriminations than any other aspect of the Versailles Treaty. Denounced as economically unsound and short-sightedly vindictive only months after the conference by John Maynard Keynes—one of the British delegates—the enormous indemnity imposed on Germany has become a tragic symbol of the excesses of democratic peacemaking.[97] More accurately, it highlights the dangers of peacemaking by nonautonomous democratic executives, as the following analysis indicates.

French Policy

During the armistice negotiations of 1918, the French stipulated that Wilson's point 8, requiring the restoration of invaded French territory, must include the payment of reparations to compensate for "all damage done to

---

94. Notes of a Meeting of the Council of Ten, January 24, 1919, *PWW*, vol. 54, 249–54; Notes of a Meeting of the Council of Ten, January 28, 1919, *PWW*, vol. 54, 318–31.

95. Notes of a Meeting of the Council of Ten, January 28, 1919, *PWW*, vol. 54, 325.

96. See Notes of a Meeting of the Council of Ten, January 30, 1919, *PWW*, vol. 54, 350–78. By the end of the day, Wilson's confidante Dr. Grayson was able to report: "When the conference adjourned that night, the president had won a complete victory; the minority had swung the majority and the mandatory system had been approved and adopted so far as it applied to African and Pacific Islands." Grayson diary, January 30, 1919, *PWW*, vol. 54, 348.

97. John Maynard Keynes, *The Economic Consequences of the Peace* (London: MacMillan & Co. Ltd., 1920). See also Étienne Mantoux, *The Carthaginian Peace; or, The Economic Consequences of Mr. Keynes* (New York: Scribner, 1952).

the civilian population of the Allies and their property." Wilson and Lloyd George approved.[98] Nonetheless, as Marc Trachtenberg has demonstrated, it was not the Clemenceau government's intention to require Germany to pay for the entire cost of the war—a course of action that the French cabinet believed would be both unrealistic and undesirable. Instead, they hoped to secure a large but manageable payment from the Germans during the postwar reconstruction period primarily in the form of raw materials and export duties, to be supplemented by liquidated German colonial holdings and confiscated property in Alsace-Lorraine and neutral countries. The balance of French reconstruction needs were to be provided by a general reconstruction fund that they hoped would be incorporated into the League of Nations.[99] The government intended to demand high reparations from the Germans at the Peace Conference, however, as a means of encouraging Wilson to establish such an international reparations fund and to continue Allied economic cooperation, as well as a ploy to secure concessions from the Germans.[100]

In line with this policy, in December 1918, the French demanded five billion francs, plus applicable interest, in repayment of the indemnity from the 1870 war. In addition, Germany was to return the amount of taxes levied by the Germans on French citizens and communities, make restitution in kind of all raw materials and equipment removed during hostilities, and pay reparations for all property destroyed or confiscated during the war. Finally, the Germans were to compensate victims for the total cost of the war in fifty-six annuities to be completed in 1975.[101] They intended to reduce these excessive demands significantly if the United States would agree to contribute to French reconstruction needs and forgive some of the French war debt.

Of course, the French strategy was out of step with French public and parliamentary opinion, which was unanimous in its determination to make the Germans pay the entire cost of the war.[102] Clemenceau banked on satisfying the public by securing the full amount needed for reconstruction. If Germany paid a significant proportion of that amount, could the French

98. See the Three Power Declaration of November 5, 1919, reprinted in *PWW*, vol. 55, 31; Bailey, *Woodrow Wilson and the Lost Peace*, 45–46.

99. Trachtenberg, *Reparation in World Politics*, chap. 1; Étienne Clementel, *La France et la politique économique interalliée* (Paris: Presses Universitaires de France, 1931), 337–48.

100. Trachtenberg, *Reparation in World Politics*, 20–27.

101. French Proposed Basis for the Preliminaries of Peace with Germany, December 1918, *FRUS*, PPC 1919, vol. 1, 372–78.

102. Miquel, *La paix de Versailles*, 425–33.

truly be upset if the balance were provided by a "Societé Financières des Nations"? The crucial goal, then, was to ensure that France received the full amount from somebody.

When French leaders realized early on, however, that the United States wanted to abandon wartime Allied financial collaboration and would not hear of a Societé Financières des Nations, Clemenceau, Finance Minister Louis-Lucien Klotz, and chief reparations negotiator Louis Loucheur faced a considerable problem. Since any shortfall in payments would have to be filled by the French people themselves—who were already taxed heavily in order to prosecute the war—rather than the international community, the public would not forgive any government that showed leniency to the former enemy. The delegates were fully aware, though, that the Germans could not possibly pay all that they owed. In these difficult circumstances, they concluded that they would have to obtain as much as they possibly could directly from the Germans to satisfy their domestic constraints, but that they should prepare to meet the shortfall through taxation. This strategy prompted the most serious clash between Clemenceau's government and the Assembly prior to the ratification debates.

In February, Klotz intimated that he would impose a capital tax in France to help finance the French budget and postwar reconstruction. Announcement of this capital levy uncorked outrage in the press and the Assembly. Complaining that "now that a blood tax had been paid, a money tax was in the offing," the center-to-right senators and deputies—who constituted more than a majority—demanded that the budget be balanced directly through reparations and indirectly through loans obtained using future reparations as security. They declared that it was unacceptable for the French public to make any additional sacrifices; it was Germany's responsibility to finance French recovery.[103] Klotz bowed to this pressure, at least rhetorically, promising "that no financial sacrifice will be asked from this nation before the basis of the enemy's indebtedness has been established." Moreover, he asserted that the government "concentrates all its attention and vigilance" to obtaining the "*réparation intégrale*" that France deserved. The right wing press was still not satisfied, ordering Clemenceau not to lose "the fertility and richness of victory."[104]

The most serious parliamentary intervention followed three weeks later. On April 10, the Senate unanimously issued a proclamation requiring "the

103. See, in particular, the speeches by Louis Dubois on March 5, 1919 and Vincent Auriol on March 7, 1919, in *JO*, March 1919, 997–1001, 1065–71.

104. Mayer, *Politics and Diplomacy*, 650–54; Miquel, *La paix de Versailles*, 436–60.

exaction from the enemy of full restitution, the reparation of damage done to persons and property, that the full cost of the war shall be charged to the enemy." The following day, three hundred members of the Assembly passed a motion associating themselves with the Senate's declaration.[105]

In the meantime, at the Peace Conference, French representatives were fighting four battles. First, they were trying to get as liberal an estimate as possible of the damage that Germany was required to reimburse. To this end, they supported the British effort to include war costs and pensions as part of the settlement, in addition to restitution for damage done.[106] Second, they tried to extend German payments over as long a period as was necessary so that the full amount would be paid, if belatedly. Therefore, Clemenceau, Klotz, and Loucheur wanted to defeat American efforts to limit repayment to whatever the Germans could pay over thirty years.[107] Third, French delegates advanced the principle of unanimity within the Reparations Commission. They desired to have a French veto on all matters concerning payment procedures and, especially, the power to postpone or forgive portions of the debt, so that the other Allied governments could not reduce the total payment without their approval.[108] Finally, they struggled against the British to retain as much of each reparation dollar for France as possible.[109] Each of these French positions was designed to get as much from Germany as possible and, more important, to satisfy the French public that they would do so.

British Policy

The hallmark of Lloyd George's position on reparations was inconstancy. He declared himself a partisan of a moderate settlement, yet he insisted that Germany pay the war costs in addition to reparations for damaged territory; he desired to set a high figure for German obligations, but he wished to allow the Reparations Commission to reduce that figure afterwards; after the British delegation proposed a much higher figure than the French, he challenged the French figure for its immoderation. These

105. Mayer, *Politics and Diplomacy,* 659–60.

106. Tardieu, *The Truth,* 292; Tillman, *Anglo-American Relations,* 244–45.

107. See Minutes of a Meeting of the Council of Four, April 5, 1919, *DCF,* vol. 1, 146–53; Norman Davis and Vance McCormick to Wilson, April 4, 1919, *PWW,* vol. 56, 598–603.

108. Minutes of Meetings of the Council of Four, April 7, 1919, *DCF,* vol. 1, 168–77; Minutes of Meetings of the Council of Four, April 10, 1919, *DCF,* vol. 1, 218–25.

109. Minutes of a Meeting of the Council of Four, March 26, 1919, *DCF,* vol. 1, 23–30.

apparent contradictions can be understood only in the context of the formidable domestic opposition the prime minister faced over the reparations issue and his desire to escape his domestic constraints through deception.[110]

As a practical matter, Lloyd George doubted that Germany would ever be able to pay for the complete restoration of Allied territory and property in addition to compensation for lives lost, let alone Allied war expenditures. He feared that requiring Germany to make this restitution would cause the Germans to refuse to sign the peace treaty and might drive Germany to bolshevism. At the same time, he was under immense domestic pressure "to exact from Germany the very last farthing that she can reasonably be called upon to pay."[111] Indeed, the British public and many on the Unionist benches were far more concerned about the reparations settlement than any other aspect of the postwar peace, demanding that the Allies "squeeze the Hun until the pips squeak."

Consequently, although he tried at times to encourage a manageable indemnity, parliamentary interventions led Lloyd George to inflate the overall amount that Germany had to pay as well as to haggle over the proportion that Great Britain would receive. As the Council of Four addressed this vexing issue toward the end of March, Unionists in Parliament and the mainstream British press united to demand a stern reparations settlement that required Germany to pay the entire cost of the war, as Lloyd George had promised prior to the election. Their campaign culminated in a minatory telegram from 370 M.P.s on April 1, charging that "[t]he greatest anxiety exists throughout the country at the persistent reports from Paris that the British delegates instead of formulating the complete financial claim of the Empire are merely considering what amount can be extracted from the enemy." The M.P.s declared that "[o]ur constituents have always expected— and still expect—that the first action of the Peace Delegates would be ... to present the Bill in full, to make Germany acknowledge the debts and then to discuss ways and means of obtaining payment."[112]

It was difficult for the prime minister to reconcile his desire for a moderate figure with the inflated public and parliamentary demands. His strategy, though, was as follows. If war costs were excluded from reparations, Great

---

110. For a similar point of view, see Antony Lentin, "Several Types of Ambiguity: Lloyd George at the Paris Peace Conference," in Cathal J. Nolan, ed., *Ethics and Statecraft: The Moral Dimension of International Affairs* (Westport, Conn.: Greenwood, 1995), 119–24.

111. Speech by Lt. Col. Claude Lowther, *Hansard,* 5th series, 113, March 17, 1919, cols. 1870–72.

112. Lloyd George, *Memoirs,* vol. 1, 374–75.

Britain would not obtain one farthing of the booty, since British territory had not been occupied. His domestic critics would call for his head if the United Kingdom were thus shut out of the reparations game despite serving as the chief financiers of the Allied war effort. Therefore, he fought spirited battles against the Americans to extract payment for the costs of the war and pensions for those who lost their lives in battle.[113] Furthermore, he and his representatives on the Reparations Commission advocated a higher total figure than the French and Americans desired because the public would object if a lower figure made it appear that Germany was being treated gingerly.[114] As he admitted to Colonel House, "he knew that Germany could never pay anything like the indemnity which the British and the French demanded," but for domestic political reasons he had to insist on an impressive sum "even if Germany could never pay it, or even if it had to be reduced later."[115]

The prime minister's own dissatisfaction with this course of action was apparent when, in the Council of Four on March 26, he repeatedly attacked the lower figure advanced by France as well beyond the German capacity to pay.[116] His final concession to public opinion was his dogged effort to secure for Great Britain as great a percentage of each reparation dollar as possible, since that was bound to please the public.[117] In all these respects, Lloyd George advanced stern reparations proposals because these aspects of the settlement would be made public in the short-run.

At the same time, he was eager to postpone the major decisions until after the Peace Conference, when public sentiment was bound to subside, so that more moderate demands could be made. In particular, on March 27,

---

113. Including pensions also had the attractive side effect of increasing the total figure of damages, which would please the public. Trachtenberg, *Reparation in World Politics,* 68–71.

114. By March 25, the British were demanding a total figure of $55 billion. In contrast, the Americans proposed a minimum figure of $25 billion and a maximum of $35 billion, while the French suggested a minimum of $31 billion and a maximum of $47 billion. *DCF,* vol. 1, 5–6n.

115. Excerpts from House diary quoted in Mayer, *Politics and Diplomacy,* 625.

116. In effect, the prime minister was undermining his own position. Minutes of a Meeting of the Council of Four, March 26, 1919, *DCF,* vol. 1, 16–22.

117. In early March, Lloyd George informed House that "he could not sustain himself with his people" if all the German reparations went to France and Belgium and none to Great Britain. Instead, he proposed that 60 percent be devoted to reparation proper, while the remaining 40 percent be allocated for war costs, in which the British would share. House to Wilson, March 7, 1919, *PWW,* vol. 54, 458–59. Later, in the Council of Four, the prime minister asked for 30 percent of each dollar, while 50 percent would go to France. French representative Louis Loucheur, however, was aghast that the British, who had not been invaded, should receive more than half of what battle-ravaged France would receive. Minutes of Meetings of the Council of Four, March 25, 1919, *DCF,* vol. 1, 5–9; Minutes of Meetings of the Council of Four, March 26, 1919, *DCF,* vol. 1, 23–30.

the prime minister embraced Klotz's plan to set only the amount of the initial payment at the conference, leaving the balance to be determined by the Reparations Commission at a later date. In the secluded confines of the Council of Four, Lloyd George explained why he approved of postponement: "I see great advantages in not announcing today the total figure of what Germany owes us. You may be sure that, whatever the figure, many people in England, as well as in France, will exclaim at once: 'It is too small!' M. Klotz's formula gives us a way to avoid discussions which might ensue in our respective parliaments."[118] From that point on, he steadfastly opposed putting a definite figure on the reparations bill not because he wanted to increase British demands, but—on the contrary—because he wanted to lower them in the future when it would be politically acceptable. He told the Council on March 29, "I call attention to the importance, from the point of view of domestic politics, of not abandoning our claim to the totality of war costs, while admitting the obligation imposed upon us by the practical necessity to limit ourselves to a more modest demand."[119] Alternatively, he suggested setting a maximum figure at the conference that would be politically acceptable in Great Britain and France, with the explicit, but private, understanding that Germany would not be expected to pay the entire amount.

On the reparations issue more than on any other issue, then, the British Government was heavily constrained by the demands of public and parliamentary opinion. Nonetheless, Lloyd George—whom historians have characterized as a manipulator and a liar[120]—did his utmost to promote moderation in the final settlement by postponing and hiding as much of the meat of the agreement as possible.

American Policy

Unlike Britain and France, the United States did not have any direct material stake in the reparations question, nor was American public opinion particularly concerned about the issue, except for a general commitment to require Germany to right the wrongs it had committed. Leading Republicans,

118. Minutes of a Meeting of the Council of Four, March 28, 1919, *DCF*, vol. 1, 49–55.

119. Minutes of a Meeting of the Council of Four, March 29, 1919, *DCF*, vol. 1, 77. On April 5, he stated more explicitly, "The English public, like the French public, thinks the Germans must above all acknowledge their obligation to compensate us for all the consequences of their aggression. When this is done, we will come to the question of Germany's capacity to pay; we all think she will be unable to pay more than this document requires." Minutes of a Meeting of the Council of Four, April 5, 1919, *DCF*, vol. 1, 146–53.

120. See Sharp, *The Versailles Settlement*, 187; Lentin, *Lloyd George, Woodrow Wilson and the Guilt of Germany*, 111–23; and Lentin, "Several Types of Ambiguity."

though, *did* desire to enforce a large indemnity on the Germans. In October 1918, for example, RNC Chairman Hays encouraged the Allies to impose "whatever reparation they may exact for the frightful outrages inflicted upon them by the accursed Huns."[121] In December, when Lodge announced the Republican majority's alternate peace aims to the Senate, he went so far as to pledge that the United States would participate in the occupation of Germany in order to guarantee payment of the indemnity.[122]

Wilson and his representatives were unimpressed with the Republican program. With no direct interests in the matter and a desire not to impose an unreasonable financial strain on Germany, they sought to adhere as closely as possible to the terms of the pre-armistice agreement, which committed the Allies to "the payment by Germany of a manageable fixed sum within a defined period of time for damages specifically done to the civilian populations of Allied countries and their property."[123] American policy, then, was committed to making the German payments "*compensatory* rather than *punitive.*"[124] In concrete terms, this meant that the United States opposed British efforts to include war costs as a category of damage to be reimbursed, since that would put an insuperable strain on the German capacity to pay. Moreover, the Americans tried to set definite and moderate amounts (not more than $30 billion) to be repaid and a specified time limit, beyond which German obligations would expire.[125]

Determination of the Settlement

The reparations negotiations were difficult and vexing because of domestic political demands. On the whole, Wilson, whose domestic audience had the least at stake, was forced to concede the most, sacrificing clarity, precision, and moderation to ease Lloyd George's and Clemenceau's domestic problems. The only American victory was the reluctant British agreement to leave war costs out of the treaty. Securing French agreement was not difficult after American legal expert John Foster Dulles emphasized that including war costs would increase the British share of the booty at the expense of

---

121. *The New York Times,* October 28, 1918.

122. Colville Barclay to Balfour, December 7, 1918, *BDFA,* Part 2, series 1, vol. 1, 5–6.

123. Tillman, *Anglo-American Relations,* 229.

124. Memo by Allyn A. Young, December 28, 1918 in Philip Mason Burnett, *Reparation at the Paris Peace Conference from the Standpoint of the American Delegation,* vol. 1 (New York: Columbia University Press, 1940), 474–75.

125. Tillman, *Anglo-American Relations,* 232–59.

France and Belgium. For reasons of domestic politics, however, the British delegation was more difficult to persuade. To satisfy the British public, Dulles worked out a compromise, whereby the Allies held the Germans liable for war costs in theory, but would not actually require their repayment because of limitations on the German ability to pay.[126]

On all other aspects of the reparations settlement, the Americans were the ones who made the important concessions. In particular, Wilson gave way on the inclusion of pensions, the specification of a fixed sum to be demanded from Germany, fixing the amount that Germany could pay and the imposition of a thirty-year time limit for reparations. To satisfy Lloyd George, who made frequent references to his domestic difficulties, the final settlement covered all damages to persons and property, including pensions.[127] Moreover, since the British leader could not agree to a definite figure of less than $55 billion, Wilson reluctantly accepted the Klotz plan to defer the final determination until the Reparations Commission met in May 1921. When American negotiator Vance McCormick objected to postponement, Wilson explained that it was necessary to accommodate the British and French desiderata "as otherwise, he was told by them, their ministries might fall and we would have no governments to make peace with for some time to come."[128] House made a similar concession to the French regarding the duration of the payments so that Clemenceau could claim to the Assembly that the Germans would pay the full amount, even if it would take fifty years to do so.[129] Since the British and French could not reach an agreement on the relative shares of reparations money each country would receive that would satisfy their respective constituencies, that too was postponed until May 1921, when the Reparations Commission was to grant each country a share proportionate to their approved claims. Once again, Lloyd George proposed this compromise because it "has the advantage of not making us announce publicly any set proportion before the necessary investigations have taken place."[130]

The final reparations settlement, therefore, met Lloyd George's most important goals. It officially held the Germans liable for Allied costs of prosecuting the war, in order to satisfy public opinion, but in practice, these

126. Ibid., 233–59; Lansing to Wilson, February 19, 1919, *PWW,* vol. 54, 210–11.

127. See the interpretive clauses to the reparations agreement printed in *PWW,* vol. 56, 602–3.

128. McCormick diary, March 31, 1919, *PWW,* vol. 56, 444.

129. Minutes of a Meeting of the Council of Four, April 5, 1919, *DCF,* vol. 1, 146–53.

130. Minutes of a Meeting of the Council of Four, April 30, 1919, *DCF,* vol. 1, 423.

moneys were waived because of limitations on the German capacity to pay. Moreover, in accordance with British domestic pressure, the final settlement covered all damages to persons and property, including pensions. In these respects, the treaty ostensibly rewarded British domestic opinion. Nevertheless, the most significant aspects of the plan—the total amount that Germany would be required to pay and the relative shares of Great Britain and France—were postponed until the Reparations Commission met in 1921 in order to defeat the public demand for vengeance.[131] Needless to say, this is not something Lloyd George brought to the M.P.s' attention when he presented the settlement to Parliament.[132] As a consequence, Lloyd George's strategy of manipulation behind the closed doors of the Council of Four worked remarkably well. During the British ratification debates, Parliament, the press, and the public were satisfied with the reparations settlement and approved the Versailles Treaty without incident.[133]

Conclusions: Weak Democratic States and the Politics of Deception

We can make several observations about the impact of public and legislative opinion on the politics of the post–World War I settlement. Most important, both the traditional realist model of democratic foreign security policy and my own autonomy model outperformed the neorealist model in this case. While neorealist hypothesis N1 asserts that democratic executives can ignore domestic opposition to conduct foreign security policy in accordance with the reasons of state—especially on such important matters as peace settlements concluding major wars—in this case, each of the three democracies were constrained by their domestic opponents (Table 4). This was particularly the case on the reparations issue, where Lloyd George and Clemenceau were compelled to press for a far more punitive financial settlement than they thought prudent because of public and parliamentary cries for vengeance. Moreover, while Wilson pursued an independent policy at the Paris Peace Conference, the Republican majority in the Senate exercised

131. Tillman, *Anglo-American Relations,* 232–59.
132. Instead, he highlighted all that Germany was officially liable for under the agreement. Prime Minister's Motion to Accept Peace Treaty, *Hansard,* 5th series, 112, July 3, 1919, col. 1215.
133. On the positive reception the House of Commons and the country gave to the treaty, which was viewed as "severe but just," see Lloyd George, *Memoirs,* 487–90; Prime Minister's Motion to Accept Peace Treaty, *Hansard,* 5th series, 112, July 3, 1919, cols. 1211–35.

its power to defeat his entire peace program because the president ignored its wishes. These findings conform more closely with both traditional realist hypothesis T1, which expects all democratic states to be domestically constrained, and my structural autonomy hypothesis A1, which expects structurally weaker democratic states to have difficulty pursuing an independent policy.

On its own, this study of the post–World War I peace settlement cannot be a sufficient test case of the relative merits of the traditional model and my structural autonomy model, since the three democracies under investigation were all endowed with comparably low levels of structural autonomy by their domestic decision-making environments (see Chapter 2). Only when we compare their performance with the politics of peacemaking after World War II, which involved two governments substantially more autonomous than these as well as one considerably more constrained, can we draw meaningful comparisons. This we will do in Chapter 4. In the meantime, however, we can make an important preliminary observation about the utility of the independence-enhancing strategies of deception, which is not captured by the traditional realist model. Indeed, the experience of peacemaking in 1919 does not fully confirm the traditional realist hypothesis that democratic states are completely captive to public opinion and are unable to pursue conciliatory policies when the public cries for vengeance. Despite constant legislative demands for an expansionist Rhineland policy, Clemenceau was able to keep the Assembly in the dark about the compromise policy he was pursuing, to make extremely unpopular concessions on the Rhineland and the Saar, and to secure ratification of the settlement in the face of near-unanimous disapproval. Across the channel, Lloyd George could not agree to a moderate reparations settlement, but he did maneuver toward a more lenient plan by appeasing the public with a stern declaration of principles, while postponing its major elements until public sentiment would subside. Thus, democratic states—even comparatively constrained

Table 4   Conflicts between domestic and leader preferences

Country	Issue	Victor
United States	Overall settlement	Senate
France	Overall settlement	Leader
France	Reparations	Mixed/domestic opinion
United Kingdom	Reparations	Mixed/domestic opinion

ones—can act with some independence from domestic preferences if they deceive domestic opponents.

Comparing the French and American experiences in 1919 reveals much about the utility of hiding, misleading, and blaming to generate more policy independence for less autonomous executives. Wilson and Clemenceau each commanded executives at the lower end of our autonomy scale, yet both leaders sought to free themselves from their democratic constraints and to maximize their personal control over foreign security policy. Both appointed mediocre foreign ministers who were inclined to bow to their patron's wishes. Clemenceau even appointed himself minister of war to maximize his influence over foreign affairs. Furthermore, both men excluded leading parliamentary figures from their Peace Conference delegations. Wilson's five-member delegation to the conference included himself, his faithful assistant Colonel House, his ineffectual Secretary of State Robert Lansing, two political nonentities in Tasker H. Bliss and Henry White, and not a single senator or prominent Republican, despite the fact that they would inevitably decide whether the treaty would be ratified. Clemenceau excluded all parliamentary and political leaders from the country's peace delegation, except his loyal cabinet ministers, snubbing the influential Aristide Briand and President Raymond Poincaré in the process. Finally, both leaders encountered the wrath and resentment of their compatriots for the treaty they brought home. If Clemenceau achieved ratification of the treaty despite almost unanimous disapproval of the final package, while Wilson's edifice crumbled in a Senate ratification vote, that can be attributed only to the French leader's willingness to use to the fullest the independence-enhancing strategies of deception available to less autonomous executives.

Clemenceau reveled in the shroud of secrecy surrounding the peace deliberations and especially the Council of Four Meetings, providing no information on the conduct of negotiations to the Assembly. On occasions when the Assembly pressed for answers and threatened to flex its muscles, Clemenceau, Pichon, and Klotz opted to mislead, telling the deputies little, except that the government was completely in accord with the chamber's priorities and was tirelessly pressing French claims to the Rhineland, the Saar, and reparations. When the treaty was publicized, the Tiger and his faithful protégé Tardieu blamed its shortcomings on the Anglo-Saxons, claiming that it was the best deal for France to which they would agree. Believing him, the deputies held their noses and voted to ratify it. Wilson's scruples and pride, however, did not allow him to mislead his opponents about his positions in the negotiations, nor to blame the Europeans for the objectionable features of the agreement.[134] He had negotiated a treaty that corresponded as closely with his own wishes as the other national leaders would allow, but would not use deception to sell it to an American public and a Republican Senate that sought harsher punishment of Germany, a greater territorial commitment to France and Poland, and no League of Nations. In fact, instead of misleading and thereby coopting his domestic opponents, Wilson wasted no occasion to challenge and humiliate them. He declared quite openly what he stood for, why it was just, and why his opponents were misguided.[135] Consequently, since the president's opponents in the Senate had no reason to believe that their preferences were affecting policy, they did not feel compelled to rubber stamp a treaty of which they did not approve, negotiated by a president who showed them utter contempt.

The implication is that less autonomous executives cannot preserve any independence in conducting international negotiations if they do not hide, mislead, and blame. If they do, however, like Clemenceau, they may be able to retain more control over policy than one would expect of a structurally constrained democracy.

Regarding the ability of democratic states to invoke domestic opposition as a means of securing concessions from their negotiating partners, we can reach the following conclusions. First, as indicated in Table 5, all three states engaged in domestic constraint projection during the 1919 Peace Conference. On balance, they were able to achieve important concessions in the process. The Rhineland question is particularly instructive in this regard. Despite the fact that Wilson and Lloyd George both adamantly

---

134. In his speech to the Senate when he presented the treaty for ratification, Wilson stated, "It was impossible to accommodate the interests of so great a body of nations ... without many minor compromises." Nonetheless, "I think that it will be found that the compromises which were accepted as inevitable nowhere cut to the heart of any principle" of the Fourteen Points. Wilson's Address to the Senate, July 10, 1919, in Ray Stannard Baker and William E. Dodd, eds., *The Public Papers of Woodrow Wilson*, vol. 1 (New York: Kraus Reprint Co., 1970), 537–52. His comments on the treaty of guarantee with France did not blame the French at all for their intransigence, but instead presented the guarantee as an "obligation of gratitude and tested friendship." Wilson's Address to the Senate, July 29, 1919, ibid., 555–57.

135. When defending the domestically unpopular League of Nations Covenant in front of the Democratic National Committee, for example, Wilson harangued the treaty's critics, charging: "of all the blind and little provincial people, they are the littlest and most contemptible.... They have not got even good working imitations of minds. They remind me of a man with a head that is not a head but is just a knot providentially put there to keep him from raveling out." Wilson's speech to the Democratic National Committee, February 28, 1919, *PWW*, vol. 55, 322–23.

opposed an extended occupation, and Wilson frowned upon French political control of the Saar, Clemenceau was able to secure important concessions by reminding the Anglo-Saxons repeatedly that his government could not survive without them. At the same time, Lloyd George and Wilson countered that their domestic opinion would not tolerate leaving troops on the continent for an extended period. As a result, Clemenceau conceded an occupation of only fifteen years with only token forces from Britain and the United States. Lloyd George was particularly successful in using domestic opposition to prevent any immediate decision on reparations that would irritate the Conservatives in his coalition. The French did not use the threat of domestic revolt successfully when addressing the Polish question because they did not press the issue vigorously, most likely because it was of considerably less importance to them than the Rhenish frontier question. Therefore, Clemenceau made only passing references to the fear of a Bolshevist revolution in France if he could not bring home a victor's peace when discussing the Polish-German border.

These findings correspond both with traditional liberal hypothesis T2 and my structural autonomy hypothesis A2, since the three democracies, which were all comparably weak states, enjoyed comparable success with domestic constraint projection in international negotiations. Because the domestic decision-making environments of the three states provided the executives with comparable levels of autonomy, we will have to wait to compare their experience with Britain, France, and the United States after World War II before we can judge which is the more powerful of these two hypotheses. We can conclude, however, that neorealist hypothesis N2 is not a useful guide for understanding the peace negotiations of 1919. After all, Wilson, the leader of the powerful United States, was continually frustrated by the weaker, war-weary Europeans and frequently gave way to them. Relative power, therefore, did not determine bargaining outcomes, as neorealists would expect.

Table 5 Domestic constraint projection in intergovernmental negotiations

Country	Issue	Outcome
France	Disposition of Rhineland	Some success
United Kingdom	Disposition of Rhineland	Some success
United States	Disposition of Rhineland	Some success
France	Polish frontiers	Failure
United States	German colonies	Some success
United Kingdom	Reparations	Success

We might also observe that domestic constraint projection can be successful only if the threat is credible. Despite their preference for more moderate peace terms, neither Lloyd George nor Wilson tried to coax Clemenceau to moderation by claiming that domestic opinion demanded it, because it would not have been credible. The public pressure on Lloyd George throughout the conference indicated that British domestic opinion was more hawkish than its leader. The same was true in the United States, where the 1918 congressional election proved that the public favored a harsher peace than Wilson desired. Moreover, the Republican majority in the Senate—who were the president's real domestic opposition—agreed with the Europeans on most aspects of the settlement and were in touch with the French throughout the peace conference.[136] Thus, while Wilson could credibly claim that the U.S. public opposed an extended occupation of the Rhineland and favored placing the former German colonies under a League mandate, he did not similarly claim that they opposed either the imposition of heavy reparations or the transfer of the Saar to France.

These observations are interesting in themselves. In order to reach definitive judgments about the hypotheses being tested in this study, though, we will have to compare the behavior of Great Britain, France, and the United States in 1919 with that of democratic executives possessing different levels of foreign security policy autonomy. To this end, the next chapter will examine the peace settlement between the Three Powers (Great Britain, France, and the United States) and Germany after World War II.

136. Indeed, Wilson rebuked Tardieu publicly in March for contacting Lodge behind his back and leaking information about the negotiations. Grayson diary, March 28, 1919, *PWW*, vol. 55, 347–49.

4

The Post–World War II
Settlement, 1945–1954

At the Yalta and Potsdam conferences, the United States, Great Britain, and the Soviet Union drafted the outlines of a punitive and comprehensive post–World War II settlement with Germany, designed to prevent the Germans from again plunging the European continent into war. Politically, this entailed the division of Germany into four occupation zones to be administered by each of the Big Three and France, who would exert complete political control over the Germans during an extended occupation until a final peace treaty was signed. The economic component of the settlement aimed at the industrial demilitarization of Germany through a program of reparations, industrial dismantling, and rigid industrial controls. Finally, Germany was to be permanently demilitarized.

Economic and strategic considerations soon caused

Western leaders to question the logic of enforcing the harsh provisions of this settlement. To begin with, since postwar Western European economic recovery was a high priority for Western governments, British and American leaders decided that it would be counterproductive to squelch German coal and steel production, which could help fuel that recovery. Moreover, the atrocious living conditions in war-ravaged Germany coupled with the harsh winters of 1946 and 1947 required the Allies to supply inordinate amounts of money and food to feed the starving German population at a time when Britain, in particular, could ill afford it. Of even greater significance, however, was the growing rift between the Soviet Union and the Western Allies. The Cold War division of Europe into East and West convinced leaders of all three Western democracies that German economic and political recovery was essential in order to keep Soviet influence out of Western Europe. After the Berlin Crisis and the Korean War highlighted the dangers of the Soviet conventional force advantage on the continent, the political and military leaders in all three countries further concluded that Western defense could not succeed without some form of West German rearmament.

As a result of these concerns, Three Power executive preferences began to diverge sharply from public and legislative attitudes. Domestic opinion in all three Western democracies was uniformly hostile to the Germans and wanted to impose harsh peace terms on them. Yet by 1947, even French leaders appreciated the need to rehabilitate the German economy. And by the autumn of 1950, the leadership of all three Western powers recognized the urgent need to rearm the Germans. The politics of the post–World War II settlement, therefore, presents an excellent opportunity to test the hypotheses about the impact of domestic opinion laid out in the Introduction. Neorealists would expect that once leaders determined that it was in their interest to rehabilitate Germany as a bulwark against the Soviet Union, they should have been able to do so immediately regardless of domestic opinion. Conversely, traditional realists would expect that when the public and the legislature desired to enforce a punitive peace, all three governments should have had great difficulty pursuing a conciliatory policy even if they believed it to be essential on national security grounds. If my model of structural autonomy is correct, however, we should expect to see a great deal of independence by the governments of the United States and Great Britain, which were identified *a priori* as having highly autonomous foreign policy executives. The highly constrained French foreign policy executive, though, should have encountered great difficulties when it tried to soften the peace terms.

Furthermore, since postwar decisions on the fate of Western Germany were largely the result of intense bargaining between the three great democratic victors of World War II, a careful study of the negotiations will allow us to test this study's second set of hypotheses, on the nature of international bargaining between democracies. To validate neorealist expectations, we would have to find that the United States—by far the dominant Western power in this period—was able to impose its preferences on the much weaker British and French. If the traditional liberal model of democratic bargaining is correct, then all three democracies should have referred to their domestic difficulties with comparable frequency and should have been comparably successful when they did so. My model of democratic autonomy would be supported if French leaders enjoyed a comparative advantage in using domestic opposition as a lever with which to extract concessions and if they resorted to domestic constraint projection more frequently.

To test these competing hypotheses, whose implications are presented in Table 6, this chapter will analyze the evolution of Three Power policies and negotiation strategies regarding the political, economic, and military settlements with Germany after World War II, beginning with the political and territorial settlement.

Table 6 Predictions of the three models for the post–World War II settlement

	Neorealist Model	Traditional Model	Autonomy Model
Domestic impact on postwar settlement policies	Minimal for all three democracies	High for all three democracies (realist)	High for France, low for Great Britain and the U.S.
Effectiveness of domestic constraint projection in multilateral bargaining	Irrelevant; power determines bargaining outcomes	High for all three democracies (liberal)	High for France, low for Great Britain and the U.S.
Frequency of constraint projection	Indeterminate and irrelevant	Frequent for all three democracies (liberal)	Frequent for France, infrequent for Great Britain and the U.S.

The Political and Territorial Settlement and
German Sovereignty, 1945–1952

Under the terms of the Yalta Agreement, Germany was divided into three zones of occupation, to be administered individually by the Soviets, the Americans, and the British until the three allies could reach a final settlement with their former enemy. From the American and British zones, an occupation zone was to be created for the French.[1] Initially, the Three Powers exerted complete control over their own zones of occupation, while they carried out programs of denazification, demilitarization, and industrial dismantling. Gradually, all three western zones allowed for greater German participation in zonal administration, as East-West tensions mounted.

Initial Attitudes

GREAT BRITAIN

Following the war, anti-German sentiment enveloped the United Kingdom. Having fought two bitter and draining wars against the Germans in thirty years, the British people harbored an intense dislike of Germany and the German people, whom they distrusted and regarded as overly militaristic. This image was compounded by the hardships endured by the British during the Battle of Britain and mounting evidence of the atrocities committed by the German Army during the war.[2] While there is little systematic polling information on British attitudes toward Germany during this period, the evidence that does exist confirms this impression. For example, in August 1945, 53 percent of Britons surveyed by Gallup reported negative feelings toward the German people, while only 25 percent professed any "sympathy" for them.[3] Even in 1947, when hatred of the Germans began to abate slightly—54 percent of British respondents with opinions claimed to be friendly toward the German people as opposed to 46 percent who

---

1. "Protocol of the Proceedings of the Crimea Conference," February 11, 1945, *Foreign Relations of the United States (FRUS), Yalta*, 978.

2. For an excellent discussion of the sources and content of British opinion toward Germany in this period, see D. C. Watt, *Britain Looks to Germany* (London: Oswald Wolff, 1965), 114–29.

3. George H. Gallup, *The Gallup International Public Opinion Polls: Great Britain, 1937–1975*, vol. 1 (New York: Random House, 1976), 117. British antipathy toward Germans was confirmed in December 1946 when 95 percent responded that they would not send any of their rationed foods to the starving population of Germany (145).

were unfriendly—an overwhelming majority doubted that Germany could become a "peace-loving, democratic nation" and expected it to threaten world peace in the future.[4] Consequently, there was heavy support in the United Kingdom for a long occupation and a peace settlement that imposed strict political, economic, and military controls on Germany in order to prevent it from starting yet another war.[5]

The political leadership, however, had different priorities. Though the Labour Government that came to power shortly after the war could hardly be labeled "pro-German,"[6] they realized quickly that a German recovery was essential in order to serve the twin objectives of British and European recovery and the reconstruction of a stable balance of power in Europe.[7] Consequently, they desired to enforce the provisions of the Potsdam Agreement without placing burdens on Germany that were too onerous, with an eye toward a rapid, if cautious, German political and economic recovery. They rejected the French plan to revise the western frontiers of Germany because of the detrimental effect it would have on the German economy. And when it became clear to the Foreign Office that the Soviet Union would always pose a threat to British interests in Germany, the Labour leadership quickly agreed, however reluctantly, on a Western strategy premised on the economic recovery, political rehabilitation, and association of western Germany with the West.[8] Thus, the Labour leadership did not allow public animosity to determine their postwar German policy.

4. Sixty-five percent of respondents with opinions expected future German aggression, while only 35 percent expected democracy to take hold. Ibid., 148.

5. Ibid., 148. Throughout the final days of the war, the British Government received an enormous amount of letters from British citizens recommending harsh peace plans designed to prevent a future German resurgence. The various plans included: transfer of German territory to other European countries, terminating German control of the Kiel canal, heavy reparations, severe industrial restrictions, a controlled, lower standard of living for Germans, and complete disarmament. See the various letters in PRO, FO371/46865–69.

6. Leading cabinet ministers, including Prime Minister Attlee and Foreign Secretary Bevin, had served in Winston Churchill's war cabinet and had supported the war effort fully. They and other prominent Labourites were only too aware of the dangers posed by German militarism and the tremendous toll Europe paid for its lack of vigilance toward Germany in the past. Indeed, Bevin said privately of the Germans to British Military Governor in Germany Brian Robertson, "I tries 'ard, Brian, but I 'ates them." Quoted in Alan Bullock, *Ernest Bevin, Foreign Secretary 1945–1951* (London: Heinemann, 1983), 90.

7. COS (46) 105 (O), April 5, 1946; CP (46) 139, April 15, 1946; CP (46) 156 (and attachments), April 15, 1946; CM (46) 36, April 17, 1946.

8. Anne Deighton goes as far as to conclude that for this reason the British cabinet was committed to a divided Germany even before the Americans were. "Towards a 'Western' Strategy: The Making of British Policy Towards Germany, 1945–46," in Anne Deighton, ed.,

Initially, in the aftermath of the war, French political leaders and the French public were in agreement on the way to treat their defeated enemy. Both believed that French security could be guaranteed only by a harsh settlement denying the Germans the economic and military resources to overturn the balance of power.[9] To meet this challenge, General de Gaulle's "thesis" on Germany, which remained the core of French policy until well into 1948, had five essential elements. First, a centralized German government should be rejected in favor of a loose confederation of German states. Second, the industrial Ruhr was to be separated from Germany and treated as a separate political entity. This region was to be occupied by an international force and its mines internationalized. Third, the left bank of the Rhine was also to be separated from Germany and divided into two or three separate states. The French were to occupy this region permanently, with the help of the Benelux countries and, possibly, Great Britain. Fourth, the Saar was also to be separated from Germany and administered by France. Sarrois mines were to become French property in compliance with the Versailles Treaty of 1919. Finally, Germany would be required to make high reparations payments in order to weaken German industry and fuel the French recovery.[10]

To be sure, there were some in the diplomatic corps, led by Ambassador to London René Massigli and Secretary General of the Foreign Ministry Jean Chauvel, who felt that de Gaulle's thesis was too harsh and, therefore, counterproductive.[11] And, in early 1946, new Premier Félix Gouin was

---

Britain and the First Cold War (New York: St. Martin's Press, 1990), 53–70; Deighton, *The Impossible Peace: Britain, the Division of Germany, and the Origins of the Cold War* (Oxford: Clarendon, 1990).

9. De Gaulle had concluded that "[t]o make France's recovery possible, the German collectivity must lose its capacity for aggression." Charles de Gaulle, *War Memoirs*, vol. 3 (New York: Simon and Schuster, 1960), 51. An August 1945 Gallup poll reported that an overwhelming 89 percent of French respondents with opinions agreed that a future war could be avoided "by keeping Germany weak and depriving her of the means of making war." George H. Gallup, *The Gallup International Public Opinion Polls: France, 1939, 1944–1975*, vol. 1 (New York: Random House, 1976), 31. In September, L'Institut Français d'Opinion Publique (IFOP) published a poll indicating that the vast majority of Frenchmen (87 percent of respondents with opinions) wanted to dismember Germany. *Sondages*, 7ième Année (1 septembre, 1945): 173.

10. de Gaulle, *War Memoirs*, vol. 3, 239–40; meeting between de Gaulle and Truman, August 22, 1945, de Gaulle, *War Memoirs*, vol. 5, 283–87; memorandum by the French delegation to the CFM, September 13, 1945, *FRUS*, 1945, vol. 3, 869–71.

11. John W. Young, *Britain, France and the Unity of Europe* (Leicester: Leicester University Press, 1984), 7; Jean Chauvel, *Commentaire: d'Alger à Berne* (Paris: Fayard, 1972), 108–10.

inclined to forgo an independent Ruhr in exchange for the international economic controls proposed by the British. But the public, the balance of the political leadership, and most important, Foreign Minister Georges Bidault, remained faithful to the general's plan, with minor elaborations.[12] Bidault rallied the cabinet to maintain a hard line on Germany and was rewarded by the electorate in June, when he rode the electoral gains of the Mouvement Républicain Populaire (MRP) to the premiership.[13]

On the political front, then, in the first year after the Allied victory, de Gaulle and Bidault pushed their policy of territorial amputation diplomatically, while General Koenig, the French military governor in Germany, resisted the creation of central German administrations in the Allied Control Council (ACC).[14] Instead, the French advocated a decentralized confederation of autonomous German *Länder* "in order to avoid rebuilding a centralized state in which the spirit of Prussian militarism would continue to predominate."[15] To this end, the French attempted to create strong *Länder* governments and encouraged separatist movements in their occupation zone. In coming years, however, the breakdown of Four Power cooperation would force French leaders to rethink their German policy and soften their position to the extent that domestic opinion allowed.

THE UNITED STATES

In the immediate aftermath of the war, American public opinion toward Germany was every bit as negative as the British and French. Throughout

12. René Massigli, *Une comédie des erreurs* (Paris: Plon, 1978), 81–82; Jacques Dalloz, *Georges Bidault: Biographie politique* (Paris: L'Harmattan, 1992), 130–31; Young, *Britain, France and the Unity of Europe,* 29–30. That the French public favored de Gaulle's call for the separation of the Ruhr over Gouin's plan for international control is indicated by a series of IFOP polls conducted in 1946. In April, 71 percent of respondents preferred separation to only 14 percent who endorsed international controls. In August, the figures were 63 percent for separation to the same 14 percent for control. *Sondages,* 9ième Année, No. 3 (1 février, 1947): 26.

13. The American Embassy attributed the MRP's electoral success directly to Bidault's popular German policy. Caffery to State Department, June 3, 1946, NARA, 851.51/6–346; Irwin Wall, *The United States and the Making of Postwar France, 1945–54* (Cambridge: Cambridge University Press, 1991), 57.

14. General Koenig to the Allied Control Council, October 1, 1945, *Documents français relatifs à l'Allemagne (DFRA)* (Paris: Imprimerie Nationale, 1947), 16; John W. Young, *France, the Cold War, and the Western Alliance, 1944–49: French Foreign Policy and Postwar Europe* (New York: St. Martin's Press, 1990), 82–83.

15. "Memorandum de la délégation française au sujet de l'Allemagne," April 25, 1946, FO371/55842. On the French plan for a German confederation, see Bevin to FO, July 10, 1946, FO371/55843.

1945 and 1946, the White House was flooded with letters from the public either supporting the Morgenthau Plan for the pastoralization of Germany,[16] advocating the division of Germany and harsh treatment or punishment of the German people, and decrying the reduction of U.S. Army rations in Europe to feed starving Germans. Considerably fewer letters asked for leniency.[17] Public opinion polls confirmed that most Americans distrusted the German people and were skeptical that they could become democratic and peace loving.[18] Consequently, the vast majority of Americans desired the territorial dismemberment of Germany, and most favored severe treatment of and rigid controls on the Germans.[19]

The American deputy military governor in Germany, General Lucius D. Clay, however, refused to let public hostility toward Germany derail his efforts to reconstruct a semblance of order in the chaos of postwar Germany. Clay "believed that his first responsibility was to get Germany 'on its

16. The Morgenthau Plan, devised by Treasury Secretary Henry Morgenthau, was a Carthaginian blueprint for postwar Germany, calling for demilitarization, prosecution of war criminals, heavy reparations payments, the removal of the Saar to France and the provinces of East Prussia and Upper Silesia to Poland, the division of the remaining portion into two autonomous and independent states, and, most infamously, the removal of all industry and technically-skilled workers from the Ruhr, "the caldron of wars." See Warren F. Kimball, *Swords or Ploughshares? The Morgenthau Plan for Defeated Nazi Germany, 1943–1946* (Philadelphia: Lippincott, 1976); Morgenthau to Roosevelt, September 5, 1944, *FRUS: Conference at Quebec, 1944,* 101–6. President Roosevelt ultimately rejected the plan in favor of the more moderate occupation blueprint, JCS 1067. "Directive to SCAEF Regarding the Military Government of Germany in the Period Immediately Following the Cessation of Organized Resistance (Post-Defeat)," September 22, 1944, *FRUS, Yalta,* 143–56; Robert Dallek, *Franklin D. Roosevelt and American Foreign Policy, 1932–1945* (New York: Oxford University Press, 1995), 472–79; and Manfred Jonas, *The United States and Germany* (Ithaca: Cornell University Press, 1984), 268–74.

17. Papers of Harry S. Truman, Official File, 198 Misc (1945–46), HSTL.

18. In a December 1945 National Opinion Research Center (NORC) poll, 66 percent of respondents with opinions doubted "that Germany will ever become a peace-loving nation," and almost 90 percent of respondents with opinions in a May 1946 NORC poll expected that "Germany would try to start another war in the next 25 years, if the allies don't watch her carefully." Roper Center at the University of Connecticut, Public Opinion On-Line (hereafter cited as *POO*), USNORC.450137, R03, December 1945 and USNORC.460142, R04, May 1946. See also USROPER.45-050, R08, October 1945, and USNORC.460241, R11A, May 1946.

19. An August 1945 NORC poll revealed that 67 percent of respondents with opinions thought that the United Nations should "break Germany up into smaller states." *POO*, USNORC.450132, R07, August 1945. In Gallup polls conducted in July and October 1945, the majority of respondents with opinions believed that the occupation regime was treating civilians in Germany "too softly" or "not tough enough," while fewer than 3 percent felt the Germans were being treated "too harshly." *POO*, USGALLUP.45-351, QKT08, July 1945 and USGALLUP.111445, RT13, November 1945. See also USGALLUP.052745, RK01, May 1945 and USNORC.450133, R07A, August 1945.

feet,'" in order to reduce the cost to taxpayers and mitigate the suffering he saw all around him in postwar Germany. He was convinced that German recovery and political rehabilitation as a democracy was an essential prerequisite for peace in Europe. Moreover, he considered that "his primary mission was the establishment of a democratic German government at the earliest possible moment."[20] As a result, he used the "disease and unrest" provision in JCS 1067—the U.S. occupation blueprint—together with the Potsdam decisions on central administrations and economic unity to rebuild Germany economically and politically, while conducting rigorous campaigns of denazification and demilitarization.[21] In the process, due to his considerable influence and the growing Soviet–American rift, other leading American officials also became aware of the need to rehabilitate the former enemy.

The first political expressions of this softer official attitude toward Germany came in the form of intense American pressure to establish the central German administrations envisioned at Potsdam and in initial American coolness to the French proposal to separate the Ruhr and Rhineland from Germany. Indeed, American leaders demonstrated their reluctance to acquiesce in any policies that threatened to render Germany economically unviable or to force the Germans to embrace the Soviet Union and communism.[22] Hence, almost from the outset, American policymakers predicated their policy toward Germany on economic and strategic concerns rather than on an effort to punish German aggression, in spite of a punitive public sentiment.

The Paris Conference of Foreign Ministers, Summer 1946: The Origins of the Bi-zone

After the Potsdam Agreement of 1945, the first significant quadrilateral discussion of Germany took place at the Conference of Foreign Ministers (CFM) in Paris from April through July 1946. The meetings revealed an

20. John H. Backer, *Winds of History: The German Years of Lucius DuBignon Clay* (New York: Van Nostrand Reinhold, 1983), 14; Thomas Alan Schwartz, *America's Germany: John J. McCloy and the Federal Republic of Germany* (Cambridge: Harvard University Press, 1991), 30.

21. Backer, *Winds of History*, 52–58.

22. See, for example, Byrnes to Caffery, November 21, 1945, *FRUS*, 1945, vol. 3, 908; Patterson to Byrnes, November 21, 1945, *FRUS*, 1945, vol. 3, 908–9; Stimson to Truman, *FRUS*, 1945, Potsdam II, 990–91; Melvyn Leffler, *A Preponderance of Power: National Security, the Truman Administration, and the Cold War* (Stanford: Stanford University Press, 1992), 68–70; and Young, *France*, 61.

unbridgeable chasm between Soviet and Anglo-Saxon views on reparations and central administrations. This left the French, who desperately wanted a Four Power settlement neutralizing all of Germany, out in the cold. Worse still for the French was that none of the other powers were willing to entertain the territorial amputations that were the cornerstone of the French German policy. However, because of extreme French domestic instability, American Secretary of State James Byrnes and British Foreign Secretary Ernest Bevin consented to the political separation of the Saar as an interim measure until a final peace settlement could be concluded.

DISCUSSIONS ON ECONOMIC UNITY

The British departed for the conference determined to reach a Four Power settlement that would treat Germany as an economic whole, as provided for at Potsdam. This meant establishing central administrations to coordinate the economy of all four occupation zones. Without them, the British zone— the most heavily populated and least agricultural—would remain unable to feed itself and would continue to impose an unbearable cost on the flagging British economy.[23] The Americans shared similar goals, although they were growing increasingly weary of Soviet intransigence and many State Department officials, including George Kennan, advocated the division of Germany so that the western zones could recover as part of Western Europe.[24] Believing that German recovery was essential, both to foster European stability and to thwart Communist influence there, Byrnes was convinced that the Four Power stalemate must be broken, lest Germany be lost.[25] British and American policies, therefore, were dictated by national imperatives rather than the public appetite for blood. Nevertheless, the secretary of state made one more appeal to the Soviets for Four Power cooperation, offering a treaty guaranteeing the demilitarization of Germany for twenty-five years in exchange for the implementation of Potsdam. The carrot, however, was accompanied by the stick; prior to the conference, he allowed Clay to suspend all reparations payments from the American zone until a decision on economic unity was reached.[26]

As expected, Soviet Foreign Minister Molotov did not cooperate. He

23. Robert W. Carden, "Before Bizonia: Britain's Economic Dilemma in Germany," *Journal of Contemporary History* 14, no. 3 (July 1979): 534–55; CM (46) 16, February 18, 1946.

24. Leffler, *A Preponderance of Power*, 117; Walt W. Rostow, *The Division of Europe after World War II: 1946* (Austin: University of Texas Press, 1981), 38–50, 62–69.

25. See, for example, Byrnes to Patterson, April 10, 1946, *FRUS, 1946*, vol. 5, 539–40.

26. This decision was taken to overcome French, as well as Soviet, intransigence. John Gimbel, *The Origins of the Marshall Plan* (Stanford: Stanford University Press, 1976), 118–19; Clay to Major Oliver Echols of the War Department, May 2, 1946, Jean Edward Smith, *The*

informed the meeting that the Soviets were reluctant to establish central administrations unless the Western powers agreed to their reparations plan—which would, in effect, devote the entire production of the Eastern zone to the service of the Soviet economy and place such a strain on the Western zones that it would be impossible for the country, as a whole, to recover.[27] Molotov also rejected Byrnes's demilitarization treaty. To add insult to injury, the Soviet foreign minister began the bidding war over Germany by declaring that Moscow wanted to revive the German economy and did not oppose the political unification of Germany.[28] Byrnes, therefore, sought to end the charade of seeking a Four Power solution by inviting any of the other three occupying states to join their zone with the American zone in the interests of West German recovery. The British cabinet did not need much persuading. While the American zone was poorer than their own, they saw in zonal fusion an opportunity to provide the British zone with timber and other resources from the American zone, as well as food and financial resources from the United States. In addition, consolidation would in the long run promote the British goal of German self-sufficiency.[29] These economic motivations dovetailed with heightened cabinet perceptions of the Soviet threat and the need to build Germany up as a barrier to communist expansion.[30] Bevin, thus, accepted the American offer and the two countries proceeded to promote recovery within the bizone, while attempting to encourage the French to add their zone to the Western lot.

The French were unwilling to follow suit. They still believed that Germany posed a greater threat to France than did the Soviet Union; thus, it

---

Papers of General Lucius D. Clay, vol. 1 (*Clay Papers*) (Bloomington: Indiana University Press, 1974), 203–4; Under Secretary of State Acheson to Byrnes, May 9, 1946, *FRUS,* 1946, vol. 5, 549.

27. In this regard, see "Discussion on Germany at the Council of Foreign Ministers," FO Minute by A. A. E. Franklin, July 11, 1946, assessing Molotov's position at the CFM—FO371/55843.

28. Molotov's speech, July 10, 1946, Beate Ruhm von Oppen, ed., *Documents on Germany under Occupation, 1945–54 (DGO)* (London: Oxford University Press, 1955), 144–47.

29. CP (46) 292, July 25, 1946; CM (46) 68, July 15, 1946.

30. In May, Bevin exhorted his cabinet colleagues that "preventing the revival of a strong aggressive Germany ... can no longer be regarded as our sole purpose, or, indeed, perhaps as our primary one. For the danger of Russia has become certainly as great as, and possibly even greater than, that of a revived Germany." CP (46) 186, May 3, 1946. Only a month earlier, the chiefs of staff had cautioned that "[o]ur policy towards Germany should be such as would not prevent us from building her up again if this becomes necessary. In addition, so that we could count on effective German assistance in the event of conflict with Russia, we should try to avoid arousing permanent German antagonism towards us." Quoted in Deighton, *The Impossible Peace,* 65–66.

was unwise to break with the USSR in order to revive Germany.[31] Besides, it would have been impolitic to side with the West over the Soviet Union without demonstrably just cause, since the pro-Moscow French Communist Party (PCF) enjoyed too much support to alienate completely.[32] Paris therefore concluded that joining the bi-zone before reaching a satisfactory agreement on the Western industrial regions, the level of industry, and the future political status of Germany would be prejudicial to French interests, risk a powerful public response, and undermine the possibility of winning Russian support for the French security propositions.[33]

FRENCH SECURITY PROPOSALS

At the Paris CFM, the French continued to press for a long occupation, territorial amputation, adequate security guarantees, and a Four Power agreement to neutralize all of Germany. It became clear early on, though, that the rift developing between the Soviet Union and the Anglo-Saxons would prevent these goals from being realized and that the conference would be a major defeat for French policy.

To make matters worse for the French, at the outset of the conference, Byrnes stated that he did not desire a long occupation of Germany.[34] Moreover, London and Washington were by now completely opposed to political separation of the Ruhr and the Rhineland. The Labour cabinet objected to an independent Ruhr since this would cut the economic heart out of the British zone and would require extraordinary financial support from a badly strained British economy that was already pumping much more than it could afford into Germany.[35] To prevent the British from becoming mired in an ever-worsening situation, Bevin—who also feared

31. See the reports of meetings between Bidault and British representatives in April 1946 in FO371/55842. In this context, it is noteworthy that in March 1947, newly elected President Vincent Auriol viewed the Treaty of Dunkirk as part of an Anglo-Franco-Soviet alliance system to contain Germany. Vincent Auriol, *Journal du Septennat*, vol. 1 (Paris: Librarie Armand Colin, 1970), 17–18.

32. Massigli, *Une comédie*, 84.

33. Ibid.; Hervé Alphand, *L'étonnement d'être: journal, 1939–1973* (Paris: Fayard, 1977), 195.

34. Bevin to FO, July 11, 1946—FO371/55844.

35. "We are spending on this zone much more than we should reasonably be required to pay, and we are getting out of it much less than we are reasonably entitled to receive," Chancellor of the Exchequer Hugh Dalton complained to the cabinet in June 1946. "And, though we are putting so much in and taking so little out, we are told that the inhabitants are nearly starving and that, unless we put more in and take less out, they will all become either Nazis or Communists." CP (46) 218, June 4, 1946.

that removing the Ruhr would leave the rump of Germany vulnerable to Soviet influence—advocated the return of the Ruhr to the future German state, but agreed that ownership of Ruhr industries should be allocated to an international authority.[36] The Americans, likewise, resisted overly punitive measures that would subvert German economic recovery or drive the German people into Soviet arms. Indeed, in his widely publicized September Stuttgart speech, Byrnes made a conscious attempt to woo the Germans, promising to keep the Ruhr and the Rhineland in Germany and committing the United States to greater German self-rule and early steps toward a democratic German provisional government.[37]

Bidault won some concessions from his English-speaking counterparts by impressing upon them the magnitude of French public hostility toward Germany and the danger that his government could be defeated by the Communists if he came out of the conference empty-handed.[38] Byrnes was reluctant to sabotage a workable plan for Western Germany to satisfy the French desire for revenge, but to allow the embattled French government at least a small victory in its territorial security policy, he agreed to exclude the Saar from the jurisdiction of central German administrations and to allow the French to administer it at least until the final boundaries of Germany were fixed.[39] Bevin, too, was concerned that domestic opposition could topple the French government and bring the Communists to power if the French security proposals for Germany were to be completely defeated. Therefore, he persuaded the cabinet to endorse the French position on the Saar, provided that France did not annex any German territory west of the Rhine.[40]

1947: A Beleaguered France Drifts Toward the West

In 1947, as Great Britain and the United States consolidated the bi-zone and Moscow remained cool toward French security aims in Germany, the

36. CP (46) 139, April 15, 1946; CP (46)156 April 15, 1946; CM (46) 36, April 17, 1946. See also the conversations between Bevin and Bidault reported in FO371/55400.

37. Byrnes' speech, September 6, 1946, *DGO*, 152–60.

38. Realizing that French domestic opposition was the only leverage he had over the Americans, Bidault frequently resorted to this sort of "blackmail." For this reason he was hated in Washington, even though American officials often accommodated him. Wall, *The United States and the Making of Postwar France*, chaps. 2 and 3, especially 57.

39. Bidault explicitly linked the need for Anglo-American support on the Saar to the need to defeat the Communists in the upcoming French elections. Memorandum of Conversation between Byrnes and Bidault, September 24, 1946, *FRUS*, 1946, vol. 5, 607–10; Bevin to FO, July 11, 1946—FO371/55844.

40. CFM meeting summaries, July 11, 1946—FO371/55844.

views of key French foreign policy officials began to diverge from domestic attitudes. The average Frenchman continued to harbor deep resentment of the Germans and remained skeptical that they could be made democratic and peace loving.[41] Hence, they continued to demand a punitive settlement and resented American efforts to curry favor with the Germans.[42] French leaders, however, were beginning to reconsider their German policies, which could not succeed without support from Washington and London.

The first confrontation occurred over the Saar during Léon Blum's brief tenure as both premier and foreign minister prior to the investiture of the first Fourth Republic president, Vincent Auriol. Blum, who believed that Germany must ultimately be rehabilitated both economically and politically, disapproved of the plan set in motion by his predecessor to establish a French border crossing between the Saar and the rest of Germany. The previous government took this step to promote Sarrois recovery without allowing French goods to move freely into Germany. Blum thought it unwise to take unilateral action in Germany when quadripartite agreements precluded any territorial changes without the ACC's approval. Despite his control of the two most powerful foreign policy posts, however, he felt powerless to prevent this popular action in the Saar.[43]

A more serious clash between France and its foreign minister over German policy developed under the next government, following the Moscow CFM of March 1947. The Moscow CFM was a turning point for Bidault (who succeeded Blum as foreign minister at the end of January) and the Quai d'Orsay.[44] At this important conference, Bidault realized that France could not rely on the Soviet Union to advance French interests in Germany. To begin with, the Soviets proved unwilling to enter into a long-term treaty on German demilitarization, which the French desperately wanted. Instead, Stalin's priorities seemed to be to establish a strong central German

41. In public opinion polls published in February 1947, 56 percent of Frenchmen surveyed reported feelings of hostility toward the German people, while only 3 percent professed sympathy. Moreover, 75 percent of respondents with opinions doubted that Germany could become a truly democratic country and 86 percent of respondents with opinions believed the Germans would again become a warmongering nation. *Sondages*, 9ième Année, No. 4 (16 février, 1947): 35.

42. A poll published in February showed that 84 percent of Frenchmen who were familiar with Byrnes's Stuttgart speech advocating the return of the Ruhr and the Rhineland to a future German state disapproved of the Secretary's comments. *Sondages*, 9ième Année, No. 3 (16 février, 1947): 26.

43. Pierre-Olivier Lapie, *De Léon Blum à de Gaulle* (Paris: Fayard, 1971), 36–38.

44. For proceedings of the conference, see *FRUS*, 1947, vol. 2, 234–390.

government, to secure Soviet involvement in any international authority controlling the industrially rich Ruhr, and to extract high reparations payments from all of Germany. While the French also wanted heavy reparations, they frantically opposed the construction of a centralized state and were reluctant to bring the Soviets so close to the Rhine. In retaliation, Molotov refused to endorse the French position on the Saar. Bidault's political associates report that his outrage at the Soviets for this spiteful act never subsided and colored his foreign policy for the rest of his career.[45] At the same time, the Western powers were much more accommodating to Bidault, as they wanted to entice France into the Western camp. Not only did Bevin and new American Secretary of State General George Marshall support the French position on the Saar, they were the only ones with the ability to relieve the severe French coal shortage that was paralyzing the French economy and threatening its political stability.

Cooperation with the West had its costs, as Bidault and the French government were well aware. The Anglo-Saxons were anxious to increase the industrial output of their occupation zones, to associate the French zone (ZOF) with their bi-zone, and to establish political institutions for all of western Germany. The initiation of the Marshall Plan in the second half of 1947 reinforced these goals for American policymakers.[46] As a result of the Soviet rebuff at Moscow, Bidault became convinced that France must go along with many of the Western plans, provided that he could slow down the pace, ensure that the future German state would have a decentralized political structure, and maintain industrial and military restrictions.[47] Although there were some members of the government—such as President Auriol and the Communists—who opposed showing leniency to the Germans, the Quai d'Orsay and a majority of the cabinet agreed with the foreign minister.[48] As part of this change of policy, the French government dropped its demand for

---

45. François Seydoux, *Mémoires d'Outre-Rhin* (Paris: Grasset, 1975), 108–10; Georgette Elgey, *La République des illusions: 1945–1951* (Paris: Fayard, 1993), 75ff. William I. Hitchcock, on the other hand, argues that French leaders had already "begun to comprehend the limits of French independence" by the time of the Moscow CFM, which augured for a Western strategy even before the conference. *France Restored: Cold War Diplomacy and the Quest for Leadership in Europe, 1944–1954* (Chapel Hill: University of North Carolina Press, 1998), 43.

46. See 140ff.

47. Dalloz, *Georges Bidault*, 168–71.

48. See Auriol's summary of Bidault's March 12, 1947 telegram from Moscow (138), the cabinet's response to a new telegram from Bidault the following day (139), the March 25 and April 9, 1947 cabinet meeting summaries (167–68, 184–86), and Bidault's April 10, 1947 letter to Auriol (757, n. 18), all in Auriol, *Journal,* 1947.

an independent Ruhr—despite its immense popularity in France—requiring instead firm international control of the area's rich industrial base.[49]

Unfortunately for Bidault, domestic political events in France conspired to make this course of action most difficult. To begin with, French Communists bitterly opposed the rehabilitation of Germany and were hostile to a policy that favored the West over cooperation with Moscow. This was no small problem for Bidault, since the PCF had polled 28 percent at the last election and was the largest party in both the coalition government and the Assembly.[50] After Socialist Premier Ramadier expelled the PCF from his cabinet on May 5, 1947, matters became even worse. Out of the government and directed by the Cominform's new Zhdanov line to oppose the 'bourgeois' government and its policy of German revival more vigorously, the Communists took advantage of political and economic instability in France to instigate a wave of debilitating strikes.[51]

In the midst of this internal chaos, Bidault made it clear to his Anglo-Saxon counterparts that he was committed to a Western policy, but that he needed both time and concessions from them in order to overcome domestic opposition. In April, Bidault assured Marshall, "I think that no-one can doubt the choice that France will make if it becomes necessary, but it is imperative that this choice is not imposed on her."[52] He stressed that "France simply needed support and time in order 'to avoid civil war.'"[53] Later, in July, the foreign minister told the American and British ambassadors in frustration, "I know full well that our zone must join yours, but I cannot do it at the mouth of a gun."[54] In particular, he insisted that no major decision be taken on Germany until after the next CFM, so that the French public would agree that no alternative was possible. Reluctantly,

---

49. Communiqué to American, British, and Soviet governments, February 1, 1947, *DFRA*, 57–64; Auriol, *Journal*, vol. 1, 738, n. 2. A January opinion poll revealed no change in the attitude of the French public toward this question: 64 percent continued to advocate the political separation of the Ruhr, while only 15 percent were satisfied with allowing the territory to remain in Germany subject to Allied control. *Sondages*, 9ième Année, No. 6 (1 avril, 1947): 68. To make matters worse, the first Assembly debate on foreign affairs after the Moscow CFM (July 25–26) was punctuated by angry invectives demanding cooperation with the Soviets and rigid controls on Germany. *Journal Officiel: Débats, Assemblée*, 25 juillet, 2542–70, and 26 juillet, 3585–612.

50. Young, *France*, 128.
51. Ibid., 165–68.
52. Dalloz, *Georges Bidault*, 171.
53. Wall, *The United States and the Making of Postwar France*, 66.
54. *FRUS*, 1947, vol. 2, 991, n. 19.

the Americans and British complied with his wishes, although Clay and other officials were growing visibly impatient.[55]

On November 25, therefore, the CFM reconvened in London for "the conference of the last chance."[56] If this meeting failed to reach a satisfactory Four Power settlement, then the French would participate in a Western condominium in western Germany. The conference started badly as Molotov dickered over procedural matters while haranguing the Western foreign ministers for seeking an imperialist peace. From Bidault's vantage point, it became clear early on that the conference would accomplish nothing, since the Soviet delegation continued to press for a strong central German government and refused to accommodate French views on the Saar. Hence, he was as anxious as Bevin and Marshall to break off negotiations and lay the blame on Stalin's doorstep, since that would free his government to pursue a Western strategy.[57] The CFM was thus adjourned on December 15 and not scheduled to reconvene. The French had at last burned their bridges to the East.

The London Accords of 1948

With the utter failure of the London CFM, France had to cast its lot with the West. The challenge for the French cabinet was to cooperate with the British and Americans while ensuring that the tri-zonal regime conformed as closely as possible to French goals. The Americans, though, had waited long enough for German recovery and were unwilling to let the French delay it further with endless negotiations. Bevin was more patient and shared French fears of political centralization, but he, too, was unwilling to make extensive concessions to the French. The Three Powers met in London during the first half of 1948 to overcome these differences and coordinate political affairs in western Germany.

The protracted discussions at London were exceedingly difficult for Bidault, who was forced to walk a fine line between the demands of his Western allies on the one hand and those of his cabinet colleagues and French public opinion on the other. The Schuman cabinet—and even President Auriol—was by this time convinced that there was no alternative to

55. *Clay Papers,* vol. 1, 385–92; Young, *France,* 157–59.

56. Michel Debré, *Trois Républiques pour une France: mémoires, 1946–58* (Paris: A. Michel, 1988), 62. For the proceedings of the CFM, see *FRUS,* 1947, vol. 2, 728–72.

57. See Marshall to Acting Secretary of State Lovett, December 8, 1947, *FRUS,* 1947, vol. 2, 754; and Marshall to Lovett, December 13, 1947, *FRUS,* 1947, vol. 2, 769.

cooperation with the West and that political and economic stability had to be restored to western Germany. They still wished to control the process as much as possible and, consequently, issued strict instructions to Bidault and the French delegation to press for decentralization and Anglo-American security guarantees as preconditions for tri-zonal fusion. Furthermore, the foreign minister was instructed to oppose the election of a West German constituent assembly to draft a constitution unless two prerequisites were met: its members had to be to be appointed by the *Länder* rather than elected on the basis of universal suffrage (which would allow the more populous regions to dominate as Prussia had in the past and would foster strong national, rather than regional, political parties), and adjustments had to be made to the *Länder* to reduce population disparities between them.[58]

Nevertheless, Bidault went to London prepared to compromise in order to prevent the Anglo-Saxons from proceeding without the French, provided that his bargain could be sold at home.[59] As he implored Ambassador Caffery, "Far from wanting to break with you we want the success of the London conference, but don't make it too hard for me. I'll have to face the Assembly and given the attitude of the Communists, the Gaullists, and the Socialists, I don't know how we will come out.... Tell your government I am on your side and in the long run I am sure we will work something satisfactory out, but at the same time, I must think about public opinion."[60] Bidault's concessions, though, were quite dear. Under stiff American pressure, he acceded to a popular election with virtually universal suffrage, and forwent a meaningful U.S. security guarantee for the time being. More important, he conceded substantial central authority for the West German legislature, giving up a central plank of French policy since 1945. In return, he got a commitment to set up some form of international authority for the Ruhr (IAR) and a military security board (MSB) to ensure that the future West German state remained demilitarized.[61]

That the Americans made these compromises is telling. It is not surprising that the French had to make concessions to the Americans, who— at least on the surface—possessed all the leverage. Only the Americans

---

58. Auriol, *Journal,* 1948, 174–80.

59. MAE Note, May 4, 1948, MAE, Secrétariat Général 1945–66, Dossiers, Allemagne, 6, 349–57.

60. Caffery to Marshall, May 25, 1948, *FRUS,* 1948, vol. 2, 281.

61. "France's German Policy," ORE 39–48, December 29, 1948, 5–6—Papers of Harry S. Truman, HSTL, PSF, Intelligence File, box 255. For the proceedings of the London conference on Germany, see *FRUS,* 1948, vol. 2, 75–145, 191–317.

commanded the military might to guarantee French security from future German and Russian threats. Only the United States controlled the financial resources to help rebuild the shattered French economy. In the final analysis, if Marshall was not satisfied with the French position, he could have acted with the British and excluded the comparatively insignificant French zone from the West Germany it was creating. Yet the United States also made noteworthy concessions to the French position. It did so because the French ironically *did* possess some bargaining power. The magnitude of French domestic political opposition to the Anglo-American line on Germany made it impossible for Bidault to capitulate to their views; he needed to demonstrate that his surrenders were hard fought and were matched by Anglo-Saxon concessions, or else he would jeopardize his own position and that of his government, while running the risk that extremists on either the right or the left would seize control of France.

Ultimately, the compromise reached was not enough to save Bidault. He tried to sell the resulting London Accords to the cabinet by stressing the concessions made to the French point of view and the consequences of rejecting what was, in effect, the final Anglo-American offer. "There is not a shadow of a chance that we can reap the benefits of Marshall aid and yet refuse a Germany that conforms to 50 percent of our views. If we want to act alone, we will lose everything," he warned his cabinet colleagues. "In order to obtain American aid, we must accept the London decisions."[62] The cabinet, however, was bitterly divided over the issue and even the normally pro-German Premier Schuman joined forces with the decidedly anti-German President Auriol to chastise the foreign minister for allowing a centralized German state.[63] The majority, however, carried the policy, which was consistent with the government's new Western orientation in Germany, and they sent the London agreement to the Assembly—although they declined to make it a vote of confidence.[64]

62. Dalloz, *Georges Bidault,* 192. At the same time, the MAE cautioned the government that previous French policy toward Germany was inconsistent with: (1) the heavy Anglo-American occupation costs, which make it necessary for them to create a self-sustaining state in their zones; (2) the difficulty of French and European recovery, which make it necessary to seek American assistance; (3) the incompatibility of European recovery with the maintenance of economic chaos in Germany; and (4) the French need for more German coal. MAE Note, June 5, 1948, MAE, Secrétariat Général 1945–66, Dossiers, Allemagne, 6, 435.

63. Raymond Poidevin, *Robert Schuman: homme d'état* (Paris: Imprimerie Nationale, 1986), 186, 190; Elgey, *République des illusions,* 386–87.

64. Auriol, *Journal,* 1948, 265–66.

Debate on the London Accords was heated, and the hostility toward Bidault for delivering "the funeral oration to a policy" of security through firm controls on Germany was palpable. The legislature finally approved the Accords on June 17 by the slimmest of margins (297–289), but it attached a number of reservations that called for the foreign minister to negotiate more vigorously for French interests in Germany as previously defined.[65] Thus, Bidault was able to force the London agreement through a hostile legislature, but only with conditions and at a very high price. Attacked from the left, the right, and even the parties of the center for his capitulation at London, he was replaced as foreign minister by Schuman, when the latter's government fell in July.[66] The lesson—that it was costly to push through unpopular agreements, regardless of their necessity—was not lost on subsequent foreign ministers, particularly when they negotiated German rearmament in the early 1950s.[67]

The Occupation Statute

As Foreign Minister, Schuman was quickly converted to the policy of limited German recovery and Franco-German *rapprochement* that Bidault had begun.[68] The first big test for this policy came as the Three Powers negotiated the Occupation Statute that would govern relations with the future West German state. Negotiations began in September 1948 at the level of the zonal commanders, but soon became deadlocked. The main political axis of disagreement was, predictably, between the French and the Anglo-Americans. In particular, the French refused to allow the Germans a right of appeal to a high court in the event of disputes between the Allied powers and the German government; they insisted that the *Länder* governments,

---

65. Young, *France,* 196–97.

66. De Gaulle denounced Bidault's efforts as "a series of retreats leading to the final surrender." *L'Année Politique, 1948,* 334–35. The PCF derided a policy to revive Germany that favored the West over the Soviet Union. In April, the Socialist cabinet ministers wrote a letter of complaint against Bidault's conduct of negotiations in London to Premier Schuman. Young, *France,* 192. The French press accused him of "putting French security in jeopardy." Even his MRP colleagues were dissatisfied with the agreement he brought home. His dismissal was inevitable. Dalloz, *Georges Bidault,* 194–97.

67. See, for example, 169.

68. It is frequently assumed that Schuman, a native of Lorraine and a fluent German speaker, originated this new policy direction. As Raymond Poidevin observes, however, the spirit of Franco-German rapprochement preceded him to the Quai d'Orsay. In fact, prior to becoming foreign minister, Schuman was a strong advocate of caution towards Germany. *Robert Schuman,* 186–90, 208.

rather than the central government, pay occupation costs to the Allies; and they demanded a unanimous voting procedure to ensure a French veto over decisions of the West German government over a wide range of subjects.[69] It appeared that the new thinking at the Quai d'Orsay would not translate into a more lenient stance on Germany.

The main reason for the discrepancy between Schuman's policy preferences and actual French policy was the existence of a large group of Gaullist officials, like Koenig, both in the military government and in the Quai d'Orsay itself. These officials, knowing that public opinion favored a hard line and believing that de Gaulle could be swept into office at any moment, attempted to obstruct conciliatory policies whenever possible and frequently kept the foreign minister in the dark about German policy.[70] As the British Foreign Office observed, "The bitter truth is that there is no unanimity among French officials in the Quai d'Orsay, no agreement between the Quai d'Orsay and General Koenig and his staff, and little or no desire on the part of the majority of French officials to carry out at present a policy which would really reconcile the Germans to the French and vice versa."[71]

By early 1949, the Foreign Office was beginning to lose patience with French intransigence and was tired of making concessions to French public opinion.[72] As one official complained:

French policy, if persisted in, is very likely to ruin the German programme, in spite of the good intentions of M. Schuman and certain other Frenchmen. *Experience has shown that in these matters the French are not really influenced by fears about security but almost always by considerations of internal politics.* There are of course times when we have got to give way to the French and decide against German interests, purely because if we do not there would be a serious risk that the present French Government would collapse.... We should however try to keep these cases to the minimum since we cannot afford to allow progress in Germany to be halted altogether

69. See summary of military governors' points of disagreements in *FRUS*, 1948, vol. 2, 615–17, 650–63; Clay to Department of the Army, November 1, 1948, *FRUS*, vol. 2, 625–26; Douglas to Acheson, February 7, 1949, *FRUS*, 1949, vol. 3, 29–31; and Riddleberger to Acheson, *FRUS*, 1949, vol. 3, 32.

70. See the report of a Schuman-Kirkpatrick conversation in Douglas to Acheson, February 7, 1949, *FRUS*, 1949, vol. 3, 29.

71. FO minute by Dean, January 26, 1949—FO371/76694. See also, Gilchrist to Dean, October 22, 1948—FO371/70530; and Murphy to Beam, *FRUS*, 1948, vol. 2, 434, note 1.

72. See the January and February 1949 minutes in FO371/76694.

by the excessive demands on relatively minor points which are sometimes put forward in order to satisfy French internal politics.[73]

Consequently, the Foreign Office encouraged Bevin to take a harder line
toward France. On the American side, Clay's patience had already been
stretched to the limit, and his attitude was viewed sympathetically in the
State Department.[74] The French were in danger of losing their influence
over German affairs.

By this time, however, Schuman had begun to assert his ascendancy over
German policy, both within the Quai d'Orsay and the cabinet. He was
assisted in this regard by progress toward a North Atlantic Treaty (NAT),
which would provide security against a resurgent Germany, thereby reducing the risks involved in German rehabilitation.[75] Schuman took matters
into his own hands and personally met with Clay on March 20, 1949 to
break the deadlock over the Occupation Statute. With "great frankness"
and a "conciliatory spirit," the French foreign minister proved willing to
simplify the Occupation Statute by listing the rights and powers reserved
to the Allies and leaving what remained to the central German government,
to apply the rule of unanimity only to amendments of the federal constitution, and to enter into negotiations immediately after the statute would
come into effect to revise it to German advantage so that Allied control
could be gradually withdrawn.[76] This meeting paved the way for a Three
Power meeting in Washington in April at which French compromises led to
British and American concessions on matters directly affecting French security.[77] As a result, the Occupation Statute and Tripartite Control Agreements
were signed and the three western zones of Germany were transformed into
an occupied state with limited governmental authority.

Between France and the Federal Republic: 1949–1952

When the Federal Republic of Germany (FRG) was established in September 1949, Allied-German relations were officially governed by the Three

73. FO minute by Dean, March 26, 1949—FO371/76694 (emphasis added).
74. See, for example, Clay to Department of the Army, November 22, 1948, Clay Papers, vol.
2, 934–36; Riddleberger to Department of State, February 11, 1949, FRUS, 1949, vol. 3, 34–36.
75. On the relationship between the NAT and the German problem, see Timothy Ireland,
Creating the Entangling Alliance: The Origins of the North Atlantic Treaty Organization
(Westport, Conn.: Greenwood, 1981); Leffler, A Preponderance of Power, 280–82.
76. Caffery to Secretary of State Acheson, March 22, 1949, FRUS, 1949, vol. 3, 115–18.
77. For a good firsthand account of the Washington meetings, see Acheson's memoranda of
March 31 to April 11, 1949, FRUS, 1949, vol. 3, 156–73. See also Auriol, Journal, 1949, 206–8.

Power Occupation Statute of April 1949.[78] In practice, however, the statute was rather vague and potentially provided for a wide range of Allied authority over German affairs.[79] Consequently, the character of its implementation depended in large measure on Three Power interpretations of the document and their attitudes toward the new West German state. Predictably, each of the three partners had different views on the proper relationship between the Allied High Commission (AHC) and the federal government. The American attitude was that "[t]he [Occupation] Statute defines the broadest limits within which the Allied High Commission will ordinarily operate." Consequently, American leaders expected the AHC to "encourage the maximum exercise of governmental authority by the Federal Republic," and "to limit intervention in German governmental affairs to the minimum deemed essential within the terms of the Occupation Statute" in order "to develop their political independence along democratic lines in close association with the free peoples of Western Europe."[80] The Americans, thus, wanted to interpret the statute as liberally as possible, while maintaining their ability to protect Allied interests and foster democracy.

The French held a far more restrictive view of the High Commission's role in German affairs, in no small part due to domestic pressure. The French public was by no means overjoyed by the new German state and continued to distrust the German people—a fact that Schuman had to bear in mind constantly and that led to continued caution in French policy.[81] Schuman argued, therefore, that the AHC should use the Occupation Statute to the fullest and play an active role in German affairs in order to prevent the development of attitudes and institutions in Germany that would endanger European integration and, by implication, French security.[82]

78. Reproduced in *DGO*, 375–77.

79. Thomas Alan Schwartz observed that it granted the Allies "a vaguely defined but essentially unlimited authority to intervene in German decision making." *America's Germany*, 44. In fact, Clay was initially infuriated by the document and accused the Allies of colonizing Germany. *Clay Papers*, vol. 2, 1090.

80. "Policy Directive for the United States High Commissioner for Germany," November 17, 1949, *FRUS*, 1949, vol. 3, 319–40.

81. Throughout the period under study, public opinion polls continued to register French distrust and dislike of the German people. See the polls reported in *Sondages* and in Jean Stoetzel, "The Evolution of French Opinion," 72–101 in Daniel Lerner and Raymond Aron, eds., *France Defeats EDC* (New York: Frederick A. Praeger, 1957), 73–74.

82. Poidevin, *Robert Schuman*, 213–15. Schuman emphasized that, though "any idea of hatred or revenge had already disappeared from French policy," it was unrealistic for the Germans to expect immediate integration into Western Europe as an equal partner. It would take time until the Germans could fully regain French confidence. Ashley-Clarke to FO, January 12, 1949—FO371/76694.

The British opted for the middle ground. Bevin informed the cabinet in November that the high commissioners were empowered to negotiate with Adenauer to bring about a gradual and satisfactory evolution of the Allied–German relationship, "provided that they all three stand firm on the essential points and do not give Dr. Adenauer any encouragement to think that he may obtain more by playing one Allied Government off against another." In his view, the Allies should bide their time until the Occupation Statute was up for review and then bring about further changes in the respective authority of the AHC and the FRG, while "binding the German Government and the German people more closely to the Western world and at the same time making adequate provision for security." The British approach was, therefore, a policy of cautious and gradual evolution.[83]

Despite Three Power disagreement, West German Chancellor Konrad Adenauer used the newly created power of the FRG to press the Allies for greater authority and political equality. To avoid alienating the Germans, Acheson and Bevin agreed to satisfy some of the chancellor's aspirations in return for concrete German steps to join the Western community.[84] Consequently, at the May 1950 North Atlantic Treaty Organization (NATO) conference in London, French representatives were outflanked by Anglo-American agreement to terminate the state of war with Germany and to revise the Occupation Statute, granting the Germans greater domestic authority and even limited control over foreign affairs.[85] Under pressure, Schuman relented, provided that the MSB and the IAR remained in place and the Germans fulfilled their commitment to enter the Council of Europe (COE). By September 1950, the state of war between the Three Powers and Germany was officially terminated.[86]

83. CP (49) 237, November 16, 1949. Bevin decided that concessions to the Germans and a transformation of relations with West Germany were necessary since they would be unable to dictate to the German people indefinitely. As he informed the cabinet early on, "We must bear in mind throughout the coming months that we have now reached a stage in Germany where we must take account of German public opinion. I do not suggest that our policy should be governed solely by what the Germans think, but even if we wished, we have no longer the power to force unpopular measures upon the Germans for very long, and our policy is much more likely to be successful if it meets with the general approval of responsible German opinion." CP (48) 5, January 5, 1948.

84. Summary of Foreign Ministers Meeting, May 12, 1950, *FRUS*, 1950, vol. 3, 1046–47. See also Acheson to Byroade, May 2, 1950, *FRUS*, 1950, vol. 3, 913–15; CP (50) 80, April 26, 1950.

85. U.S. Delegation to Marshall, May 4, 1950, *FRUS*, 1950, vol. 3, 923–26. Tripartite Meeting Summary, May 10, 1950, in Roger Bullen and M. E. Pelly, eds., *Documents on British Policy Overseas* (DBPO) (London: Her Majesty's Stationery Office), series 2, vol. 1, 10–13; CP (50) 80, April 26, 1950; CM (50) 29, May 8, 1950.

86. Acheson to Webb, May 9, 1950, *FRUS*, 1950, vol. 3, 1013–18; U.S. Delegation to

By then, however, political events had overtaken the pace of Western concessions to the FRG. After the outbreak of the Korean War in June 1950 obliged the Anglo-Americans to enlist a German contribution to Western defense, Adenauer's bargaining power vis-à-vis the Three Powers increased exponentially.[87] Domestic political opposition to rearmament within West Germany strengthened the chancellor's appeal for political concessions. After all, the German people could not be compelled to participate in Western defense; they would have to agree voluntarily. In order to secure their agreement, substantial concessions to the concepts of German equality and sovereignty would be necessary. Furthermore, Acheson viewed greater German sovereignty as essential if the Germans were to have the will to resist the Soviets. Consequently, the U.S. government was increasingly disposed to treat the FRG as an ally rather than an occupied state.[88]

Seizing this political opportunity, Adenauer demanded, as preconditions for a German contribution to the Western defense effort, "[c]omplete restoration of German sovereignty in the administration of justice" and the negotiation of a contractual agreement to end the occupation and restore full sovereignty and equality to the FRG.[89] These demands alarmed the French and unsettled the British, who were concerned about possible Soviet responses to what would amount to a violation of the Potsdam Agreement. Acheson, though, was willing to enter into contractual arrangements with the federal government provided several conditions were met. Most important, he required German commitments to participate in both Western defense and the Schuman Plan, to join the institutions of the western liberal trading order, and to undertake various domestic commitments required by the Three Powers. In addition, the Germans would have to accept certain voluntary limitations on the nature of their defense establishment and military production. If the Federal Republic could accept these provisions, Acheson was prepared to treat the contractual settlement as a peace treaty between West Germany and the West.[90]

Webb, May 12, 1950, *FRUS*, 1950, vol. 3, 1044–51; Communiqué by Three Foreign Ministers, September 19, 1950, *DGO*, 517–20.

87. For a discussion of the negotiations leading to a German defense contribution, see below 156–173.

88. NSC 71/1, July 3, 1950; Bonnet to MAE, December 16, 1950, MAE, EU 1944–60, Allemagne, 190.

89. Adenauer's *aide-mémoire* is included in McCloy to Acheson, November 17, 1950, *FRUS*, 1950, vol. 4, 780–84; François-Poncet to MAE, November 17, 1950, MAE, EU 1944–60, Allemagne, 189.

90. Acheson to McCloy, December 12, 1950, *FRUS*, 1950, vol. 4, 797–99.

When the three foreign ministers addressed the German demands at the December 1950 Brussels defense conference, the Europeans were still wary. Schuman stated that he agreed with the principle of German equality, but "if equality means automatic and complete removal of restrictions and servitudes on the Germans, then we must be careful." He professed that he had no objections to contractual arrangements, if that meant subjecting most Three Power decisions on Germany to negotiations with the FRG. Nonetheless, he "did not believe it was possible to put total relations with Germany, particularly matters relating to troops, on a contractual basis and supplant the occupation regime because the basis of relations with Germany is covered by four power agreements." Bevin similarly cautioned that, while relations with Germany could in general be premised on German equality, there would have to be exceptions to that rule. The three ministers agreed, though, to study the issue in the coming year.[91]

French domestic difficulties continued to hold up negotiations, though. While Schuman was personally amenable to delegating greater authority to the Germans, he faced a French public that distrusted the Germans and feared a revival of German nationalism. Acheson's linkage between German sovereignty and German rearmament was particularly troublesome, since the French people, on the eve of the June 1951 elections, overwhelmingly opposed the latter, perceiving any German military capability as a serious threat to French security.[92] Caught between strong American pressure to meet the German demands and formidable domestic opposition to German sovereignty, Schuman had little choice but to proceed slowly and secure adequate safeguards to assure the French public that Germany could not again threaten French security. He insisted, therefore, that the German rearmament question had to be settled satisfactorily before German sovereignty could be restored. In this manner, the Allies could bind the future German military establishment tightly within the Western European framework so that it could not be used as a national instrument by a newly independent German state. For if the FRG were granted sovereignty before the conclusion of military arrangements, there could be no guarantees that the Germans

---

91. Parodi to French representatives to Bonn, London, Washington, and New York, December 21, 1950, EU 1944–60, Allemagne, 190; U.S. Delegation Meeting Minutes, December 19, 1950, *FRUS*, 1950, vol. 4, 803–13.

92. Acheson Memo, July 6, 1951, *FRUS*, 1951, vol. 3, 813–14. For French attitudes toward German rearmament, see below 159.

would accept the principle of supranational control or, for that matter, that they would agree to participate in Western defense at all.[93]

Furthermore, although the Quai d'Orsay was willing to place some aspects of Allied-German relations on a contractual basis, it would not relinquish the principle of Allied supreme authority.[94] Finally, the French continued to pursue Four Power negotiations with the Soviet Union to attempt to settle the German question without resort to either rearmament or the premature restoration of German sovereignty, although this precondition was dropped shortly after the French election when preliminary Four Power ministerial-level talks in Paris quickly reached deadlock and were permanently adjourned.[95]

The Germans objected vociferously to the French scheme, countering that the restoration of German sovereignty and equality must precede rearmament.[96] In order to overcome the Franco-German stalemate, the U.S. State Department concluded that sovereignty and rearmament had to be pursued jointly.[97] Consequently, while talks in Bonn and Paris were underway on defense arrangements, the AHC began talks with German representatives to draft contractual agreements that would replace the existing basis of relations between the occupying powers and the FRG.

In the fall, Three Power negotiations made substantial progress. The new French government, with the election securely behind it, made a number of important concessions to the Anglo-American position.[98] As French

93. Bruce to Acheson, February 19, 1951, *FRUS,* 1951, vol. 3, 1463–64.

94. Parodi to French representatives to Bonn, London, Washington, and New York, December 21, 1950, EU 1944–60, Allemagne, 190; Bruce to Acheson, January 8, 1951, *FRUS,* 1951, vol. 3, 1446–49.

95. Schuman did not expect a new CFM to yield any tangible benefits and pursued this option only to satisfy public opinion before the election that all alternatives to German rearmament would be fully explored before the French government would allow it. Lapie, *De Léon Blum à de Gaulle,* 362–63; Seydoux, *Mémoires d'Outre-Rhin,* 166–67; Minutes of Tripartite Meeting, December 19, 1950, *FRUS,* 1950, vol. 4, 810–11. For records of the failed Four Power meetings in Paris, see *FRUS,* 1951, vol. 3, 1086–162.

96. CM (51) 12, February 8, 1951; Acheson to McCloy, February 14, 1951, *FRUS,* 1951, vol. 3, 1014–16; McCloy to Acheson, January 5, 1951, *FRUS,* 1951, vol. 3, 1317–21; Konrad Adenauer, *Memoirs 1945–53* (Chicago: Henry Regnery, 1965), 322–28.

97. Acheson to Paris Embassy, June 21, 1951, *FRUS,* 1951, vol. 3, 786–89; Acheson and Lovett to Truman, *FRUS,* 1951, vol. 3, 849–52. Although the threat of a Soviet response and Bevin's death dampened British enthusiasm for German rearmament, they agreed to the American strategy. Morrison to Acheson, August 17, 1951, *FRUS,* 1951, vol. 3, 1174–75.

98. Foreign Ministers Meeting, September 13, 1951, *FRUS,* 1951, vol. 3, 1272–78. For the revised drafts of "Instructions from the Three Foreign Ministers to the Allied High Commission" and "the Agreement on General Relations with the Federal Republic," see *FRUS,* 1951, vol. 3,

parliamentary agitation over the rapid pace of German rehabilitation began to grow in early 1952, however, Schuman's willingness to compromise abruptly ended. The foreign minister required explicit provisions within the contractual agreements prohibiting Germany from producing not only weapons of an unconventional character (atomic, biological, and chemical—the so-called ABC weapons), missiles, military aircraft, and naval ships, but also civilian aircraft and all heavy military equipment (e.g., gun barrels and propellants).[99] Adenauer wanted these restrictions in the European Defense Community (EDC) Treaty rather than the contractuals to avoid a visible restriction on German sovereignty, but the French argued that they had to be explicitly included in the contractuals—which delimited the authority of the West German state—in order "to satisfy French public opinion that [the] German menace will be removed."[100] As pro-German French High Commissioner André François-Poncet lamented to the AHC, "However one may try, it was impossible, particularly for [the] Fr[ench] public, to formulate policy without taking into account past experience with Ger[many]."[101]

Anglo-American pressure compelled Adenauer to accept a wide range of voluntary restrictions on German military production that would be both written into the EDC Treaty and the subject of an exchange of letters at the time of the signing of the contractuals.[102] Nonetheless, the French insisted on as many extra "voluntary" restrictions in April 1952 as they could convince the other powers to accept and tried to hold onto whatever control they could maintain on Germany in order to pacify an increasingly bellicose National Assembly.[103] To overcome French obstruction, Acheson demanded that the pace of negotiations be accelerated. He threatened that if the agreements were not signed by May 9, 1952, he would be unable to convince Congress and the American public to provide European security appropriations.[104] This threat did not have the desired effect, though, as last-minute French demands extended negotiations in Bonn until May 25.

1197–214. The November concessions are included in "Draft Agreement on General Relations," November 17, 1951, *FRUS*, 1951, vol. 3, 1592–97.

99. Schuman to Acheson, January 29, 1952, *FRUS*, 1952–54, vol. 5, 7–11.

100. Bruce to Acheson, February 3, 1952, *FRUS*, 1952–54, vol. 7, 7–9.

101. McCloy to Department of State, February 6, 1952, *FRUS*, 1952–54, vol. 7, 9–12.

102. Meeting Summaries, February 18–19, 26, 1952, *FRUS*, 1952–54, vol. 5, 66–77, 163–67; Acheson to Truman, February 21, 1952, *FRUS*, 1952–54, vol. 5, 80–86.

103. See, for example, McCloy to Department of State, May 2, 1952, *FRUS*, 1952–54, vol. 7, 45–47.

104. Acheson Memorandum, April 8, 1952, *FRUS*, 1952–54, vol. 7, 24–25; Acheson to McCloy, April 11, 1952, *FRUS*, 1952–54, vol. 7, 25–28.

At long last, the Bonn Contractuals were signed on May 26, putting Three Power relations with Germany on a contractual basis, rather than an occupation footing. The high commissioners were to become ambassadors once the contractuals and the EDC Treaty with which they were linked were ratified. The French delayed their EDC ratification vote until 1954, when it was defeated in the Assembly. The contractual agreements (slightly modified in the FRG's favor) thus did not enter into force until 1955, after a new European defense arrangement was concluded in October 1954.[105]

THE SAAR

Another perpetual source of inter-Allied irritation—not to mention Franco-German antagonism—was French policy on the status of the Saar.[106] Having failed to secure Allied agreement to separate the region permanently from Germany, in 1949 the French cabinet proposed Sarrois entry into the COE.[107] Bevin and Acheson objected on the grounds that it would unnecessarily provoke the Germans and might cause the FRG to stay out of the organization.[108] Schuman made it clear to his allies, however, that public and governmental attitudes made it impossible for the French government to permit German entry before comparable Sarrois admission was allowed. Furthermore, because of French sensitivity on this matter, Schuman would have to consult the National Assembly before he could officially endorse German entry.[109] In light of these developments, Bevin endorsed simultaneous German and Sarrois admission, and the United States did not protest.[110]

For the same reason, the Anglo-Saxons did not react strongly when, on March 3, 1950, the French concluded conventions with the Saar government

105. See 172–73.
106. The definitive work on the Franco-German struggle over the Saar remains Jacques Freymond, *The Saar Conflict* (New York: Frederick A. Praeger, 1960).
107. Auriol, *Journal,* 1949, 402, 612, n. 21 and n. 22; Adenauer, *Memoirs,* 203, 211–12.
108. Douglas to Acheson, July 25, 1949, *FRUS,* 1949, vol. 3, 478–79; Acheson to Douglas, July 29, 1949, *FRUS,* 1949, vol. 3, 479–80.
109. Bruce to Acheson, October 29, 1949, *FRUS,* 1949, vol. 3, 491–92. Indeed, leading cabinet members, such as Bidault—who had recently rejoined the cabinet—and Jules Moch, would accept FRG membership in the COE only if the Saar joined first. Auriol, *Journal,* 1949, 401–6. Schuman, himself, was not happy about this policy, since he recognized that German entry into the COE was a desirable means of "turning her away from the East as well as from all economic and, as a consequence, military expansionism." Quoted in Poidevin, *Robert Schuman,* 213–14.
110. See Acheson to Douglas, October 31, 1949, *FRUS,* 1949, vol. 3, 492–94. Associate member status was conferred to the Saar only "on the understanding that the definitive status of the Saar shall await the peace settlement." Acheson to Webb, November 11, 1949, *FRUS,* 1949, vol. 3, 306–8.

on the region's autonomy, economic relations between France and the Saar, the fifty-year lease of Saar mines by France, and the control of Saar railroads.[111] Adenauer protested strenuously, but the only support that Acheson or Bevin offered him was an AHC statement promising that the status of the Saar could be reversed if the final peace treaty stipulated that the Saar was to be returned to Germany. With this less than satisfactory commitment, the Bundestag reluctantly voted to enter the COE, thereby defusing the crisis.

It erupted again at the end of 1950, however, when French High Commissioner for the Saar Gilbert Grandval transmitted a Sarrois *Landtag* resolution desiring independent admission of the Saar into the European Coal and Steel Community envisioned by the Schuman Plan. Schuman was reluctant to ignite a confrontation that would endanger Adenauer's ability to participate in the Schuman Plan and, therefore, affirmed to the German leader that the final status of the Saar would be determined by Franco-German negotiations.[112] For this act, Schuman was criticized by Grandval and important figures within the French cabinet such as Auriol, Bidault, and Finance Minister Maurice Petsche.[113]

After the June 1951 election brought a government coalition of the further Right to power, Schuman was increasingly isolated within a legislature that favored a hard line toward Germany and the Saar settlement. In January 1952, after Schuman was attacked in the Assembly for his weak policy in the Saar, the new French government violated Schuman's commitment to Adenauer. To emphasize that the Saar was an independent country associated with France rather than Germany, the French announced that Grandval was being made the French ambassador to the Saar, the Saar would have diplomatic representation in Paris, and Sarrois representatives would be attached to French diplomatic missions abroad.[114] Furthermore, on the government's authority, Grandval used his power to scrutinize the formation of political parties, thereby reducing the participation of pro-German groups in Saar politics and causing an immense outcry in Germany.[115]

111. The first three of these agreements are reproduced in *DGO*, 469–82.

112. Poidevin, *Robert Schuman*, 282–84; Adenauer, *Memoirs*, 333–35. For details on the Schuman Plan, see 152ff.

113. When Grandval threatened to resign over Schuman's "sell-out" of the Saar, these powerful figures in the cabinet would not allow the foreign minister to accept his resignation. Moreover, they criticized Schuman for his handling of the Saar affair. Auriol, *Journal*, 1951, 147, 183.

114. Poidevin, *Robert Schuman*, 332; Adenauer, *Memoirs*, 402–3.

115. McCloy to Department of State, January 30, 1952, 1952–54, vol. 7, 1403–5.

Though Acheson was concerned about the effect that the French actions could have on the entire Western project, which was premised on Franco-German cooperation, he once again refrained from pressuring Schuman over the matter because of the latter's domestic difficulties. Acheson and Eden offered their good offices, but remained aloof from Franco-German negotiations.[116] Under these circumstances, a resolution of this complex issue was unlikely in 1952, given the state of public and governmental opinion in France. The issue, therefore, remained unresolved until 1954, when renewed pressure to finalize Western defense arrangements required a bilateral Franco-German settlement of this contentious matter.[117]

Conclusion: Structural Autonomy and Executive Policy Independence

Two counterintuitive findings of this case study of Three Power political and territorial settlement policies toward Germany after World War II can be explained only with the structural autonomy model of democratic foreign policy and interdemocratic negotiations advanced in Chapter 1. First, when the preferences of the foreign policy executives of the three Western democracies clashed with public and parliamentary opinion, British and American leaders could largely ignore domestic opposition to pursue policies aimed at restoring German political stability. French leaders, conversely, were paralyzed by domestic opposition and, consequently, pursued a much tougher line toward Germany than they thought prudent after 1947. Second, while it is not surprising that French leaders made numerous concessions to the more powerful Anglo-Saxons, it is very surprising that the Americans, who held all the political and economic trump cards, frequently made concessions to the French point of view. Each of these observations merits further consideration.

Table 7 lists the conflicts between domestic opinion and governmental preferences over the direction of policy toward Germany in the three countries during the period under study. In the initial period, 1945–46, domestic opinion in Great Britain and the United States was markedly anti-German. Yet both governments resisted French calls for territorial amputation and pursued policies designed to restore German political stability in order to serve their economic and geopolitical interests. The French, conversely,

116. Acheson to Schuman, February 4, 1952, *FRUS*, 1952–54, vol. 7, 1406; Bruce to Acheson, February 6, 1952, *FRUS*, 1952–54, vol. 7, 1408–9.

117. For details on the bilateral negotiations that resolved the Saar conflict, see Freymond, *The Saar Conflict*.

Table 7   Conflicts between domestic and leader preferences

Country	Year	Issue	Victor
Great Britain	1945–46	Overall German policy	Leaders
United States	1945–46	Overall German policy	Leaders
France	1947	Policy toward Saar	Domestic opinion
France	1948	London agreements	Leader, but at high cost
France	1948–52	Overall German policy	Mixed results

were unable to ignore domestic pressure. In 1947, public and parliamentary opinion made it impossible for Blum to prevent the erection of a border between Germany and the Saar. The following year, Bidault secured Assembly approval of the unpopular London Accords, but paid a high political price for doing so. From then on, domestic opinion served as a brake on French policy. Though the trajectory of Schuman's policy was toward restoring rights and authority to the FRG, at each step of the way he was forced to haggle over details and slow down progress toward a final agreement on German sovereignty in order to satisfy his domestic critics. As a result, the contractual agreements were delayed until May 1952.

Of course, even the government of the French Fourth Republic—identified as the least autonomous in this study—possessed some measure of policy independence that allowed Bidault to push through the unpopular London Accords and permitted Schuman to secure eventual, if reluctant, agreement to the Bonn Contractuals. This limited policy independence was won by hiding executive preferences from the French public and the National Assembly and, more important, by blaming the Allies for the unpopular compromises, even if Bidault and Schuman also believed they were necessary. Nonetheless, this observation should not obscure the larger point that the domestic impact on policy was infinitely greater in France than it was in Great Britain or the United States, where it played almost no role. In a structurally constrained state, such as the French Fourth Republic, there were important limits to the French executive's ability to generate independence through the politics of deception, as Bidault's ouster demonstrates. Thus, this case study supports my structural autonomy model's hypothesis A1 that the ability of a democratic state to pursue a conciliatory peace settlement when encountering domestic opposition depends on the degree of structural autonomy it possesses. Neorealist hypothesis N1 falls short because it cannot explain why the French were unable to soften their position toward Germany, even when they were convinced that important national interests

Table 8   Domestic constraint projection in intergovernmental negotiations

Country	Year	Issue	Outcome
France	1946	French security proposals	Very limited success
France	1947	General German policy	Limited success
France	1948	General German policy	Limited success
France	1950	Saar	Success
United States	1952	May 9 deadline for contractual agreement	Failure

were at stake. Similarly, traditional neorealist hypothesis T1 is undermined by the ease with which British and American leaders brushed aside domestic opposition to pursue a policy of German rehabilitation.

Furthermore, as my hypothesis A2 predicted, when the Three Powers negotiated the political settlement with Germany, it was mainly the French who begged for concessions in order to pacify domestic opinion (see Table 8). Moreover, even though the French did not get everything they asked for when they employed domestic constraint projection, they did succeed in wrangling a number of concessions from their English-speaking partners that the Anglo-Americans were not inclined to grant. These included: acceptance of interim French separation of the Saar; the creation of the IAR and the MSB; a delay of bi-zonal policies that would inflame French opinion; Anglo-American pressure on Adenauer's West German government to accept a wide range of security controls in the contractual agreements; and Sarrois admission into the COE. These concessions are all the more noteworthy when one considers that the Americans held all the political, economic, and military cards. France's only bargaining power was its domestic weakness.

Conversely, the United States, which should have been able to dictate its terms to the weaker Europeans according to neorealist hypothesis N2, engaged in constraint projection on only one occasion, to no avail. In 1952, a frustrated Acheson invoked congressional pressure in an attempt to secure an early deadline for the signature of the contractual agreement. He failed, even though his appeal was directly linked to a threat that Congress might cut off aid to Europe in the absence of an agreement. The British did not attempt domestic constraint projection in any significant way when negotiating this issue area of the settlement. Thus, we are unable to make judgments about the likelihood that such entreaties would have met with success. Their reluctance to engage in constraint projection, however, might indicate that the British were less confident about their prospects for success, as hypothesis A2 suggests. Thus, for the political/territorial issue area of the settlement, hypothesis A2 clearly outperformed both hypothesis N2 and traditional liberal hypothesis T2—positing that all democracies would utilize domestic constraint projection with comparable frequency and comparable success.

The political and territorial settlement indicates, then, that the French foreign policy executive was far more constrained by domestic opinion than the other two democracies. Public and parliamentary opposition hampered the French government's ability to undertake specific actions that it favored, caused it to oppose agreements that its leaders preferred, and generally affected the timing of policy changes. At the same time, it assisted French leaders in securing concessions from their allies.

Industrial Dismantling and the Control of German Industry, 1945–1952

Another complex series of issues arising out of the war pertained to the economic settlement with Germany. Beyond the mere question of reparations to the ravaged nations of Europe, the Allies were motivated in large part by the fear that if the Germans were allowed to resume their pre-war levels of industry, they would once again dominate the continent both economically and militarily. Therefore, for peace and stability to endure, it was widely accepted that German industry had to be subjected to strict controls, all weapons production had to cease, and industrial plants producing militarily strategic goods, such as steel, in excess of the country's peaceful needs should be dismantled.

As Cold War competition for Germany heated up, many Western leaders feared that these punitive measures might undermine the construction of a stable democracy in Western Germany and might ultimately force all of Germany into the Soviet camp. Instead, they wished to loosen the restrictions on German industry and cut back on dismantling, while maintaining sufficient controls over German military capability. How to balance these two objectives, though, became the source of sustained and bitter disagreement between the Western powers. In addition, at various times, the issue of industrial controls placed each of the three governments at odds with its domestic opinion, which believed that renewed German industrial strength would breed renewed German militarism. In the end, the Allies resolved the matter by creating European institutions that harnessed German industrial production for the economic health of Western Europe.

At Potsdam, the Big Three agreed to extract reparations payments from Germany primarily by dismantling industrial plants that produced weapons and war-related materials and by removing capital equipment. In addition, whatever industrial capability they allowed Germany to retain was subjected to strict controls.[118] This plan served four purposes. First, it allowed the European allies, particularly the French, to rebuild their shattered industrial bases with German equipment. Second, it avoided the costly debacle that resulted from the extraction of reparations from current production after World War I. Third, it was consistent with the Allied determination to afford the Germans a standard of living no higher than neighboring countries. Finally, industrial dismantling would prevent the Germans from rebuilding their military might and once again threatening European security.[119]

The Soviet Union did not adhere to this agreement and obtained exorbitant reparations from current production and capital goods in their occupation zone.[120] The three Western zones initially followed this plan, until Cold War exigencies and fears that it was crippling the German economy and interfering with European economic recovery caused the Allies to reconsider.

Initial Attitudes, 1945–1946

After the war, public opinion in all three countries wanted to punish Germany with severe economic restrictions. In Great Britain, as noted earlier, public antipathy toward Germany was very strong, and there was widespread support for strict controls on German industry, heavy reparations payments to victims of German aggression, and a controlled, lower standard of living for the German people.[121] Significantly for the Labour Government,

---

118. The Potsdam Agreement on reparations is reproduced in *DGO*, 46–47.

119. Schwartz, *America's Germany*, 67–68; Bruce Kuklick, *American Policy and the Division of Germany* (Ithaca: Cornell University Press, 1972), 198–202; Manuel Gottlieb, *The German Peace Settlement and the Berlin Crisis* (New York: Paine Whitman, 1960), 32–34, 42.

120. The Soviets so completely plundered their zone that even the bath fixtures from the American delegation headquarters at Potsdam had been removed! James F. Byrnes, *All In One Lifetime* (New York: Harper & Brothers, 1958), 290.

121. See 109–110. See also, Alec Cairncross, *The Price of War* (Oxford: Basil Blackwell, 1986), 129; and the many letters in the Government's public correspondence file, FO371/46865–69.

the influential Trades Unions Congress, representing all of the United Kingdom's trade unions, echoed this demand for economic punishment, declaring, "[t]he crimes of the German people have to be paid for, and all surpluses over and above a minimum required for the nutrition of the German people will be used for the benefit of the peoples they have so greatly wronged."[122] The French public heartily concurred and, in fact, advocated the removal of all heavy industry from Germany, making it an agricultural state.[123] Even the American public, which had suffered least in the war, overwhelmingly called for the control, limitation, or elimination of German industry.[124]

For the first two years of the occupation, French leaders shared this public hostility toward the Germans.[125] Therefore, in line with de Gaulle's thesis on Germany, postwar French economic policy toward Germany was guided by two main objectives: German economic disarmament, and the transfer of German resources and equipment to France in order to accelerate French economic recovery. Consequently, the French advocated high reparations, extensive industrial dismantling in the military sector and related industries, strict industrial controls on all sectors of the German economy, and the utilization of German laborers for French reconstruction projects. In addition, as a matter of justice, the French government demanded that the German standard of living should be maintained below that of its wartime victims.[126]

The British and American governments, however, held much more lenient views than public opinion. To be sure, the central figures of the Labour Government were keenly aware of the role that German industry had played in the militaristic regimes of Imperial and Nazi Germany. Their socialist principles made them particularly sympathetic to public calls to dismantle the industrial strength of German capitalists. Nonetheless, the

---

122. "Germany After the War," *The Times*, February 10, 1945, 1. Quote from CP (46) 8, January 7, 1946.

123. In an IFOP poll published in September 1945, 86 percent of respondents with opinions favored this extreme course of action. *Sondages,* 7ième Année (1 septembre, 1945): 173.

124. In an October 1945 Gallup poll, an overwhelming majority of American respondents called for some form of limitation, control, or removal of German industry. *POO,* USGALLUP.45-358, QK06, November 1945. In addition, 54 percent of respondents with opinions advocated the removal of all heavy industry from Germany. *POO,* USGALLUP.45-358, QT06A, November 1945.

125. See 110-11.

126. This position is laid out in MAE note, *Direction générale des affaires economiques,* July 7, 1945, Y/363. See also Young, *France,* 58–59; Benjamin U. Ratchford and William D. Ross, *Berlin Reparations Assignment* (Chapel Hill: University of North Carolina Press, 1947), 94–95.

cabinet's priorities were to reestablish a European balance of power and to foster a postwar European—and thereby British—economic recovery. In addition, they desired limited German self-sufficiency to reduce the staggering amounts of food and money that Great Britain would have to pour into their occupation zone. In the first year alone, the British bill for their zone was £80 million, and it threatened to grow unless a concerted effort was made to jump-start the German economy.[127] For this reason, Bevin concluded "that any policy of excessive de-industrialisation would be likely to defeat our own ends."[128]

The British Government, therefore, eschewed the imposition of heavy reparations from current production since these might be difficult to enforce and the Allies might have to finance their payment, as they had following World War I.[129] They advocated reparations in the form of surplus machinery and manufacturing plants only. Significantly, they argued that the primary goal of industrial dismantling should be the industrial disarmament of Germany rather than the payment of reparations to the victims of German aggression; thus, dismantling should not reduce German industrial capacity below the levels required to meet their peaceful industrial needs.[130]

Faced with the daunting task of postwar European reconstruction, American decision makers similarly concluded soon after the cessation of hostilities that they needed to revive the German economy rapidly, despite the public desire to punish the Germans. As Clay repeatedly cabled, European recovery depended on the production and export of German coal, which, in turn, depended on the revival of the German economy as a whole and the amelioration of living conditions in Germany.[131] The foreign policy executive—particularly Truman, Stimson, and Byrnes—agreed. Truman wrote to Churchill in June, "From all the reports which reach me I believe that without immediate concentration on the production of German coal we will have turmoil and unrest in the very areas of Western Europe on which the whole stability of the continent depends."[132] Consequently, he

---

127. Carden, "Before Bizonia"; CM (46) 16, February 18, 1946.

128. CP (45) 160 and Annex, September 10, 1945.

129. CM (45) 7, June 11, 1945; Deighton, *The Impossible Peace*, 32.

130. CP (45) 160 and Annex, September 10, 1945; CM (45) 31, September 13, 1945; Watt, *Britain Looks to Germany*, 53–55; Cairncross, *The Price of War*, 72–75, 104–9; Bullock, *Ernest Bevin*, 22.

131. See, for example, Clay to John Hildring, Head of the War Department's Civil Affairs Division, July 5, 1945, *Clay Papers*, vol. 1, 46–49; and Clay to John J. McCloy, Assistant Secretary of War, June 29, 1945, *Clay Papers*, vol. 1, 43–44.

132. Truman to Churchill, June 24, 1945, *FRUS*, Potsdam, vol. 1, 612.

ordered the Supreme Headquarters, Allied Powers Europe (SHAPE) to make its top priority the production and export of 25 million tons of coal by April 1946.[133] Moreover, since JCS 1067 prevented the War Department from spending money on the supplies and equipment necessary to increase coal production, U.S. policymakers decided that the money received in payment for Ruhr coal exports should pay for these imports before reparations could be paid.[134] Thus, like the British, the Americans opted early for German economic recovery rather than economic castration. In deference to public opinion as well as French and Russian sensibilities, though, this remained an unstated policy objective.

The Level of Industry Agreement

The first big test of Western policies toward the German economy came in the latter half of 1945, during quadrilateral talks on the implementation of the Potsdam Agreement. Aside from the dispute over the creation of central economic administrations for all of Germany, the key area of disagreement concerned the level of industry to be allowed in Germany and, in particular, the permitted level of steel production. When the ACC addressed this issue in December 1945, the British, insistent that the Germans should be permitted to produce an ample amount of coal and steel to fuel postwar reconstruction and promote German self-sufficiency, recommended an annual steel output of 11.5 million tons.[135] This position was thwarted, however, by French and Russian sternness toward the Germans. The French—who were less interested in German economic recovery since resource removals actually made their occupation zone a source of profit—were adamant about restricting the German level of industry to the lowest reasonable amount.[136] Thus, French representatives initially required a limit of no more than 7 million tons of German steel *per annum.*[137] They readily revised their estimate

133. Truman to Eisenhower, July 26, 1945, *FRUS, Potsdam,* vol. 2, 1028–30; Leffler, *A Preponderance of Power,* 65.

134. Leffler, *A Preponderance of Power,* 65. This was ideal for Clay, who believed that reparations should not be allowed to interfere with German economic recovery. Schwartz, *America's Germany,* 30; Clay to McCloy, June 29, 1945, *Clay Papers,* vol. 1, 41–42.

135. Annex to CP (45) 160, September 10, 1945.

136. On French occupation policy, which featured wholesale removal of coal, timber, industrial equipment, and electricity, see Frank Roy Willis, *The French in Germany* (Stanford: Stanford University Press, 1962); and Marc Hillel, *L'Occupation Française en Allemagne* (Paris: Balland, 1983).

137. Murphy to Byrnes, December 22, 1945, *FRUS, 1945,* vol. 3, 1484–86.

downward in January 1946 when the Soviet Union argued that 5.8 million tons of steel production annually was adequate.[138]

The initial American position reflected a genuine desire to compromise with the Soviet Union in order to secure Molotov's support for central administrations. Clay advocated 7.8 million tons of steel production because it represented a middle ground between the Russian and British proposals at the time.[139] American negotiators were adamant, though, that no reparations could be taken from plants producing light consumer goods and other industries necessary to maintain a peacetime economy, as this would undermine the German economic recovery they sought to achieve. Consequently, they maintained that any figures mentioned in the plan relating to peaceful industries were to be interpreted as estimates, rather than limits enforceable through reparations.[140]

Faced with more rigid Allied positions, the British reduced their demands to 10 million tons and then later to 9 million tons before agreeing, much to their chagrin, to restrict overall German industrial capacity to between 50 and 55 percent of the 1938 level, including an allowable steel production limit of 5.8 million tons per annum with a production capacity of 7 million tons in March 1946.[141] The Foreign Office feared that the "lower the level of industrial activity, the less rapidly will Germany gravitate either towards the west ... or towards democracy, which will appear more of a luxury." It, therefore, attached several conditions to the Level of Industry Agreement, most important of which was based on its insistence that economic unity

138. Murphy to Byrnes, December 31, 1945, *FRUS*, 1945, vol. 3, 1499–502; Murphy to Byrnes, January 8 and 11, 1946, *FRUS*, 1946, vol. 5, 481–84; Clay to Byrnes, January 31, 1946, *Clay Papers*, vol. 1, 154–55. The French were amenable to a high level of German coal production, provided the bulk of German coal was allocated for export, but this was less a sign of leniency than it was a reflection of a severe French shortage of that critical commodity. Even before the war, the French had depended on German imports to meet their coal needs; after the war had ravaged the French coal industry, reconstruction—and the new Monnet Plan for industrial expansion—depended on ample supplies of German coal. Young, *France,* 88–89; Philippe Mioche, *Le Plan Monnet: Genèse et élaboration* (Paris: La Sorbonne, 1986); Hitchcock, *France Restored,* 29–40.

139. Murphy to Byrnes, December 22, 1945, *FRUS*, 1945, vol. 3, 1484–86; Clay to Hilldring, January 29, 1946, *Clay Papers*, vol. 1, 153.

140. Cairncross, *The Price of War,* 126; Ratchford and Ross, *Berlin Reparations Assignment,* 137.

141. Cairncross, *The Price of War,* 107–8; "Control Council Plan for Reparations and the Level of Post-War German Economy," March 28, 1946, *DGO,* 113–18; Karl Hardach, *The Political Economy of Germany in the Twentieth Century* (Berkeley and Los Angeles: University of California Press, 1976), 92–93.

had to be achieved before the agreement could take effect. This allowed them to pursue an independent policy in the Ruhr in the interim.[142]

After the Anglo-American agreement on zonal fusion in the summer of 1946, the British were able to work toward West German economic self-sufficiency together with the Americans. In the meantime, U.S. declaratory policy toward the German economy changed dramatically. Until September 1946, despite Clay's efforts, American officials refrained from committing themselves publicly to German economic recovery. In his September Stuttgart speech, however, Byrnes announced that while the United States remained committed to the Potsdam Agreement, "[t]he German people were not denied, however, the possibility of improving their lot by hard work over the years. Industrial growth and progress were not denied them." Moreover, he identified German recovery as essential for European recovery and, therefore, an American priority. He declared:

> While Germany must be prepared to share her coal and steel with the liberated countries of Europe dependent on these supplies, Germany must be enabled to use her skills and her energies to increase her industrial production and to organize the most effective use of her raw materials. Germany must be given a chance to export goods in order to import enough to make her economy self-sustaining. Germany is a part of Europe and recovery in Europe, and particularly in the states adjoining Germany, will be slow indeed if Germany with her great resources of iron and coal is turned into a poorhouse.[143]

Thus, after the Stuttgart speech, priming the German economy became a stated priority of U.S. policy, rather than an unspoken one.[144] Of the Three Powers, then, only the French pursued a highly punitive economic settlement in the first year of the occupation, despite domestic hostility toward Germany in all three countries.

France, the Bi-zone, and the Marshall Plan, 1947–1948

During the first year of the bi-zone, Washington and London increased their commitment to stimulate the West German economy. The exceptionally

---

142. Deighton, "Towards a 'Western Strategy'," 61; Cairncross, *The Price of War*, 147–48.
143. The text of Byrnes's speech is reproduced in *DGO*, 152–60.
144. Backer, *Winds of History*, 135; Leffler, *A Preponderance of Power*, 120.

harsh winter of 1946–1947 had exacerbated the poor living conditions in Germany and had obliged the British, who occupied the most heavily populated zone, to pump even more food and money into the country to avert widespread starvation.[145] The immense burden this placed on a flagging British economy heightened London's urgency to restore the bi-zone's economic health, with an eye toward making it self-sufficient.[146] The Americans shared the British desire to make western Germany economically viable and agreed to increase the permitted bi-zonal level of industry—particularly for the steel sector—in an effort to help both countries climb out of their financial sinkhole in Germany. Negotiations to this end began in Berlin between their military governors. At the same time, the Anglo-Americans attempted to persuade Paris to administer its occupation zone together with the bi-zone.

Bi-zonal cooperation did not iron out all the wrinkles in Anglo-American relations, and several significant differences of opinion remained that made negotiations slow and often tedious. To begin with, the British wanted the reluctant Americans to assume a greater share of financial responsibility for Germany, since the British economy was considerably weaker and under tremendous strain.[147] Of more enduring concern, the two countries disagreed on the disposition of the Ruhr industries. The Labour cabinet, in whose zone they were located, intended to nationalize ownership of the most important industries and return them to German authorities, "subject to such international control that they cannot again be a threat to their neighbours." This policy was designed to give the German people a stake in increased production, while allaying French fears of German industrial and military revival.[148] The Americans steadfastly opposed socialization of the Ruhr industries, which they felt was too risky at a time when bi-zonal stability depended on a substantial increase in coal production.[149] They preferred to return the industries to private German ownership. Another important difference was that the British, like the French, wanted to maintain permanent industrial limits, particularly on German steel production,

145. Schwartz, *America's Germany*, 31; Cairncross, *The Price of War*, 151.

146. Watt, *Britain Looks to Germany*, 54–55.

147. See Murphy's memorandum summarizing a meeting between Byrnes and Bevin, November 20, 1946, *FRUS*, 1946, vol. 5, 640–42.

148. *Parliamentary Debates (Hansard)*, 5th series, vol. 427, col. 1515, October 1946; Bullock, *Ernest Bevin*, 319–20.

149. Patterson to Marshall, June 13, 1947, *FRUS*, 1947, vol. 2, 1151–53; Meeting between Marshall, Patterson, and Forrestal, June 19, 1947, *FRUS*, 1947, vol. 2, 927–28; Memorandum of Marshall-Clayton conversation, June 20, 1947, *FRUS*, 1947, vol. 2, 929.

while the Americans would consider production ceilings only for the duration of the occupation.[150] Finally, the British were firmly committed to carrying out the industrial dismantling and reparations settlement, while the Americans started to have second thoughts in 1947.

Anglo-American differences, however, paled in comparison to the widening gulf between French economic security goals in Germany and the Anglo-American desire to resuscitate the German economy. The announcement of the Marshall Plan was an American attempt to narrow this gap, and it had an enormous impact on Three Power relations in Germany.

THE MARSHALL PLAN

In a June 5, 1947 commencement address to Harvard University graduates, Secretary of State Marshall called attention to "the dislocation of the entire fabric of the European economy" caused by World War II and asserted that the United States had an obligation to rebuild it in the interest of world peace. He announced Washington's commitment to a reconstruction effort, whose purpose would be "the revival of a working economy in the world so as to permit the emergence of political and social conditions in which free institutions can exist." Marshall emphasized, though, that since it was primarily a European problem, it was up to the Europeans to take the initiative in designing a plan to meet their needs.[151] Bevin and Bidault, desperate for reconstruction aid, jumped on the opportunity and called for a conference among interested nations to discuss European needs and to organize a program together with the United States. In only a few months, this effort produced an intricate European Recovery Program (ERP), or "Marshall Plan," to relieve the most urgent needs of the European participants.[152]

From the outset, the western zones of Germany were included in the ERP. In fact, John Gimbel maintains that the primary purpose of the ERP was to overcome French resistance to German recovery by giving them a stake in German economic revival. Thus, he argues, "the Marshall Plan originated as a crash program to dovetail German economic recovery with a general European recovery program in order to make German recovery politically acceptable in Europe and the United States."[153] Whether he is correct or

---

150. Lovett to Hoffman, December 3, 1948, *FRUS,* 1948, vol. 2, 837; British Embassy in Washington to State Department, December 4, 1948, *FRUS,* 1948, vol. 2, 838–41.

151. Marshall's Harvard Speech, June 5, 1947, *FRUS,* 1947, vol. 3, 237–39.

152. Gimbel, *Origins of the Marshall Plan,* 6–17; Young, *France,* 151–54; Bullock, *Ernest Bevin,* 404–27. For details of the Marshall Plan's operation, see Herbert Carleton Mayer, *German Recovery and the Marshall Plan* (Bonn: Edition Atlantic Forum, 1969), 19–23.

153. Gimbel, *The Marshall Plan,* 4.

whether, as others have speculated, the program was intended primarily as a means of promoting general European stability and containing communism, the allocation of Marshall aid to Germany had profound implications for the U.S. government's German policy and subsequent Three Power decisions. It would, after all, be irrational to continue pumping vast sums of money into Germany if the Three Powers were to maintain onerous restrictions on German industry and continue reparations deliveries that would obstruct a meaningful recovery. Indeed, the American financial commitment through the Marshall Plan, together with a growing public perception of the Soviet threat, converted the American public to the cause of German economic reconstruction.[154] Moreover, since the plan's administrators viewed German coal and steel as essential to broader European recovery, they could not tolerate excessive restrictions in these areas. It was, therefore, no coincidence that soon after the announcement of the Marshall Plan, the Americans took bold steps to increase the bi-zonal level of industry, and urged the British and French to reconsider the pursuit of economic security through industrial dismantling.

FRANCE VERSUS THE BI-ZONE

Although the failed Moscow CFM of March 1947 left the French with no alternative to collaboration with Great Britain and the United States in western Germany, they were still unwilling to join their occupation zone to the Anglo-American bi-zone without satisfactory guarantees that French economic and security interests in Germany would be adequately met.[155] Bidault privately admitted to American representatives in July 1947 that "the reconstruction of Germany is an element of European reconstruction," but he insisted that German needs "must not take precedence" over French.[156] Nor could the French government appear to the French public as abandoning its rigid economic security plan for Germany. Therefore, they continued to press for strict controls and ceilings on heavy industry, completion of the industrial dismantling and reparations programs, and an adequate supply of German coal to meet French recovery needs. They did, however, abandon their futile attempts to separate the Ruhr and the Rhineland from Germany and instead reformulated their policy to require

154. In a June 1948 NORC poll, for example, 68 percent of respondents with opinions approved of American efforts to build up German industry. *POO*, USNORC.480159, R16A, June 1948.

155. Y/128, June 18, 1947.

156. Caffery to Marshall, July 11, 1947, *FRUS*, 1947, vol. 2, 983–86.

international ownership and control of the Ruhr industries—the hotbed of German industry.[157] These priorities placed the French in a protracted struggle with their Anglo-Saxon counterparts whose primary objective was to make Western Germany economically viable so as to reduce their financial burden.

The inter-Allied clash of priorities manifested itself quite vividly in a July 1947 dispute over industrial policy. After Marshall aid was earmarked for Germany, Clay and Robertson agreed to increase bi-zonal industrial output and to place the Ruhr coal mines at the disposition of German businessmen. Furthermore, they raised the bi-zonal ceiling on steel output from 5.8 million tons to 10.7 million tons (11.1 million tons for all three western zones) and lifted all output ceilings in the consumer goods sector. The French protested in vain that these were matters to be determined by Four Power agreement, rather than by unilateral declaration.[158] Bidault objected violently, not so much to the substance of the Anglo-American decision as to the effect it would have in France. He worried that it would strengthen the hands of the French Communists, who maintained that cooperation with the West would only lead to a revived German menace. In a letter of protest to Bevin and Marshall that the cabinet urged him to write, Bidault warned that the joint action would "appear to French public opinion as justifying the position taken by Mr. Molotov and that adopted within France by the adversaries of the French Government" that the Marshall Plan was aggressive and intended to give German recovery precedence over French recovery. He stressed that "[t]he Government of the French Republic would be placed in an unexpected and untenable situation if the decisions which are now contemplated were confirmed" and his own position would be placed in grave jeopardy. He then told the American Ambassador to Paris that "he fully realizes our position and realizes that France must eventually go along with us but at [the] same time emphasizes in [the] strongest possible terms [the] impossibility of [the] average Frenchman doing so at this juncture."[159]

Convinced that Bidault's domestic political concerns were genuine, Marshall wrote to Bevin that "the attitude of the French Government cannot be disregarded in this matter." He suggested, therefore, postponing the

---

157. Communiqué to American, British, and Soviet governments, February 1, 1947, *DFRA*, 57–64; Caffery to Marshall, July 11, 1947, *FRUS*, 1947, vol. 2, 983–86.

158. On the Clay-Robertson agreement and its aftermath, see Young, *France*, 156–59; Gimbel, *Marshall Plan*, 225–40; Wall, *The United States and the Making of Postwar France*, 77–80; Clay to Assistant Secretary of War Petersen, July 16, 1947, *Clay Papers*, vol. 1, 383–84. For the text of the plan, see *DGO*, 239–45.

159. Caffery to Marshall, July 18, 1947, *FRUS*, 1947, vol. 2, 996.

announcement of the Clay-Robertson decisions until after the French had an opportunity to express their views.[160] Bevin concurred "that if these proposals were to be approved and published the French Government would find themselves in a position of great difficulty, which might result in their resignation."[161] Hence, they granted Bidault a short reprieve.[162] In addition, in order to mitigate the domestic consequences in France of the new bi-zonal level of industry agreement, the two governments made more German coal and coke available to France and agreed to give "sympathetic consideration" to the French proposal for an international authority to ensure European access to Ruhr production.[163]

At the extended London conference in early 1948, the British and Americans, true to their words, considered the French demand for an international body to control and distribute Ruhr production. The French wanted to vest ownership of Ruhr mines and industries in an authority composed of American, British, French, and Benelux representatives, which would manage and distribute their production domestically and internationally.[164]

The British and Americans held very different views. Sir William Strang, representing Bevin at the conference, made it clear early on that HMG would not approve any scheme for international ownership or management of the Ruhr—which Bevin feared would interfere with coal production and increase the appeal of communism to the German public—but would agree to international control of allocation and distribution.[165] The Americans, too, believed that rigid and punitive controls might drive the Germans into the Soviet camp. Marshall was convinced, however, that some concession to French public opinion on the Ruhr was necessary or else the French

160. Clay was so enraged by this decision that he threatened to resign. General Eisenhower had to intervene personally to persuade him to remain in Germany. See *Clay Papers,* vol. 1, 385–92.

161. CM (47) 63, July 23, 1947; CP (47) 209, July 22, 1947.

162. Marshall to Bevin, July 19, 1947, *FRUS,* 1947, vol. 2, 997; Bevin to Marshall, July 21, 1947, *FRUS,* 1947, vol. 2, 1000.

163. Lovett to Douglas, August 27, 1947, *FRUS,* 1947, vol. 2, 1063–64; CM (47) 76, August 20, 1947. For the text of a Three Power communiqué of August 28 on the revised level of industry agreement, see *DGO,* 238–39. The text of the August 29 revised bi-zonal plan is in *DGO,* 239–45.

164. Caffery to Marshall, August 13, 1947, *FRUS,* 1947, vol. 2, 1029–31; Cabinet meeting, February 21, 1948, Auriol, *Journal,* 1948, 106–7; Douglas to Marshall, February 26, 1948, *FRUS,* 1948, vol. 2, 92–94. French public opinion still preferred the outright separation of the Ruhr and would certainly not countenance allowing the Germans to operate the mines independently. *Sondages,* 9ième Année, No. 6 (1 avril, 1947), 68.

165. CP (48) 5, January 5, 1948; Douglas to Marshall, February 26, 1948, *FRUS,* 1948, vol. 2, 92–94.

government would be unable to agree to the broader political agenda for Germany that was the main focus of the conference.[166] The end result was a watered-down provisional statement of principles that would form the basis of an IAR after further negotiation.[167]

On the eve of the November 1948 conference to finalize an agreement on the IAR, the French were hit by another bi-zonal bombshell. To solve the Anglo-American dispute over nationalizing or privatizing the Ruhr industries, Clay and Robertson reached a compromise on November 10, drafting Law 75, which allowed the Germans themselves to decide on their future ownership.[168] The French were infuriated since they had still hoped to reach an agreement on international ownership at the conference, as the National Assembly had insisted when it reluctantly ratified the London Accords in June.[169] Schuman, the new foreign minister, personally approved of the substance of the new law, but objected to the timing of the announcement, which left him in an awkward position.[170] The proclamation of Law 75 "unleashed emotions" in France and caused "a veritable groundswell of public outrage that Schuman could not ignore."[171] To soften the domestic political repercussions of this decision in France, Marshall and Bevin allowed the French to participate in the bi-zonal "Essen Groups," which supervised the steel industry during the occupation period, and accepted French demands for limited international management and strict control of the German-owned Ruhr mines.[172]

AMERICAN PRESSURE TO RECONSIDER REPARATIONS[173]

The Marshall Plan and the 1947 level of industry agreement also called into question the logic of industrial dismantling. After all, the reparations

166. Marshall to U.S. Embassy in London, March 4 and April 28, 1948, *FRUS,* 1948, vol. 2, 122–23, 206–7.

167. *FRUS,* 1948, 285–88, 290–91; CP (48) 78 and Annexes, March 7, 1948; Young, *France,* 192.

168. For the text of Law 75, see *DGO,* 335–43.

169. Cabinet meeting, November 10, 1948, Auriol, *Journal,* 1948, 516–17, 654 n. 59.

170. He told Caffery that "he realizes full well that a good part of French policy towards Germany is not realistic (but the French people in general do not realize that); he knows furthermore that France will have to abandon at least some of her positions in connection with Germany." But these policy changes would have to be timed correctly to minimize the public reaction. Caffery to Lovett, *FRUS,* 1948, vol. 2, 479.

171. Poidevin, *Robert Schuman,* 210–11; Young, *France,* 207–8.

172. Minutes of Foreign Ministers Meeting, November 19, 1948, *FRUS,* 1948, vol. 2, 517–22; CP (48) 304, December 20, 1948; Young, *Britain, France and the Unity of Europe,* 133; Bullock, *Bevin,* 636–39.

173. For a brief, but excellent treatment of the dismantling dispute, see Schwartz, *America's Germany,* 67–83.

plan was politically rather than economically rational; it was designed to disarm Germany industrially, rather than to reduce Allied occupation costs. Once the United States committed itself to providing the financial impetus for German and European recovery, however, Congress grew increasingly concerned about the economic irrationality of industrial dismantling, and many congressmen agitated for a dramatic reduction in, if not a complete halt to, reparations deliveries.[174]

Unlike in other aspects of occupation policy, British policy on reparations was closer to the French than to the Americans. Both the British and French governments argued that continued industrial dismantling was the most reliable means to restrain German military potential and ensure that German recovery did not outstrip the convalescence of France and other European nations.[175] Thus, it was more difficult for Marshall to negotiate a change in Allied reparation policy. The revised level of industry plan, however, gave him an opportunity to cut back on dismantling, while complying with British and French demands that reparations be resumed. Since the reparations settlement was intended to remove plants in excess of allowed German production capacity, the near doubling of German steel production limits and similar measures in bi-zonal consumer sectors would necessitate the withdrawal of hundreds of plants from the reparations list. Consequently, the revised list submitted by the bi-zonal occupation governments to the Inter-Allied Reparations Agency (IARA) in October 1947 listed only 682 plants—a dramatic reduction from the previous figure of 1,636.[176] Having agreed to the revised level of industry, the British had little choice but to go along, although they insisted that the remaining plants had to be completely dismantled.

The October reduction was not enough for Washington. At the behest of Congress, Marshall established a cabinet technical mission to study the reparations issue further to determine if any of the plants scheduled for demolition should be spared on the grounds that they produced goods that were in short supply.[177] The British and French agreed to refrain from dismantling plants under consideration by the cabinet mission until the

174. John Gimbel, *The American Occupation of Germany* (Stanford: Stanford University Press, 1968), 176–77; Backer, *Winds of History,* 216. In an open report to Truman on food conditions in Germany, former President Herbert Hoover went so far as to call for an end to dismantling and the removal of all restrictions on German industry. For the text of his report, see *The New York Times,* March 24, 1947, 4.

175. CP (48) 5, January 5, 1948; Auriol, *Journal,* 1948, 562.

176. *FRUS,* 1947, vol. 2, 1126–28; Gimbel, *American Occupation of Germany,* 177–78.

177. See *FRUS,* 1948, vol. 2, 708–33; State Department Memorandum, January 20, 1948, *FRUS,* vol. 2, 711–16.

committee submitted its report in July 1948.[178] The report advocated that 315 whole plants and 16 partial plants should be retained in the interests of world supply.[179] The cabinet later reduced this number to 163 whole plants and 1 partial plant in the hope of securing British and French agreement.[180] This was still not sufficient for Marshall Plan Economic Cooperation Administration (ECA) Administrator Paul Hoffman, who initiated a separate ECA technical commission (the so-called Humphrey Commission) to study the same question. Once again, Marshall asked the Western Europeans to suspend their dismantling operations pending the ECA commission's report.[181]

Despite the presence of a more receptive foreign minister, however, the French government would not yield on this sensitive issue. Schuman personally rejected the logic of industrial dismantling, which he believed was counterproductive and risked inflaming German nationalism.[182] His views, though, were light-years ahead of French public opinion and the attitudes of key French legislators, so French policy remained committed to industrial restrictions and dismantling.[183] Across the channel, Bevin found himself in the dilemma he always faced: the German economy had to be rebuilt, but not at the expense of creating a new German military threat or, worse, of leaving German plants for the Soviets to utilize.[184] Not only did he want to "steer a middle course" between the Americans and the French, he also sought the middle ground in a cabinet that included such advocates of German recovery as Lord Pakenham and Sir Stanford Cripps and those such as Hugh Dalton and Aneuran Bevan who were notoriously suspicious of Germany.[185] He also had to contend with a sizeable group in Parliament and the country as a whole who would regard the interruption of the dismantling program as a sellout.[186] He was very reluctant to agree, therefore,

178. Douglas to Marshall, June 2, 1948, *FRUS*, 1948, vol. 2, 754–56.

179. Technical Commission Report, July 1948, *FRUS*, 1948, vol. 2, 778–88.

180. Cabinet Reparations Committee to Truman, August 9, 1948, *FRUS*, 1948, vol. 2, 790–92.

181. Marshall to Bevin, September 16, 1948, *FRUS*, 1948, vol. 2, 808.

182. Poidevin, *Robert Schuman*, 212; Auriol, *Journal*, 1949, 173.

183. See, for example, Auriol, *Journal*, 1948, 360; Schuman to Marshall, October 6, 1948—NARA, State Department Decimal File, 740.00119 EW/10-648. In keeping with this policy, on August 25, the French government declared its intent to continue reparations deliveries from the western zones of Germany. Auriol, *Journal*, 1949, 670, n. 60.

184. Bevin to Marshall, September 7, 1948, *FRUS*, 1948, vol. 2, 806.

185. CM (48) 82, December 20, 1948; Hugh Dalton, *The Political Diary of Hugh Dalton, 1918–40, 1945–60*, Ben Pimlott, ed. (London: Jonathan Cape, 1986), 445–46; Young, *Britain, France and the Unity of Europe*, 133.

186. Marshall to Douglas, August 26, 1948, *FRUS*, 1948, vol. 2, 798; Memorandum by James Hendrick, ECA, *FRUS*, 1948, vol. 2, 820–21.

to interrupt plant removals in the British zone during the Humphrey Committee investigation and he did so—along with the French—only under extreme U.S. pressure.[187] Pressure to stop the dismantling program, though, would only increase in the following year.

Softening the Restrictions, 1949

In 1949, pressure from the ECA, the U.S. Congress, and the Germans themselves kept the economic illogic of industrial dismantling on the political agenda and continued one of the most difficult and protracted Three Power disputes of the postwar era. Meanwhile, as the political restrictions on the German people were being eased concurrently with the establishment of the FRG, the Three Powers also had to consider whether the industrial controls in place in Germany were all necessary or enforceable. By the end of the year, both aspects of the economic settlement were substantially revised in the Germans' favor.

INDUSTRIAL DISMANTLING

In December 1948, the Humphrey Committee's report recommended sparing 167 of the 381 factories it studied from dismantling to further the goal of European recovery.[188] Meanwhile, German dissatisfaction with plant removals began to grow. In August 1948, the *Land* government of Württemberg-Hohenzollern had resigned in protest of industrial dismantling. More worrisome, workers in the British zone—where the bulk of the dismantling took place—grew impatient, and a series of violent confrontations with British troops ensued.[189] Since this was the first open defiance of the Allied occupation authorities of any consequence, it was imperative to meet some of the German concerns lest the legitimacy of Allied rule and the governability of the Germans be undermined. Hence, the Americans pushed for further reductions in the Allied dismantling program and tried to slow down its overall pace. The Europeans, though, feared that growing German independence and the impending West German government would make it impossible to complete German industrial disarmament if it were to be delayed any longer.[190] In the spirit of cooperation that surrounded the

187. See correspondence in *FRUS*, 1948, vol. 2, 796–830; Cairncross, *The Price of War*, 185.

188. Douglas to Marshall, December 15, 1948, *FRUS*, vol. 2, 850–51.

189. Schwartz, *America's Germany*, 69; Auriol, *Journal*, 1949, 669, n. 40.

190. Bevin to Marshall, September 7, 1948, *FRUS*, 1948, vol. 2, 804–7; Douglas to Acheson, February 9, 1949, *FRUS*, 1949, vol. 3, 552–53; Auriol, *Journal*, 1949, 207.

Washington talks of April 1949, the Three Powers reached a compromise agreement. With the NAT and the IAR to provide security against a German resurgence, the Europeans agreed to retain 159 of the 167 plants that the ECA committee wanted to spare. In return, the Americans agreed to complete the removal of the all the remaining plants.[191] The deal was difficult for Schuman to sell to the French cabinet and the public, despite his linkage of French compromises to Acheson's willingness to assist the French government in pursuit of its security interests.[192]

The Washington agreements failed to settle the issue, however. Despite the number of plants that had been reprieved, the German people grew increasingly resentful of Allied plant removals and protested more vociferously. Dismantling became an important issue in the first FRG election campaign in the fall of 1949, and both of the major candidates, Adenauer and Kurt Schumacher, pleaded with John J. McCloy, the future American high commissioner, to reconsider the policy.[193] Persuaded by McCloy, Acheson reopened the question at a September 15 meeting in Washington with an appeal to his European counterparts to halt dismantling not only because of the detrimental effect it had on German morale, but also because of American public opinion. "There is wide criticism in the United States whenever a plant is pulled down. We are under strong pressure to change the policy." Schuman was unimpressed, countering "that he understood what the public opinion in the United States was and that it was equally difficult in France on this problem." He stressed that "the question of abandoning dismantling would cause serious and immediate trouble in France." Bevin added that the British public was also committed to dismantling. Consequently, he and Schuman refused to budge, maintaining that the question had already been settled in April. With great reluctance, Acheson consented to let dismantling continue.[194]

Within two months, the Allies reopened the issue yet again, this time, ironically, at Bevin's insistence. The foreign secretary was concerned that British authorities in Germany were singled out for derision by the Germans because the bulk of the factories being dismantled were in the British

191. For the text of the agreement, see *DGO,* 386–89.

192. Auriol, *Journal,* 1949, 173, 207.

193. Schwartz, *America's Germany,* 69–72; McCloy to Acheson, September 13, 1949, *FRUS,* 1949, vol. 3, 594–96.

194. Memorandum by Acheson, September 15, 1949, *FRUS,* 1949, vcl. 3, 599–603; Dean Acheson, *Present at the Creation: My Years in the State Department* (New York: Norton, 1969), 326–27.

zone. He feared that recent union agitation in the British zone would lead to renewed confrontations between German workers and British troops over dismantling. Therefore, he urged Acheson and Schuman to consider scaling back plant removals in return for meaningful security commitments from Adenauer's government.[195] Acheson was quite pleased, but the French cabinet maintained that only the removal of surplus German industrial production could guarantee French security. Indeed, the Socialists in the cabinet were "hostile toward anything that looked like a concession" since they believed that would encourage German nationalistic tendencies.[196] Nonetheless, at the November Paris conference, an isolated Schuman agreed to suspend all remaining dismantling operations, except for plants universally agreed to be "war plants," if the Germans agreed to cooperate with the IAR and the MSB, and if the ceiling on German steel production were to remain intact. In addition, Bevin and Acheson prevailed upon Schuman to drop his demand for German compensation to IARA members for lost reparations.[197] To the horror of Moch and other French ministers, the resulting agreement with the FRG, the Petersberg Protocols of November 22, went even further, halting all dismantling in Berlin and reprieving several synthetic oil plants previously considered "war plants."[198]

INDUSTRIAL CONTROLS

As a direct result of the reduction in industrial dismantling, the Three Powers found it necessary to reconsider the levels of industrial production to be allowed in Western Germany. The Four Power Prohibited and Limited Industries (PLI) agreement of 1946 and its 1947 upward bi-zonal revision hinged on the assumption that dismantling and industrial limitations were complementary, such that manufacturing plants in excess of the agreed-upon limits would be removed from Germany. Consequently, the Americans hoped—and the British and French feared—that sparing plants would raise German production allowances. A pitched diplomatic battle thus erupted in November 1948 and raged until November 1949 over the matter.

195. Bevin to Acheson, October 28, 1949, *FRUS, 1949*, vol. 3, 618–21; Bullock, *Ernest Bevin*, 736–37; CP (49) 237, November 16, 1949; CM (49) 67, November 17, 1949. On union unrest in the British zone, see Schwartz, *America's Germany,* 75–76.

196. Cabinet Meeting, November 8, 1949, Auriol, *Journal*, 1949, 403–6.

197. CM (49) 67, November 17, 1949; Acheson, *Present at the Creation,* 337–39.

198. For the text of the Petersberg Protocols, see *DGO*, 439–42. On Moch's castigation of Schuman, admonishing that "concessions lead to other concessions" and "this is artichoke politics," see Cabinet Meeting, November 22, 1949, Auriol, *Journal,* 1949, 419.

There were three principal points of disagreement: the duration of industrial controls, the list of industries subject to restriction, and the all-important level of German steel production. Regarding the duration of a new PLI agreement, the initial American position was that no restrictions would be maintained after the conclusion of a Four Power peace treaty with all of Germany. If, however, such a settlement were indefinitely delayed, the Three Powers would lift them earlier, in the interest of German recovery.[199] The British countered that the restrictions were imposed for security reasons and, therefore, should endure at least until the conclusion of a peace treaty, regardless of whether the reduction in industrial dismantling would leave surplus production capacity in Germany. The French, moreover, demanded permanent industrial controls, which would remain in place even beyond a peace treaty. The British, too, wanted to extend the prohibitions — although not the production ceilings — into the post-control period.[200] The disagreement over the materials to be restricted was just as important. The Europeans wanted to restrict or prohibit German production of a broad array of goods both to prevent a future German military menace and also to limit German economic competition with their own producers of these materials.[201] The Americans, though, wished to restrict only those industries directly affecting European security, which they wanted to define as narrowly as possible.[202] In practical terms, the Allies disagreed over whether or not to restrict shipbuilding and the production of synthetic rubber, synthetic oil, ball and roller bearings, and several categories of machine tools.[203] Finally, though the Europeans remained committed to an annual tri-zonal steel production ceiling of 11.1 million tons, many influential Americans wanted a substantial increase.[204]

199. See, for example, Douglas to Marshall, December 8, 1948, *FRUS*, 1948, vol. 2, 843–45.

200. CP (48) 203, August 13, 1948; CP (48) 303, December 20, 1948; Cairncross, *The Price of War*, 183; Murphy to Marshall, November 17, 1948, *FRUS*, 1948, vol. 2, 832–33; Clay to Royall, December 7, 1948, *Clay Papers*, vol. 2, 946–47.

201. The French, in particular, were quite concerned that if industrial restrictions were to be eased German recovery would outpace French recovery. Auriol, *Journal*, 1948, 562.

202. CP (48) 303, December 20, 1948; Acheson to Douglas, February 6, 1949, *FRUS*, 1949, vol. 3, 550–51. Clay, in particular, was unwilling to compromise, grousing, "Security against Germany lies in the intent to enforce security and not in artificial restrictions of industries essential to normal commerce." Clay to Department of the Army, December 20, 1948, *Clay Papers*, vol. 2, 958–59.

203. CP (48) 303, December 20, 1948; CP (49) 23, February 7, 1949.

204. The Humphrey Committee argued that an increase to 13.5 million tons was necessary and "insignificant" to security calculations. Douglas to Marshall, December 7, 1948, *FRUS*, 1948, vol. 2, 841–43. Clay also wanted an increase in steel production to allow for exports. Clay to Department of the Army, November 22, 1948, *Clay Papers*, vol. 2, 931–32.

The disagreement on steel production was swiftly resolved. The State Department, fearing Western European public and governmental reactions, pledged its commitment to an 11.1 million ton limit.[205] Negotiations on the other two matters, however, ran into difficulties throughout the winter of 1948–49, as the Three Powers disagreed on even the the scope of matters to be discussed. Bevin and Schuman decided that negotiations on a new PLI agreement must be linked to talks on industrial dismantling, so that they could make concessions on the latter in exchange for American concessions on the more important industrial controls.[206] Acheson, however, was unwilling to link the two matters both because he feared the tedious nature of the PLI negotiations would delay an agreement on the Humphrey Committee report and also because he feared having to compromise on the former to get an early dismantling agreement. In fact, the Secretary of State was inclined to postpone the PLI negotiations, much to the chagrin of the British and French who wanted to resolve the matter before the establishment of a West German state would make the imposition of industrial controls very difficult.[207] After a month of runaround, Acheson warned Bevin that the two matters would have to be delinked because he could not continue to withstand congressional pressure for a rapid and satisfactory resolution to the dismantling dispute. Moreover, he threatened that Congress might express its displeasure by cutting off aid to Great Britain, France, and other countries receiving reparations.[208] This gambit failed, however, when Bevin responded that HMG would face its own internal difficulties if it complied with American pressure and would prefer to risk a reduction in Marshall aid than face Parliament with nothing to show but a capitulation on industrial dismantling.[209] Frustrated, Acheson agreed to link the two subjects, provided the talks lasted no longer than four to five days.[210]

When the PLI talks formally began in March, Acheson pushed for a three-year duration for all prohibitions and limitations and urged his colleagues to free as many industries as possible from these controls. Bevin and Schuman, though, demanded nothing less than a five-year duration, after which the restrictions could be eased if the Three Powers agreed.

205. Lovett to Hoffman, December 3, 1948, *FRUS, 1948,* vol. 2, 836–38.

206. CP (49) 23, February 7, 1949; CM (49) 10, February 8, 1949.

207. Douglas to Acheson, February 23, 1949, *FRUS, 1949,* vol. 3, 555–56; Young, *France,* 206; Acheson to Douglas, February 6, 1949, *FRUS, 1949,* vol. 3, 550–51.

208. Acheson to Douglas, March 4, 1949, *FRUS, 1949,* vol. 3, 559.

209. Douglas to Acheson, March 7, 1949, *FRUS, 1949,* vol. 3, 559–60; Bullock, *Ernest Bevin,* 662–63.

210. Acheson to Douglas, March 11, 1949, *FRUS, 1949,* vol. 3, 560–63.

Moreover, they insisted on restrictions on German shipbuilding, synthetic oils, ball and roller bearings, machine tools, electronic valves, and a host of other industries. These differences—particularly over shipbuilding and the duration of the agreement—were significant, and the negotiations lasted several weeks. Nonetheless, both sides compromised to reach a deal by early April, although the French insisted that details could not be released until after their local elections, lest the Communists gain from their concessions.[211] The agreement included most of the bans that the Europeans requested, together with restrictions that reflected a genuine compromise between the Europeans and the Americans—a fact which irritated Clay and the Department of Defense (DoD). It stipulated that the prohibitions would remain in force until a peace settlement, while the limitations would endure only until January 1, 1953.[212]

The April PLI agreement was revisited in the autumn of 1949 due to American pressure to cease industrial dismantling. Since the Americans agitated for the retention of the remaining synthetic rubber and oil plants, as well as many steel installations, it seemed that the prohibition and restriction of these manufactures would have to be lifted. Bevin and Schuman were adamant, though, that the excess plants could not produce prohibited or restricted materials and that the essentials of the PLI agreement—particularly the steel production limit—should remain intact for reasons of security and public opinion.[213] As the Quai d'Orsay noted, "It is undeniable that authorizing Germany to exceed the 11,100,000 limit would constitute for France—more from the point of view of public and parliamentary opinion than for reasons of security principles or commercial competition—a delicate matter."[214] Thus, aside from a relaxation of the controls on German shipbuilding, the PLI agreement was largely untouched by the Petersberg Protocols.[215]

---

211. See the American notes of these negotiations in *FRUS,* 1949, vol. 3, 557–92.

212. Ibid.; CP (49) 76, April 5, 1949. For the text of the Agreement, see *DGO,* 380–86. On Clay's objections, see teletype conference between Voorhees and Clay, March 17, 1949, *FRUS,* 1949, vol. 3, 105–13.

213. CP (49) 237, November 16, 1949; CM (49) 67, November 17, 1949.

214. MAE Note sur des affaires économiques et financières, August 7, 1950, MAE, EU 1944–60, Allemagne, 184.

215. Sir Alec Cairncross writes that the ban on synthetic rubber and oil disappeared as part of the November agreements. *The Price of War,* 187. There would appear to be no support for this assertion in either the text of the agreements or the British and American records of the talks. See McCloy to Acheson, November 22, 1949, *FRUS,* 1949, vol. 3, 343–48.

The Schuman Plan, Western Defense, and German Industry:
1950 and Beyond

If French decision makers learned anything from the 1947–1949 negotiations on reparations and the PLI agreement, it was that they could not count on any tripartite agreements to last. Both the Germans and the Americans were dissatisfied with the industrial controls that the Three Powers continued to impose on the FRG. It was likely that, as they had done with the dismantling issue, the Americans would continually reopen the issue and gradually chip away at the restrictions until nothing of consequence endured. Worse still for the French, the British began to press for an increase in German steel production and a general easing of economic restrictions as a prelude to the May 1950 foreign ministers meeting in London.[216] Finally, the Anglo-Americans remained committed to bi-zonal Law 75 allowing the German government to determine the future ownership of the Ruhr coal and steel industries. The French economic security platform was in jeopardy unless the French could find a way to bind German industrial power that the Americans would accept.

On May 9, 1950, with this concern in mind, the French government announced the Schuman Plan to integrate French and German coal and steel production in the interests of Franco-German reconciliation and European security. Other European states would be welcome to join the new Coal and Steel Authority. The plan would bind the most threatening sectors of the German economy to supranational European institutions that would regulate production and distribution. An international framework would solve problems of overt discrimination against Germany, since the supranational authority would also regulate French industries.[217] A supranational European framework would also reconcile French public opinion with the eventuality of German economic resurgence. At this last task, in particular, the plan was quite successful and by 1952, a French public that in 1950 did not want France to have cordial relations with Germany overwhelmingly endorsed the Schuman Plan.[218]

216. U.S. Delegation to Acheson, May 3, 1950, *FRUS,* 1950, vol. 3, 918–20; U.S. Del. to Acheson, May 4, 1950, *FRUS,* 1950, vol. 3, 923–26; CP (48) 80, May 8, 1950.
217. Jean Monnet, *Memoirs,* Richard Mayne, trans. (London: Collins, 1978), 284–94; Massigli, *Une Comédie des Erreurs,* 185–202; Wall, *The United States and the Making of Postwar France,* 189–94; Schwartz, *America's Germany,* 101–5; *DBPO,* series 2, vol. 1, xiii. For an explanation of the Schuman Plan stressing economic rather than political factors, see Poidevin, *Robert Schuman,* 244–56.
218. A February 1950 Gallup Poll revealed that 55 percent of decided French voters

The Schuman Plan, then, promised to solve the problem of German industry over the long-term. Following the North Korean invasion of South Korea in June 1950, Allied concerns about the inadequacy of Western European defenses added new urgency to the American quest to lift restrictions on German industry in the shorter-term. Fearing that the Soviets would try the same sort of challenge by proxy forces in Europe, the Americans found Western European defenses woefully unprepared and desperately short of manpower and materiel, both of which the Germans could supply. They therefore proposed that the PLI agreement be reviewed and eased at the September 1950 NATO meetings in New York.[219] Acheson found the British most willing to oblige and met with comparatively little resistance from the French, who agreed to renegotiate the PLI agreement in order to forestall concessions on a German defense contribution, which would be far more difficult for the French public to swallow.[220] Moreover, agreement on the Schuman Plan had already begun to overcome French domestic opposition to German industrial revival. As a result, in September 1950, the Three Powers agreed to negotiate a significant upward revision of the PLI agreement.[221]

Negotiations were still slow going until the completion of a treaty in April 1951 to establish the high authority of the European Coal and Steel Community envisaged by the Schuman Plan. In the context of this plan, the French proved willing to remove all restrictions on the German steel industry, as well as other industries not producing weapons or other heavy military equipment.[222] Furthermore, in the fall of 1951, the Three Powers agreed to replace the Allied right to control German industry with voluntary undertakings by the West German government not to produce certain

---

opposed cordial relations with Germany. Several months later, after the Schuman Plan was announced, supporters of the plan outnumbered opponents by almost two to one. Gallup, *Gallup International Public Opinion Polls: France,* vol. 1, 141, 144. By September 1952, an IFOP poll indicated that 79 percent of decided French voters supported the Schuman Plan. Stoetzel, "The Evolution of French Opinion," 94.

219. See, for example, Acheson to Bruce, August 1, 1950, *FRUS,* 1950, vol. 3, 172–74; U.S. Delegation Position Paper, August 30, 1950, *FRUS,* 1950, vol. 3, 1275–76.

220. Bevin to Sir Oliver Franks, September 6, 1950, *DBPO,* series 2, vol. 3, 18–20; CP (50) 199, September 4, 1950; CM (50) 56, September 6, 1950; MAE, Note Direction d'Europe, August 29, 1950, MAE, EU 1944–60, Allemagne, 185. See 156–193 for a discussion of Allied policies toward German rearmament.

221. *FRUS,* 1950, vol. 3, 1291.

222. William Diebold, Jr., *The Schuman Plan* (New York: Frederick A. Praeger, 1959), 68; Acheson, *Present at the Creation,* 389.

types of military goods.[223] Allied control over German industry was at last terminated.

Conclusion: Structural Autonomy and Domestic Constraint Projection

In the immediate postwar period, domestic opinion in all three countries opposed German economic rehabilitation at least as much as it disapproved of restoring German political and territorial integrity. Nonetheless, as my structural autonomy model would expect, the three governments varied in their ability to ignore domestic opposition when national leaders believed it was in their interests to rebuild German economic strength both to foster a broader European recovery and to help resist communism. British and American leaders quickly displayed their ability to soften the restrictions on German industry when they wished to do so. The French government, however, was more constrained. After 1947, when France's new western orientation and the Marshall Plan made German recovery an essential precondition of French recovery, Bidault and Schuman were unable to shift French policy accordingly. Instead they continued to resist German economic revival until the Schuman Plan provided a European framework that satisfied the French public's desire for safeguards against German independence. Furthermore, the French executive did not increase its independence meaningfully by practicing the politics of deception in this issue area, although they were able to make minor concessions to the Allies on the bi-zonal level of industry on the condition that the agreement was to be hidden from the public.

Table 9 illustrates the comparative policy independence of the United States and Great Britain, and the cat-and-mouse game that the French foreign minister had to play with public and parliamentary opinion. The only aberration occurred in 1948 and 1949, when the Attlee Government appeared to have difficulty with an open termination of reparations deliveries and the elimination of restrictions, particularly on the shipbuilding industry, because of public opinion.[224] Nonetheless, in October 1949, when

223. See Draft Instructions from the Three Foreign Ministers to the AHC, September 10, 1951, *FRUS*, 1951, vol. 3, 1199–200; *FRUS*, 1951, vol. 3, 1703–10.

224. It is not entirely clear that this represented a significant divergence between executive and public opinion, since Bevin, himself, seemed somewhat committed to both these policies. See, e.g., CP (49) 23, February 7, 1949. Nonetheless, in light of stated Government preferences to revive the German economy and lift the unnecessary restrictions upon it, it would appear that the Government was more inclined to forgo these industrial controls than the public. See CP (48) 5, January 5, 1948.

Table 9   Conflicts between domestic and leader preferences

Country	Year	Context	Victor
United Kingdom	1945–46	German recovery	Leaders
United States	1945–46	German recovery	Leaders
France	1948	Ownership of Ruhr mines	Mixed/domestic opinion
France	1947–50	German recovery	Domestic opinion
United Kingdom	1948–49	Reparations and PLI	Mixed/domestic opinion
United Kingdom	Nov. 1949	Reparations and PLI	Leaders

conditions in Germany heightened the need for these concessions, Bevin was able to endorse them freely.

Thus the politics of the postwar economic settlement conforms more closely to my hypothesis A1 than to the neorealist or traditional realist alternatives. Neorealist hypothesis N1 cannot explain French paralysis when faced with powerful economic and strategic incentives to rebuild the German economy. By the same token, the ease with which the British and American governments shifted to a policy of German economic revival despite domestic opposition casts doubt on traditional realist hypothesis T1. Only hypothesis A1 can explain why the structurally constrained French executive was hampered by domestic hostility toward Germany while the autonomous British and French foreign policy executives could resist it.

The economic settlement after World War II can also teach us more about the utility of highlighting domestic opposition in intergovernmental negotiations, since more attempts at domestic constraint projection were made in this issue area than any of the other issue areas in this study. As Table 10 indicates, all three governments resorted to this bargaining tactic. Though they did not get everything they wanted through domestic constraint projection, French leaders used their domestic opposition effectively to delay the announcement and implementation of Anglo-American plans to increase the bi-zonal level of industry, to secure French participation in the bi-zonal steel supervision body and Anglo-American consent to limited international management and control of the Ruhr mines, and to prevent the Americans from reopening the PLI agreement and bringing the reparations program to a complete halt, as they wished to do in 1948 and 1949. Both times that Acheson attempted to use congressional dissatisfaction as a lever to halt industrial dismantling and production ceilings, however, he

Table 10   Domestic constraint projection in intergovernmental negotiations

Country	Year	Context	Outcome
France	1947	Level of industry	Some success
France	1948	Ownership of Ruhr industries	Some success
United Kingdom	1949	PLI-dismantling linkage	Success
United States	1949	PLI-dismantling linkage	Failure
France	1949	Reparations	Some success
United Kingdom	1949	Reparations	Success
United States	1949	Reparations	Failure
France	1949	PLI	Success

was thwarted by similar French and British claims. The American failure at domestic constraint projection is particularly noteworthy, given that they used this tactic hand-in-hand with implicit threats to cut the Europeans off from vital American economic support.

It is more difficult to draw meaningful conclusions about the British use of domestic constraint projection. Bevin tried it on two occasions in order to thwart Acheson's own reference to American domestic opposition as a reason to bring the reparations program to a halt and to decouple the PLI and dismantling talks. His success tells us something about the comparative ability of the two governments to use this ploy credibly. Since the British did not use the domestic opinion gambit against the French, we cannot make a similar comparison of their respective abilities to employ it successfully. Moreover, the second time Bevin employed domestic constraint projection, he did so in tandem with Schuman. Thus it is difficult to determine whether his success in continuing the dismantling program can be at all attributed to British public and parliamentary opposition, or whether the domestic difficulties of the much less autonomous French regime would have won out regardless of British preferences.[225] The most we can conclude, therefore, is that the British were more successful than the Americans at converting domestic opposition into international political gains.

Negotiations in this issue area, then, provide good support for my bargaining hypothesis A2, since the structurally constrained French employed domestic constraint projection quite effectively, the Americans could not, and the British did so effectively only when attempting to influence the more

225. We do not have a similar problem disentangling French success from the British, since we have many other instances of French success, even when employing domestic constraint projection against both the British and the Americans.

autonomous American executive or when they attempted this tactic together with the French. The neorealist model and its hypothesis N2 cannot explain why the postwar Western hegemon, the United States, was constantly stymied and delayed by the considerably weaker Europeans. Finally, this issue area provides little support for the traditional liberal hypothesis T2, since American leaders could not use their domestic opposition to their advantage, despite being every bit as democratic as the French.

On the whole, then, the economic settlement policies of the Three Powers after World War II provide us with a good deal of support for my structural autonomy model of democratic foreign security policy. There was considerable variance in the three democracies' ability to pursue a generous settlement when the public and powerful parliamentary forces wanted to punish the former enemy, as well as in the efficacy with which they manipulated domestic pressures at the international bargaining table. Moreover, this variance is consistent with the relative structural autonomy of the three states as determined in Chapter 2. The next section will present the most powerful test of our hypotheses: the German rearmament question after World War II.

German Rearmament, 1950–1954

Perhaps the most difficult decision undertaken by the Three Powers after World War II was to rearm the FRG and allow their former enemy to contribute to the defense of Western Europe. Since German militarism had plunged the world into war twice in the first half of the century, it was widely agreed that world stability depended on keeping Germany permanently demilitarized. Even after Europe divided along Cold War lines, most in the West were unwilling to consider utilizing German forces as a bulwark against the Soviet Union. The governments of the Three Powers, though, gave serious consideration to German rearmament starting in 1950, and after four years of arduous negotiations, reached agreement to include West German troops within NATO, subject to voluntary restrictions.

At the Potsdam conference, the United States, Great Britain, and the Soviet Union agreed to demilitarize Germany and dismantle all industrial capability devoted to munitions production. The French, having suffered three times in seventy years at German hands, were only too pleased to agree to these provisions. The Three Powers remained unequivocally committed to keeping Germany demilitarized until the 1948 Soviet challenge in Berlin drew the attention of Western military and political leaders to the uncomfortably large conventional force advantage that the Soviet Union enjoyed in Europe. Moreover, after the detonation of the first Russian atomic bomb in 1949, the West would no longer be able to rely on American atomic weapons to deter a Soviet attack in Europe. Consequently, the military establishments of all three countries became convinced that Western European security might be impossible without a German military contribution.[226]

In late 1949, amidst rampant press rumors that German rearmament was imminent, the three governments issued stiff denials. Nonetheless, spurred by the onset of the Korean War, the issue burst onto the international agenda in 1950 and demanded the Three Powers' immediate attention.

Before the Korean War: Initial Attitudes

As early as 1948, British military leaders—most notably Chief of the Imperial General Staff Field Marshal Viscount Montgomery—warned the Attlee Government that a continental defense effort could not succeed without a German defense contribution.[227] The Soviet Union and its allies possessed an overwhelming numerical superiority, which the token Allied forces in Germany could not counter.[228] Moreover, due to a deteriorating financial situation, it was unclear whether Great Britain would be able to maintain troop levels as they were.[229] After Moscow successfully exploded its first atomic weapon in 1949, American military leaders similarly concluded that, given the state of Western unreadiness, if war were to occur in 1950, the USSR would be able "to overrun Western Europe, with the possible exceptions of the Iberian and Scandinavian Peninsulas."[230] The DoD and the Joint Chiefs of Staff (JCS) therefore advised Truman that "the appropriate

226. David Clay Large, *Germans to the Front: West German Rearmament in the Adenauer Era* (Chapel Hill: University of North Carolina Press, 1996), 32–38; Robert McGeehan, *The German Rearmament Question* (Urbana: University of Illinois Press, 1971), 16–17.

227. P.R.O., DEFE 4/10, JP (48) 16 (Final), January 27, 1948; Viscount Bernard Law Montgomery of Alamein, *The Memoirs of Field-Marshal the Viscount Montgomery of Alamein, K. G.* (New York: Da Capo, 1958).

228. Saki Dockrill, *Britain's Policy for West German Rearmament, 1950–55* (Cambridge: Cambridge University Press, 1991), 7.

229. U.S. Intelligence assessments speculated that Britain might attempt to cut defense costs by, among other things, reducing its troop commitment to Germany. ORE 93–49, December 23, 1949, Papers of Harry S. Truman, HSTL, PSF, Intelligence File, box 257.

230. NSC-68, April 14, 1950, *Documents of the National Security Council, 1947–1977 (DNSC)* (Maryland: a Microfilm Project of University Publications of America Inc., 1980).

and early rearming of Western Germany is of fundamental importance to the defense of Western Europe against the USSR." They feared that if the Germans were not allowed to participate in their own defense, not only would important German defense resources be lost to the West, but Germany could once again cause an international threat, "either independently or with the USSR primarily." They strongly urged Truman to pressure the Europeans to accept the urgent need for a German military contribution.[231] Even French military leaders acknowledged that Western defense would be difficult, if not impossible, without German participation,[232] and that, even rearmed, "Germany no longer represented any danger, either immediately or in any foreseeable future."[233]

For a variety of reasons, not least of which was strong public opposition in all three countries to rearming the Germans, the political establishments of each of the Western powers maintained their steadfast opposition. In Great Britain, where Bevin personally viewed a German military contribution as both necessary and inevitable, the Government nevertheless condemned the idea because of the dreadful effect it would have on opinion at home and in France.[234] Indeed, despite Opposition Leader Winston Churchill's public endorsement of a German contribution to a European Army, a large majority of the British public opposed the idea and the British press was almost unanimous in its disapproval.[235] This public uneasiness

231. NSC-71, June 8, 1950, HSTL, PSF, NSC files, meetings, meeting 60, July 6, 1950.

232. Georges-Henri Soutou, "France and the German Rearmament Problem, 1945–1955," in R. Ahmann, A. M. Birke, and M. Howard, ed., *The Quest for Stability: Problems of West European Security, 1918–1957* (London: Oxford, 1993), 497; Pierre Guillen, "Les Chefs militaires français, le réarmement de l'Allemagne et la CED, 1950–1954," *Revue d'histoire de la deuxième guerre mondiale et des conflits contemporains* 33 (1983): 3–33. Indeed, as early as winter 1948, Generals Ely and Stehlin issued a memorandum to Schuman demanding German rearmament. Georgette Elgey, *La République des contradictions, 1951–1954* (Paris: Fayard, 1968), 215.

233. McGeehan, *The German Rearmament Question,* 17. See also Peter Calvocoressi, *Survey of International Affairs, 1949–1950* (London: Oxford University Press, 1953), p.155. By the end of 1949, notable military figures such as Général Delattre de Tassigny began to express these views publicly. "Le Bulletin de l'Etranger," *Le Monde,* December 7, 1949.

234. Massigli to the MAE, March 17, 1950, MAE, EU 1944–60, Allemagne, 183, 78–79; *Parliamentary Debates (Hansard),* 5th series, vol. 473, "House of Commons Official Report, session 1950," col. 324, PRO, ZHC2/981; Massigli to Schuman, April 14, 1950, MAE, EU 1944–60, Allemagne, 183, 140. Bevin's personal conviction that a German military contribution was desirable is expressed in his private correspondence and confidential cabinet reports. In particular, see Bevin to Morrison, December 31, 1948, FO371/76527; CM (50) 29, May 8, 1950; CP (50) 80, May 3, 1950.

235. In the popular press, only *The Economist* endorsed the idea. Massigli to the MAE, November 28, 1949, MAE, EU 1944–60, Allemagne, 182, 58. Indeed, until December 1950,

was well represented at the heart of the Labour party where prominent Labourite R. H. S. Crossman and influential Cabinet Ministers Dalton and Bevan distrusted German power and were outspoken critics of German rearmament.[236] Thus it was politically expedient to avoid the issue.

The U.S. State Department also rejected German rearmament as premature on political grounds and dangerous on strategic grounds. In a June 1950 memo to the president, Acheson advised that NSC-71—the DoD plan for German military renewal—was "decidedly militaristic and in my opinion not realistic with present conditions." In his view, Germany was not well enough integrated into the Western political orbit yet and Western opinion had not advanced to the point that it would accept a German military. Until the Korean War, Truman was inclined to agree, indicating in his hand-written comments that the DoD report was "wrong as can be."[237] Consequently, American policy pronouncements prior to the Korean War steadfastly denied that German rearmament was even being considered.[238]

Not surprisingly, most French politicians and foreign policymakers also refused to consider the question. Although some, like Paul Reynaud, hailed an eventual German contribution to a European Army as a necessary measure to secure Western Europe from a Soviet attack,[239] most government members, including Schuman—the most "pro-German" of French politicians—drew the line at German rearmament.[240] On strategic grounds, they feared that rearmament would lead to German independence and either a

---

a majority of Britons resolutely opposed German rearmament. See, for example, Gallup, *The Gallup International Public Opinion Polls: Great Britain,* 229. For Churchill's European Army plan, which Attlee called "irresponsible," see Massigli to the MAE, March 17, 1950, MAE, EU 1944–60, Allemagne, 183, 78–79. As Massigli noted, however, the Churchill plan "is far from unanimously approved" by the Conservative party. Massigli to MAE, April 1, 1950, MAE, EU 1944–60, Allemagne, 183, 108.

236. R. H. S. Crossman, "Open Letter," *The Times,* April 10, 1950; Dalton, *Political Diary,* 425; and Michael Foot, *Aneurin Bevan,* vol. 2 (London: Davis-Poynter, 1973), 305–7, 319.

237. Acheson to Truman, June 16, 1950, HSTL, PSF, NSC files, meetings, meeting 60, July 6, 1950.

238. In February 1950, for example, McCloy announced that "Germany cannot be allowed to develop political conditions for a military status which would threaten other nations or the peace of the world. That means there will be no German army or air force." Undated FO Brief, filed March 30, 1950, FO371/85087; Wahnerheide to FO (German Section), February 7, 1950, FO371/85087. This American line was confirmed by Acheson and other American representatives. See Massigli to MAE, April 1, 1950, MAE, EU 1944–60, Allemagne, 183, 110; Bonnet to Schuman, April 13, 1950, MAE, EU 1944–60, Allemagne, 183, 138; and telegram 341 Saving from Sir Oliver Franks, Washington, to FO, June 8, 1950, FO371/85088.

239. Schuman (signed by Seydoux) to André François-Poncet, January 20, 1950, MAE, EU 1944–60, Allemagne, 183, 25–26.

240. Poidevin, *Schuman,* 306–9.

renewed German military threat or, even worse, a German-Russian combination. Alternatively, German rearmament might provoke the USSR and spark a war for which the West was ill prepared. Finally, the creation of German military units might strengthen the hands of those American advocates of withdrawal from Europe due to the high costs of the occupation.[241] The gravity of these strategic considerations was matched by compelling domestic political reasons to prevent German rearmament. The French people were hostile toward Germany in general and steadfastly opposed to German rearmament.[242] The public and parliamentary outcry over press reports in 1949 that the Americans were considering a German military contribution was so great that it created a parliamentary crisis, which the Government survived only by initiating a vote of confidence categorically denying the possibility of German rearmament. The episode confirmed that "[i]n the present climate of opinion in France no French Government can agree to any proposal involving the rearmament of Germany," since the magnitude of public opposition could easily threaten the survival of the fragile governing coalition.[243]

The Impact of the Korean War

The invasion of South Korea by North Korean forces on June 25, 1950 dramatically altered the stakes in the German rearmament debate. It demonstrated to the West that the Soviet Union, its allies, and its proxies were not averse to using force to achieve their objectives and were liable to exploit Western weakness wherever it was manifest. For many in the West, the Korean situation closely paralleled the German one.[244] Both countries

241. Note, DE, November 18, 1949, MAE, EU 1944–60, Allemagne, 182, 24–25; Auriol, *Journal,* 1949, 463–64; MAE Note, DE, April 18, 1950, MAE, EU 1944–60, Allemagne, 183, 155; MAE Note, DE, April 27, 1950, MAE, EU 1944–60, Allemagne, 183, 163.

242. A February 1950 Gallup poll asked Frenchmen if France should have "cordial relations" with Germany. Fifty-five percent of all decided respondents responded negatively. Gallup, *The Gallup International Public Opinion Polls: France,* 141.

243. Kirkpatrick Memorandum, December 15, 1949, FO371/76650. The text of the vote of confidence declared: "The National Assemby confirms that it must remain out of the question for the Federal Republic of Germany to become a signatory of the Atlantic pact and the reconstruction of an armed force must remain forbidden throughout all German territory." Kirkpatrick Minute, November 29, 1949, FO371/76650. On French public and parliamentary protests, see Harvey to FO, November 23, 1949, FO371/76650; meeting between Acheson and Bonnet, December 1, 1949, HSTL, PDA, Memoranda of Conversations.

244. Massigli reported, for example, that many British leaders "were struck by the apparent analogies between the situation in Korea and that of Germany." Dispatch 1245 from Massigli to Schuman, August 2, 1950, MAE, EU 1944–60, Allemagne, 184, 126–27.

were artificially divided by the Cold War. Western defenses in both countries were inadequate. Most importantly, the Soviets had armed the North Koreans in much the same way as they had the East German Volkpolizei, a Soviet-equipped paramilitary force masquerading as an alert police.[245] Consequently, in the aftermath of the invasion, British and American advocates of rearming the Germans were able to sway government policy and bring the issue to the forefront of the Allied agenda.

The war had an immediate effect on American policy. Although Acheson still feared that "a proposal to rearm Germany would be a divisive force on Western opinion, certainly in countries like France and Norway, and not least in the United States,"[246] at a July 6 NSC meeting Truman ordered the DoD and the State Department to begin preparations for German rearmament.[247] This was a bold move, considering that public opinion polls during the first two months of the Korean War showed that most Americans still wanted to keep the Germans disarmed and opposed rebuilding German military strength as a defensive buffer against Russia.[248] It was not until late August—a-month-and-a-half after Truman committed himself to German rearmament—that public opinion swung around to favor a German military contribution.[249] This change, which followed strong endorsements by leading newspapers, freed American policymakers from further domestic opposition over the matter.[250] Nonetheless, Truman's decision to proceed with German rearmament in early July, when the public was still quite

245. In the summer of 1950, the Volkpolizei numbered over fifty thousand troops, including three armored and seven artillery units. These figures were expected to grow as the Soviets stepped up recruitment and military training. CIA Memorandum, July 7, 1950 and Intelligence Memorandum No. 322, August 21, 1950, HSTL, PSF, CIA Files, Memoranda 1950–52.

246. Acheson to Truman, June 30, 1950, PHST, HSTL, PSF, NSC files, meetings, meeting 60, July 6, 1950; NSC-71/1, July 3, 1950, PHST, HSTL, PSF, NSC files, meetings, meeting 60, July 6, 1950.

247. Meeting summary of the sixtieth meeting of the NSC, July 8, 1950, PHST, HSTL, PSF, NSC files, meetings, meeting 60, July 6, 1950.

248. George H. Gallup, The Gallup Poll: Public Opinion 1935–71, 2 vols. (New York: Random House, 1976), 914; POO, USNORC.500282, R02, June 1950. Indeed, as French Ambassador Henri Bonnet observed, the U.S. government had been criticized by the American press and the American public not for its German policy, but for its China policy. Those who were upset with its German policy complained not about its opposition to German rearmament, but about its policy of industrial dismantling. Bonnet to Schuman, April 13, 1950, MAE, EU 1944–60, Allemagne, 183, 134.

249. Gallup, The Gallup Poll: Public Opinion 1935–71, 932.

250. See, for example, the Gallup polls of December 1950 and January 1951, and the NORC surveys of January and October 1951. Gallup, The Gallup Poll: Public Opinion 1935–71, 951, 962; and POO, USNORC.510298, R16, January 1951 and USNORC.510313, R15.

hostile to it, indicates that when the stakes were high, the American foreign security executive would act independently of domestic opinion.

The Korean War also had an important but subtler impact on British policy. While HMG remained officially opposed to a German military force,[251] it admitted privately that German rearmament was essential, and began incremental steps in that direction.[252] First, the British launched an initiative to establish a federal German border police of one hundred thousand and an expanded frontier police force to meet the threat posed by the Volkspolizei.[253] Then, following the U.S. lead, they began organizing and arming a German labor police in their zone.[254] By late August, British High Commissioner in Germany Sir Ivone Kirkpatrick called for one hundred thousand German troops under Allied command to augment the Allied occupation forces.[255] The Foreign Office took these incremental steps despite continued British public and parliamentary hostility to German rearmament.[256]

The changed international environment also had a profound effect on French leaders. Even prior to the Korean War, some influential French diplomats and politicians, including Massigli and Reynaud, began to contemplate a German military contribution to Western defense, despite their residual distrust of Germany. The Korean War converted others in the Quai d'Orsay to this position, which was gaining ground in governmental circles.[257] By

251. During the August 1, 1950 defense debate in the House of Commons, Defence Minister Shinwell asserted that German defense was assured by the occupation forces stationed on German soil. Any change to this policy, including the institution of a German military contribution, could only be made with Three Power agreement. Furthermore, the priority was to arm NATO members. Massigli to Schuman, August 2, 1950, MAE, EU 1944–60, Allemagne, 184, 122–23.

252. See François-Poncet to MAE, July 13, 1950, MAE, EU 1944–60, Allemagne, 183, 38; Bevin to Harvey, September 5, 1950, *DBPO*, series 2, vol. 3, 9–13.

253. Meeting between Bevin and J. Holmes, U.S. Chargé d'Affaires, September 4, 1950, *DBPO*, series 2, vol. 3, 5; Air Marshal Elliot to Bevin, September 8, 1950, *DBPO*, series 2, vol. 3, 22–24.

254. Bérard to the MAE, August 4, 1950, MAE, EU 1944–60, Allemagne, 183, 141–42.

255. CM (50) 56, September 6, 1950; François-Poncet to MAE, August 24, 1950, MAE, EU 1944–60, Allemagne, 185, 47–50.

256. According to Massigli, very few in the House of Commons and the House of Lords spoke out in favor of German rearmament in the wake of the Korean invasion. Most were behind the Government's refusal to consider it. Massigli to Schuman, August 2, 1950, MAE, EU 1944–60, Allemagne, 184, 122–27. On British public attitudes, see note 265.

257. Indeed, the MAE's Direction d'Europe had observed as early as April that growing voices in French governmental circles were becoming convinced that it was "absurd, in the face of the Soviet danger, to impose a trusteeship regime on Germany that prevents it from making an indispensable contribution to the defence of Europe." Note, Direction d'Europe, April 12, 1950, MAE, Secrétariat Général 1945–66, Dossiers, Allemagne, 6, 49–50; Massigli

August 1950, the French recognized that the Soviet Union represented a more serious and more immediate threat than did Germany and, consequently, that the best method to secure Western Germany against a Soviet challenge was to allow German reserve units of the various *Länder* to serve under Allied command.[258] Moreover, they feared that extreme obstinance could lead the Anglo-Saxons to rearm the FRG without French participation. Therefore, French goals changed from preventing German rearmament to limiting it.[259] Nonetheless, unlike their Anglo-American counterparts, they felt powerless to reverse official French opposition to German rearmament because of the public uproar that would inspire.[260] Hence, they opted for subterfuge. In order to overcome their vulnerability to domestic opposition, French leaders needed to make it appear that any concessions they made to German rearmament were initiated by the Anglo-Saxons and forced on the French government over its staunch objections. Thus, the Quai d'Orsay continued to oppose publicly any notion of German rearmament,[261] while secretly hinting to its allies that the French position was malleable. Significantly, the State Department *Weekly Review* reported at the end of August:

---

to Schuman, March 17, 1950, MAE, EU 1944–60, Allemagne, 183, 80. One high profile convert was Bidault, who declared his support for a German defense contribution within Churchill's EA plan, albeit after the Allies had time to rebuild their forces. Furthermore, the French Ministère de la Défence Nationale, which was much more openly favorable to some form of German military commitment than the Quai d'Orsay, sent Pierre Renaud, Secrétaire Général Adjoint de la Défence Nationale, on "a mission to Bavaria to explore the possibilities that Germany offers in the domain of rearmament." Louis Roche (French Observer in Bavaria) to Armand Berard (Deputy High Commissioner in Germany), August 9, 1950, MAE, EU 1944–60, Allemagne, 184, 192–94.

258. MAE, Note, Direction Générale des Affaires Politiques, September 6, 1950, MAE, EU 1944–60, Allemagne, 185, 231–35.

259. MAE Note, August 5, 1950, MAE, EU 1944–60, Allemagne, 184, 150–51; MAE Note, Direction d'Europe, Sous-Direction d'Europe Centrale, August 10, 1950, MAE, EU 1944–60, Allemagne, 184.

260. An October 1950 Gallup poll, for example, revealed that an overwhelming majority of the French wanted to exclude Germany from any European Army, and those in France who believed that German rearmament would increase French security (24.7 percent of decided respondents) were outnumbered by more than two to one by those who feared it would decrease French security (55.6 percent). Gallup, *The Gallup International Public Opinion Polls, France,* 144. Thus, in late August, the MAE could cable French diplomatic representatives in Bonn, London, and Washington, stating, "The government agrees with you ... that the moment has not yet come to renounce our position that there is no question, today, of envisaging the recreation of a German army." Nonetheless, this language indicates that there might be such a time in the near future. Direction d'Europe to Bonn, London, and Washington, August 23, 1950, MAE, EU 1944–60, Allemagne, 185, 32–33.

261. See the public statement reported in MAE Circulaire 183 IP, July 26, 1950, MAE, EU 1944–60, Allemagne, 183, 68–69.

The French Foreign Office has informed Embassy Paris that a recent French statement to the effect that the French remained opposed to German rearmament and to the abrogation of limitations on certain German industries was merely a 'routine' statement in response to press queries and was not intended to prejudice London Study Group consideration of the Prohibited and Limited Industries' Agreement. The Foreign Office spokesman added, however, that the French position on the subject at the Study Group meeting will be 'tough'.[262]

Thus, the French traveled to the September foreign ministers meeting in New York much less reluctant to rearm Germany than they wanted their public to be aware.

The Fall 1950 Foreign Ministers Meeting, the Pleven Plan, and the Spofford Compromise

Acheson hosted the September NATO meetings in New York intent on securing Anglo-French acceptance of German participation in Western defense. He opened with the Pentagon's "one package" proposal, making American agreement to increment troop levels and provide a unified Allied command contingent upon German rearmament. The Pentagon insisted on this linkage since it did not want to commit troops to a mission that did not have reasonable prospects for success, and they believed European defense could not succeed without German divisions. To make the pill easier for the French to swallow, Acheson required only agreement in principle on the inclusion of German military units, which could take place after a sufficient delay to allow the French to build up their own forces first.[263] Bevin was convinced by the logic of the American position and he believed that the defense of Europe should be mounted as far east as possible; thus, he persuaded his Government to endorse the plan, at least in principle, despite strong opposition within the cabinet.[264] This was a bold move for the Government, since British public opinion still opposed German rearmament.[265]

262. State Department, *Weekly Review,* August 30, 1950, 16, HSTL, Papers of Harry S. Truman, WHCF, Confidential File, Box 59.

263. PDA, Princeton Seminars, October 10–11, 1953, reel 6, track 1, 7, HSTL.

264. The cabinet agreed to endorse the American plan only reluctantly, and insisted that general Western rearmament precede the furnishing of German units. CM (50) 58, September 14, 1950; CM (50) 59, September 15, 1950.

265. An October Gallup poll indicated that 54 percent of decided British respondents opposed rearming Western Germany. Gallup, *The Gallup International Public Opinion Polls: Great Britain,* 229.

Schuman confirmed that the French government also appreciated the necessity of a German defense contribution. He emphasized that they would be willing to agree in principle to German rearmament, provided that the whole affair was kept secret.[266] Acheson, however, would not hear of a secret agreement on the matter. Moreover, there was sufficient opposition at the September 16 French cabinet meeting—primarily from Defense Minister Jules Moch and the Socialists—to prevent the French from agreeing even secretly to incorporate German units.[267] Denied this avenue of escape from domestic opinion, the French government opted to stall while it searched for a way to resolve its domestic political dilemma. Schuman enumerated the tremendous risks involved in rearming the Germans and proposed other ways for the Germans to assist Western defense—including a limited federal German police force, increased nonmilitary industrial production, employment of German labor battalions to build a defensive line, and even utilization of German volunteers by the Allied armies of occupation.[268] Moreover, he insisted that even if, in the future, the French government were to approve of German rearmament in principle, it could take place only after all other Western European powers armed first and required integration of the smallest units possible, rather than at the divisional level.[269] Thus, the French government publicly resisted the principle of German rearmament for domestic political reasons, although they would shortly embrace the principle privately without achieving Schuman's preconditions.[270] The

266. Sir Gladwyne Jebb to Minister of State Kenneth Younger, September 16, 1950, *DBPO*, vol. 3, 63. The day before, Massigli told Attlee that "the French Government would not be able to accept any mention in a public communiqué of the principle of German rearmament. As to the principle itself, their attitude was not entirely negative." 63, n. 2. This was consistent with the MAE's assessment that "it is possible to envision the participation of a German contingent to a European Army, or rather an Atlantic one. It is clearly not the French government that opposes the creation of such an army, which the most qualified representatives of the French parliament supported at the Assembly of the Council of Europe only a few weeks ago." "Rearmament Allemand," MAE Note, September 10, 1950, MAE, EU 1944–60, Allemagne, 185, 284–85.

267. *DBPO*, vol. 3, 63, note 2.

268. PDA, HSTL, Princeton Seminars, October 10–11, 1953, reel 6, track 2, 7; CM (50) 59, September 15, 1950; Jebb to Younger, September 17, 1950, *DBPO*, 67–68.

269. Jebb to Younger, September 23, 1950, *DBPO*, series 2, vol. 3, 89–97.

270. In October, for example, the MAE informed its embassies abroad that "as far as the principle of German participation in Western defence is concerned, the French government is entirely in agreement." Of course, they recognized that "French public opinion . . . will never understand if we wish to proclaim our willingness to recreate a German army, when everyone knows that the Allies cannot quickly rearm themselves." MAE, Direction Politique (Pactes) to French Embassies, October 9, 1950, MAE, Secrétariat Général 1945–66, Dossiers, Allemagne, 6, 257.

government's New York "filibuster," however, effectively prevented Three Power agreement on the matter and bought time until the French government countered the American proposal with the Pleven Plan at the end of October.

Inspired by Jean Monnet, the Pleven Plan called for France, Italy, and the Benelux countries to retain their own national armed forces, but place divisions under the control of a separate NAT force coordinated by a European defense minister. The Germans would contribute several battalions to this force, but would not be allowed to retain national troops outside the European Army (EA).[271] This and the French requirement that the Germans accept the Schuman Plan as a precondition made the plan unpopular with the Germans, the British, and the Americans, since it relegated the FRG to an obviously inferior status.[272] For this reason, however, the Pleven Plan was a success in the French Assembly, where it helped the government win a critical vote of confidence in late October. In effect, this was "a vote *against* the rearmament of Germany rather than *for* the European Army."[273]

The Americans viewed the Pleven Plan as a deliberate French attempt to postpone the issue by advancing a plan that was militarily unviable and acceptable to no one. They feared, however, that rejecting the plan outright might cause the French government to collapse; therefore, they applauded the French initiative and suggested that the plan merited study.[274] In December, U.S. representative Charles Spofford offered a compromise plan at the NATO defense ministers' conference in Brussels. Given the urgent need to rearm Germany in a timely manner, Spofford proposed an interim agreement to allow German Regimental Combat Teams (RCT) of five thousand to six thousand men to fight alongside Allied divisions under the authority of the Allied High Command while the Three Powers continued to study the Pleven Plan with an eye to a permanent solution. In return, Acheson dropped the "one package" position and offered a U.S. military commander (General Dwight D. Eisenhower) and six American divisions even before a definitive agreement on German participation was reached.[275]

---

271. Declaration du Gouvernement français sur la création d'une armée européenne, October 24, 1950, AN, Les Papiers de René Pleven, 560AP45, dossier 1.

272. CM (50) 69, October 30, 1950; HSTL, PDA, Princeton Seminars, December 11–13, 1953, reel 1, track 1, 5.

273. Soutou, "France and the German Rearmament Problem," 499.

274. HSTL, PDA, Princeton Seminars, December 11–13, 1953, reel 1, track 1, 5.

275. Acheson to Spofford, November 16, 1950, *FRUS, 1950*, vol. 3, 471–72; U.K. Deputy to the North Atlantic Council to Bevin, November 20, 1950, *DBPO*, series 2, vol. 3, 274–77.

Events in Korea and Germany, however, conspired against the Spofford compromise. By December 1950, the war in Korea had started to go badly for the United States, the Russians warned against rearming Germany in violation of the Potsdam Agreement, and the German public rejected a military program. As a result, the British lost their nerve. In a meeting with Pleven and Schuman in London, Bevin voiced concerns that, since Washington needed to devote military resources to the Far East, it would be very dangerous to provoke the Russians by creating a German military force without maintaining the means to defend it.[276] Under these circumstances, the British Government approved the Spofford compromise only in principle, stipulating that, since a Four Power meeting was ultimately necessary to determine the future of Germany, it was unwise to reach too hasty a settlement of the German defense problem.[277]

Schuman and Moch were able to accept the Spofford compromise since the German reaction doomed it from the start. Under fire from Protestant leaders, the German government rejected the very idea of rearmament. Moreover, Adenauer informed the French government in advance that the Germans could never accept the plan since it would not allow the FRG the equality of rights that it demanded;[278] therefore, there was no danger that the Brussels agreement would lead to German military units in the foreseeable future.[279]

Thus, the French government effectively thwarted resolute American and British efforts to rearm Germany in the fall of 1950, because of their domestic opposition.

The European Defense Community (EDC) Treaty

During the first half of 1951, the French continued to frustrate American efforts to enlist a militarily viable German contribution to Western defense. In military advisors meetings in Bonn, the French representatives claimed

276. Compte Rendu, December 2, 1950, AN, Les Papiers de René Pleven, 560AP45, dossier 1. See also Bevan's December 14 report to the cabinet. CM (50) 86, December 14, 1950.

277. Parodi to French embassies in Atlantic Pact countries, December 21, 1950, MAE, EU 1944–60, Allemagne, 190.

278. Kirkpatrick to Bevin, December 12, 1950, DBPO, series 2, vol. 3, 354–56. On the Protestant leaders' objections, see Bérard to the MAE, October 17, 1950, MAE, EU 1944–60, Allemagne, 187; François-Poncet to the MAE, November 1, 1950, MAE, EU 1944–60, Allemagne, 188.

279. MAE Note, Direction d'Europe, December 5, 1950, MAE, EU 1944–60, Allemagne, 189.

that they lacked governmental authority to meet German demands for a contribution at the division level—rather than the militarily inferior RCT—to equip German units with heavy armor, and to place German troops on equal footing with the others. Consequently, after months of negotiations, no agreement was reached.[280]

Meanwhile, the EA talks in Paris initially fared no better. Despite a serious effort by French delegation leader Hervé Alphand to make progress in these negotiations, French public opinion conspired against a rapid resolution of even the principles that would underlie a European defense force. With an election scheduled for June 17, 1951, the government refused to negotiate on the critical questions of the size of the EA's basic unit and level of military integration until afterwards—even though Schuman himself was "wholly receptive to a militarily workable unit rather than a politically palatable one"[281]—lest they be compelled to compromise and face defeat at the polls. Moreover, fearing public outrage if it proceeded with German rearmament while it was still possible to reach a final settlement with Moscow that would keep Germany demilitarized, the government wanted a four power CFM before agreeing to enlist German military units.[282] At the same time, Paris rejected interim utilization of German contingents, contending that a provisional solution would impede the construction of an EA with adequate safeguards.[283] French domestic politics, therefore, managed to impede progress on all fronts.

These delays frustrated American strategists immensely, as they were anxious to field a viable European defense force as soon as possible. Washington never liked the "unrealistic and undesirable" EA plan and tolerated these negotiations only to make it possible for the French to agree to an interim contribution.[284] But the talks were deadlocked, with no prospect for German units in sight. Nonetheless, Acheson resisted the temptation to pressure the French to proceed with an interim defense plan because he did not want to destabilize the fragile French government.[285] Nor could the Americans count on British support to help them overcome French intransigence. The Labour Government had grown frightened of provoking

280. For the text of the AHC Report on the meetings, see FRUS, 1951, vol. 3, 1044–47.
281. Acheson, Present at the Creation, 552.
282. Bruce to Acheson, April 18, 1951, FRUS, 1951, vol. 3, 782.
283. Acheson to Bruce, June 28, 1951, FRUS, 1951, vol. 3, 803; Bruce to Acheson, July 3, 1951, FRUS, 1951, vol. 3, 805–12.
284. Acheson to American diplomatic offices, January 29, 1951, FRUS, 1951, vol. 3, 760–62; Acheson to Bruce, March 17, 1951, FRUS, 1951, vol. 3, 781–82.
285. Acheson to Bruce, June 28, 1951, FRUS, 1951, vol. 3, 801–5.

a Soviet response and, therefore, was content to let negotiations founder in Paris over what they believed was an unworkable plan for an EA.[286] In addition, Acheson was unwilling to coerce the Germans to accept French terms, since the Truman administration as a whole lacked confidence in the EA formula.

By the autumn of 1951, however, three notable pro-EA American officials—McCloy, Ambassador to France David Bruce, and new convert to the EA, Supreme Allied Commander, Europe (SACEUR) Eisenhower—had begun to generate enthusiasm for the EDC back in Washington.[287] As a result, the United States embarked upon an arm-twisting campaign that helped to overcome the deadlock. They spurred the French on by threatening to rearm Germany directly within NATO if an EDC treaty were not reached.[288] McCloy applied parallel pressure on the Germans, urging them to cooperate with the French plan despite its warts. The new American attitude toward the EDC had another welcome side effect; it caused the British to reconsider their opposition to the plan.[289] Thus, renewed American interest in the EA changed the negotiating climate in the latter half of 1952.

The French election of June 17 helped Washington overcome French intransigence. After these elections, Pleven formed a government of the right, excluding Socialists—and, notably, the anti-EDC Jules Moch—from the cabinet for the first time ever in the Fourth Republic. Without fear of immediate electoral reprisal, this new government made several noteworthy concessions to the German position at the EA conference. In particular, it agreed to let SHAPE recommend the size of the basic unit and subsequently accepted an armored *groupement* only marginally smaller than a

286. Indeed, Attlee's February 12, 1951 address to the House of Commons imposed four time-consuming conditions that had to be met before German armed forces could be raised. "Policy of the Labour Government Towards the Rearmament of Germany," FO Paper for Eden, December 19, 1951, FO371/97905. Meeting these conditions would effectively postpone German rearmament for a period of years.

287. See, for example, Eisenhower's cable to Acheson in July 1951, in which he states that after discussions with Bruce and McCloy, "I am convinced that the time has come when we must all press for the earliest possible implementation of the European Army concept." Department of the Army (Eisenhower) to Acheson, July 1951, HSTL, PSF, NSC files, July 1951. Large, *Germans to the Front*, 125–29; Schwartz, *America's Germany*, 223–24; Bruce to Acheson, July 3, 1951, *FRUS*, 1951, vol. 3, 805–12; Stephen Ambrose, *Eisenhower*, 2 vols. (New York: Simon and Schuster, 1988), vol. 1, 506–8; Bruce to Acheson, July 18, 1951, *FRUS*, 1951, vol. 3, 838–39.

288. Soutou, "France and the German Rearmament Problem," 501.

289. CM (51) 58, September 4, 1951; CM (51) 56, July 30, 1951; CP (51) 233, July 24, 1951; CP (51) 240, September 1, 1951; Dockrill, *Britain's Policy for West German Rearmament*, 76–78.

U.S. division.[290] Nonetheless, the Pleven government held firm on several points. First and foremost, it would not allow German entry into NATO, despite Bonn's insistence, due to domestic fears that NATO membership would grant the Germans a truly national army within an alliance that could be dragged into offensive operations to regain their eastern provinces.[291] Second, Great Britain had to join the EDC in order to guarantee that Germany could not escape its constraints. Finally, the French required safeguards against German militarism, including restrictions on German weapons production and a guarantee against German secession from the EA.[292]

These demands were problematic. The Germans disapproved of the inferior status implied by restrictions on NATO entry and weapons production. The British, meanwhile, refused to join the EDC since the supranational character of the organization would jeopardize British independence, their ties to the British Commonwealth, and, above all, their special relationship with the United States.[293] Nevertheless, American pressure compelled Adenauer to make important concessions to the French position.[294] The British, too, tried to satisfy French demands to some extent, declaring in September 1951 that "the Government of the United Kingdom desires to establish the closest possible association with the European continental community at all stages of its development."[295]

290. Bonsal (American Chargé in France) to Acheson, September 3, 1951, *FRUS*, 1951, vol. 3, 878–79; Bruce to Acheson, October 3, 1951, *FRUS*, 1951, vol. 3, 883–85. Jacques Fauvet, "Birth and Death of a Treaty," 128–64 in Lerner and Aron, *France Defeats EDC*, 128–29.

291. Memorandum of a meeting between Acheson and Schuman, September 6, 1951, PDA, Memoranda of Conversations, HSTL; Report to Gouvernement by Hervé Alphand, May 10, 1952, MAE, EU 1944–60, Allemagne, 1067; Auriol, *Journal*, 1952, 105–6.

292. Poidevin, *Robert Schuman,* 320–26; Soutou, "France and the German Rearmament Problem," 500–501; Acheson to Truman, November 30, 1951, *FRUS*, 1951, vol. 3, 1730–32.

293. Churchill echoed these concerns to the cabinet after becoming prime minister in October. C (51) 32, November 29, 1951; Dockrill, *Britain's Policy for West German Rearmament,* 80–81; Anthony Seldon, *Churchill's Indian Summer: The Conservative Government, 1951–1955* (London: Hodder & Stoughton, 1981), 26–30.

294. See, in particular, the reports of the foreign ministers meetings in November 1951 and London in February 1952; Large, *Germans to the Front,* 135–41.

295. Declaration of the Foreign Ministers of France, the United Kingdom, and the United States, September 14, 1951, *DBPO*, series 2, vol. 1, 723–24. Churchill reaffirmed this commitment after returning to office in the fall. Government Communiqué of December 18, 1951, *DBPO*, series 2, vol. 1, 796n; Sir Anthony Eden, *Full Circle: The Memoirs of Sir Anthony Eden* (London: Cassell, 1960), 31–35. Eden justified these concessions to the French by telling the cabinet that "the more positive form Great Britain's association . . . can take, the more likely the [French] Assembly is to approve." John W. Young, "German Rearmament and the European Defence Community," in John W. Young, ed., *The Foreign Policy of Churchill's Peacetime Administration* (Leicester: Leicester University Press, 1988), 82.

The crucial test for the French EDC policy came in mid-February 1952 when the National Assembly voted on the EDC plan. The vigorous, heated debate in the legislature illustrated the extent of opposition to the EA and fear of German rearmament in any form.[296] The Assembly approved the plan by a majority of forty votes (327 to 287), but attached no fewer than fourteen conditions that had to be met before the government could proceed.[297] Notably, it required: an Anglo-American guarantee in case Germany violated the terms of the treaty; active British participation in the EDC; an agreement that no EDC member (especially not the Germans) could possess more armed forces in Europe than the French; a provision that Germany would never be allowed a German national army or general staff and would not be admitted into NATO. The very large minority who voted against the plan included many members of the Socialist party and the Government "pro-EDC" parties (Radical, and MRP), reflecting the widespread feeling among the French public that a final attempt should be made to reach an accord with Moscow on a neutralized, demilitarized Germany. That is not to imply that the French public and their representatives brooked illusions about Soviet intentions; they simply feared Germany more.[298]

In the event, the government proceeded with EA negotiations and secured many of the revisions requested by the National Assembly, including a declaration by Eden that he would sign a mutual assistance treaty between the United Kingdom and the EDC.[299] The only real concession the French had to make on the military side was to convene joint NATO-EDC meetings so that the FRG could attend NATO meetings without suffering overt discrimination. The EDC Treaty of May 27, 1952, therefore, represented a considerable victory for French policy.

The Treaty Unravels, May 1952–August 1954

The public and political response to the EDC Treaty in France was strong and negative at all ends of the political spectrum. Within weeks of its

296. Hervé Alphand, *L'Etonnement d'être* (Paris: Fayard, 1977), 227.

297. For a complete list of these conditions, see Alphand's Report, May 10, 1952, MAE, EU 1944–60, Allemagne, 1067.

298. Fauvet, "Birth and Death of a Treaty," 131; Harvey to Strang, April 8, 1952, FO371/97905.

299. Eden, *Full Circle*, 44. In his May 10, 1952 Report to the Government, Alphand commented that all changes made to the treaty since the February vote brought the final treaty closer to Pleven's original plan, and that progress was made on all fourteen of the Assembly's conditions. MAE, EU 1944–60, Allemagne, 1067.

signature, General De Gaulle, President Auriol, Radical leader Edouard Herriot, and, paradoxically, a host of Gaullists and Communists condemned the treaty.[300] To complicate matters further, French public opinion welcomed the Soviet note on Germany in the spring of 1952 as an avenue to explore before committing irrevocably to German rearmament.[301] In that inhospitable climate, Premier Antoine Pinay and Schuman—both strong advocates of German rearmament within the EDC—delayed the ratification vote in the vain hope of extracting concessions, such as British association with the EDC and an American guarantee against German secession, to make the deal more palatable for the French public.[302] Moreover, to reassure domestic critics, the French government refused to commence a ratification debate until the Federal Republic ratified both the Bonn Contractuals and the EDC Treaty.[303]

In January 1953, prospects for ratification took a decided turn for the worse as Pinay's short-lived government was defeated by the Assembly and René Mayer formed a new cabinet with the support of the Gaullists. Mayer was a staunch partisan of the treaty, but had to maneuver carefully within the constraints of his coalition.[304] Disliking the supranational constraints of the EDC, the Gaullists demanded that the treaty be loosened to allow France the right to withdraw whatever forces it wished from the EA without asking for permission from other signatories.[305] Furthermore, they insisted on modifications to the EDC Treaty to confer the same status on French forces in Germany that British and American forces enjoyed and to prevent the EDC's weighted voting scheme from undermining Franco-German equality.[306] Mayer also tried to link support for the EDC to greater U.S. support for the crumbling French position in Indochina and continued to

300. Poidevin, *Robert Schuman*, 327–28; Soutou, "France and the German Rearmament Problem," 504–5; Dunn to Acheson, October 20, 1952, NARA, Decimal File, 751.001/10-2052.

301. Memorandum of Ministerial Talks, June 27, 1952, PDA; Memoranda of Conversations, HSTL; Meeting between Acheson and Schuman, June 28, 1952, PDA, Memoranda of Conversations, HSTL; Georges-Henri Soutou, "La France et les notes soviétiques de 1952 sur l'Allemagne," *Revue d'Allemagne* 20 (1988): 261–73.

302. Poidevin, *Robert Schuman*, 329; Memorandum of a conversation between Acheson and Eden, November 12, 1952, *FRUS*, 1952–54, vol. 5, 696–98; Acheson to Dunn, September 6, 1952, *FRUS*, 1952–54, vol. 5, 690–92.

303. Dunn to Department of State, June 20, 1952, NARA, Decimal File, 740.5/6-2052.

304. Fauvet, "Birth and Death of a Treaty," 137; Meeting between Eisenhower, Dulles, and Belgian Foreign Minister Van Zeeland, March 16, 1953, *FRUS*, 1952–54, vol. 5, 773–75.

305. As it was, the treaty provided for the removal of troops only in the event of internal disorder. See HSTL, PDA, Princeton Seminars, December 11–13, 1953, reel 1, track 1, 6.

306. Dunn to Department of State, January 15, 1952, NARA, Decimal File, 740.5/1-553.

request British association with the EDC.[307] He argued that these amendments were necessary in order to secure National Assembly approval of the treaty. Even more damaging than these revisions was the Gaullist requirement that the intractable Franco-German dispute over the Saar be resolved as a precondition of ratification. The Gaullists were effectively and self-consciously delaying both the EDC and the Bonn contractuals indefinitely.[308] When pro-EDC Joseph Laniel formed yet another French cabinet in June 1953, he adhered to Mayer's conditions.[309]

Eisenhower, the new American president, and Secretary of State John Foster Dulles feared that accepting the French amendments would not hasten French ratification, but would only embolden the French to demand further changes.[310] They warned the French that the "EDC [is] so important in American eyes that [the] American people would not support aid to France if they were given [the] impression that France [was] resorting to dilatory tactics in order to postpone ratification [of] this vital document."[311] The threat went unheeded, however, as Mayer and Bidault—who had personally suffered in 1948 for pushing an unpopular agreement through the Assembly due to American pressure—feared their own domestic response to an unpopular treaty more than American impatience. As a result, the United States urged the other five EDC signatories to accept many of the French supplementary protocols.[312]

The French also achieved a closer British association with the EDC. In February 1953, arguing that the French assembly would defeat the treaty without consequential British support, Bidault proposed exempting the British from the supranationality of the EDC if it participated in the organization and agreed to keep British troops in Europe.[313] In order to ease

307. Bruce to State Department, March 12, 1953, European Defense Community, Box 14, AS, Papers of Dwight D. Eisenhower as President, 1953–61, DDEL.

308. Indeed, the Americans believed that the French preconditions were primarily delaying tactics rather than serious concerns. See, for example, Gruenther to Eisenhower, February 7, 1953, General Alfred Gruenther 1954 (4), Box 16, Administration Series, Papers of Dwight D. Eisenhower as President, 1953–61, DDEL; and Meeting between Dulles and Eisenhower, March 24, 1954, Dulles Papers, Eisenhower Library Collection, White House Memoranda, Princeton.

309. Laniel to Eisenhower, October 8, 1953, FRUS, 1952–54, vol. 5, 820–21.

310. Bruce to Department of State, February 27, 1953, FRUS, 1952–54, vol. 5, 741–43.

311. Dulles to Bruce, March 26, 1953, FRUS, 1952–54, vol. 5, 781–84.

312. FRUS, 1952–54, vol. 5, 775; Dillon to Dulles, September 20, 1953, FRUS, 1952–54, vol. 5, 811.

313. Auriol, Journal, 1953–54, 54; Dunn to Dulles, February 16, 1953, FRUS, 1952–54, vol. 5, 730–32.

French parliamentary difficulties, the British reluctantly agreed to consult with EDC members before altering their European forces and to propose a thirty-year extension of the NAT to make it coterminous with the EDC.[314] Not surprisingly, the French were disappointed and pressed for a firmer commitment.[315] In response, the British cabinet also granted a degree of technical military collaboration between the British military establishment and the EDC powers and the creation of a British mission to the EDC commisariat.[316] Although these commitments still fell short of the full British commitment to the EDC Treaty that the French desired, they represented a significant victory for French diplomacy. They were insufficient, however, to sway the tide of French parliamentary opinion and secure the treaty's ratification.

In June 1954, the Assembly made Pierre Mendès-France both premier and foreign minister. Unlike his predecessors in both posts, however, Mendès-France did not commit himself unequivocally and publicly to the EDC. Indeed, every indication suggested that the new premier actually preferred a NATO solution—which would include American and British power as a counterbalance to the Germans—to an EDC framework leaving France alone with Germany.[317] He demanded yet another round of treaty revisions, telling the Americans that the EDC should not be passed by a small majority over a large, embittered minority. Moreover, he implored Dulles that these changes were necessary to win a large enough majority in the Assembly to override the vote in the Council of the Republic, which would certainly oppose the EDC.[318]

Ironically, by the time the French became completely disenchanted with the EDC, the Americans had been so thoroughly converted to the EA concept that they would not hear of a NATO solution.[319] Thus, they used all

314. C (53) 73, February 20, 1953; CC (53) 14, February 24, 1953; CC (53) 15, February 26, 1953.

315. Auriol, *Journal,* 1953–54, 78.

316. C (53) 332, November 20, 1953; CC (53) 32, May 19, 1953; CC (53) 72, November 26, 1953.

317. Churchill to Dulles, August 24, 1954, John Foster Dulles August 1954 (1), Box 2, Dulles-Herter Series, Papers of Dwight D. Eisenhower as President, 1953–61, DDEL.

318. Dillon to Dulles, June 21, 1954, John Foster Dulles June 1954 (2), Box 2, Dulles-Herter Series, Papers of Dwight D. Eisenhower as President, 1953–61, DDEL. Meeting between Dulles, Mendès-France, and MacArthur, July 13, 1954, John Foster Dulles July 1954 (1), Box 2, Dulles-Herter Series, Papers of Dwight D. Eisenhower as President, 1953–61, DDEL.

319. Soon after Eisenhower took office in January 1953, Dulles met with leading State Department officials and the JCS to discuss American options in the event that the Europeans failed to ratify the EDC Treaty. The Secretary was surprised to hear that General Bradley

the diplomatic leverage they could muster through a variety of channels to coerce the French and influence both the timing and the outcome of their ratification vote. On one plane, Dulles warned the French that the American people were dissatisfied with stalled progress toward an EA and would not permit further delay. Hence, if the EDC were not ratified quickly, the United States, perhaps with British agreement, would unilaterally restore German sovereignty and rearm the Federal Republic without French participation.[320]

In June 1954, Churchill and Eden visited Washington for a conference with Eisenhower to which the French were deliberately not invited so that they would conclude that their obstruction was leading to isolation. At this meeting, Eisenhower persuaded Churchill to use all his diplomatic clout to influence Mendès-France to ratify the Treaty.[321] In Paris, U.S. Ambassador Douglas Dillon added to the American barrage, charging that the French had only one unpleasant alternative to the EDC. "Shall the inevitable rearmament of Germany be a controlled rearmament within a European Defense Community," he asked, "or shall there be recreated once again an independent German National Army?"[322] Dulles underscored this threat, frequently referring to an "agonizing reappraisal" of American policy, which could prompt the United States either to rearm Germany unilaterally or to retreat to a peripheral defense strategy.[323] In late July, Dulles engineered a Senate declaration calling upon Eisenhower to take direct action to grant

---

believed German entry into NATO was preferable to the EA formula and declared that "[f]rom the political standpoint, EDC is much to be preferred." Memorandum of Discussion, January 28, 1953, *FRUS*, 1952–54, vol. 5, 711–17. In August, Eisenhower approved NSC 160/1, stating, "The United States should support with all available means the creation of the European Community and the ratification of the EDC Treaty. No satisfactory substitute for this solution has yet been found." NSC 160/1, August 13, 1953, *DNSC*.

320. Dulles to U.S. Embassy in Paris, May 18, 1954, *FRUS*, 1952–54, vol. 5, 956–57; Meeting between MacArthur and Laniel, April 14, 1954, Dulles Papers, Eisenhower Library Collection, White House Memoranda, Princeton; Meeting between Dulles, Hagerty, and the President, April 19, 1954, Dulles Papers, Eisenhower Library Collection, White House Memoranda, Princeton.

321. Churchill to Dulles, August 24, 1954, *FRUS*, 1952–54, vol. 5, 1077; Eden to Dulles, August 24, 1954, *FRUS*, 1952–54, vol. 5, 1078–79.

322. Speech by Dillon to the Anglo-American Press Association in Paris, June 29, 1954, p.7, J. F. Dulles Personal Papers, Correspondence, Douglas Dillon, 1954, Princeton. Dulles wrote Dillon on July 6, 1954, saying his speech was "an excellent statement of our position."

323. Bonnet to the MAE, March 29, 1954, MAE, EU, 1944–60, Généralités, CED, 27; John Foster Dulles Oral History Collection, Princeton University, René Mayer, 6; John Foster Dulles Oral History Collection, Princeton University, Ogden Reid, 3–4; Press and Radio News Conference summary, June 15, 1954, 5, John Foster Dulles Papers, Correspondence, European Defense Community, 1954, Princeton University; *FRUS*, 1952–54, vol. 5, 868.

the FRG sovereignty unless France ratified the EDC Treaty in a timely manner.[324] The Senate had already cut off all aid to France and Italy until they ratified the EDC Treaty under the terms of the Richards Amendment of July 1953.[325]

Despite this overwhelming Anglo-American pressure, Mendès-France continued to delay the ratification vote because the French public never truly accepted that the dangers of German rearmament could be effectively contained.[326] Public antipathy to German remilitarization strengthened the hands of the parliamentary opposition to the EDC—even those, such as the Gaullists, who favored German rearmament by other means.[327] In such a hostile and turbulent domestic environment, the prospects for ratification were slim. Mendès-France attempted to secure eleventh hour concessions to sweeten the deal for France, including a shorter treaty duration, the right to rescind the treaty if the United States or Great Britain were to withdraw their troops from Europe, the requirement of a unanimous vote on all matters not explicitly stipulated by the treaty, and integration of only those troops in the forward zone—thereby freeing all French troops outside of Germany.[328] The other Western leaders, however, had grown weary of French dickering, and under intense Anglo-American pressure, the premier could no longer delay the inevitable; on August 30, 1954, the National Assembly defeated the EDC Treaty by a sound margin (264 votes for, 319 against). The most powerful opponents of the treaty all expressed distrust of German power and deemed it irresponsible to rearm the nation that had "invaded us in 1792, in 1814, in 1815, in 1870, in 1914, and in 1940."[329]

324. The resolution was passed on July 27. Dulles's orchestration is documented in a Memorandum for the President on his conversation with Senators Knowland and Ferguson and Congressman Halleck on July 21, 1954, Dulles Papers, Eisenhower Library Files, Subject Series, Princeton.

325. This amendment linked military assistance to EDC signatories from fiscal year 1954 funds directly to ratification of the treaty. For the text of this amendment, see Dulles to Bruce, July 13, 1953, FRUS, 1952–54, vol. 5, 796.

326. In a July 1954 IFOP survey, for example, 66 percent of decided French respondents reported that German rearmament was a danger under any form, while 28 percent believed that it required acceptable safeguards. Stoetzel, "The Evolution of French Opinion," 84.

327. As Jean José Marchand points out, the French press contributed to this problem by conflating two separate, but related, issues: rejection of the EDC and rejection of German rearmament. It is possible that the EDC might have survived a ratification vote if the public were made aware that Germany would contribute to Western defense one way or another. "A Tableau of the French Press," in Lerner and Aron, France Defeats EDC, 102–23.

328. Bonnet to the MAE, August 13, 1954, MAE, EU, 1944–60, Généralités, 76.

329. Alexander Werth, Lost Statesman: The Strange Case of Pierre Mendès-France (Ann Arbor: University of Michigan Microfilms, 1980), 183.

The NATO Solution, September–October 1954

The French rejection of the EDC sparked a flurry of international negotiations as Dulles and Eden desperately sought a means of rearming the Germans to which the French could agree quickly. The British and Germans
clearly preferred German entry into NATO. Dulles initially groused that
Congress and the American public required a supranational framework,
but he had to accept the fact that a revival of the EDC was not possible.[330]
Thus Dulles continued to threaten American disengagement from Europe
if Mendès-France did not work quickly and in good faith to find an acceptable alternative to the EDC.[331] Furthermore, to heighten a sense of urgency
and isolation amongst French leaders, the secretary of state cut off all
Mutual Defense Assistance Program aid to France, avoided France on a tour
of European capitals, and publicly empathized with Adenauer's frustration.[332] Eden, meanwhile, took the initiative in calling a Nine Power conference in London in late September to consider his own plan for German
entry into NATO within the European framework of the Brussels Treaty
(BT) Organization.

The agreement finally reached in London brought Italy and the FRG
into the Western European Union (WEU) under the BT, which was revised
to include additional safeguards against a rebirth of German militarism.
Moreover, Adenauer issued a unilateral guarantee renouncing the FRG's
right to produce ABC weapons, guided missiles, heavy warships, long-range
artillery and strategic bombers on German soil. In addition, the WEU military forces were put directly under the authority of SACEUR, whose powers
were enhanced to control their integration, deployment, supply, and inspec-
tion in order to "make it impossible for any single member nation to use its
armed forces in Europe for nationalistic adventures."[333] Finally, to allay
French fears, Eden pledged not to remove British forces from the Continent
without the approval of a majority of BT signatories, and Dulles promised
to advise Eisenhower to extend the same guarantees to Europe as he had

330. Eden, *Full Circle*, 162–64.
331. Dulles immediately warned the French that "[t]he French negative action, without the
provision of any alternative, obviously imposes on the United States the obligation to reap-
praise its foreign policies." Statement by Dulles, August 31, 1954, *FRUS*, 1952–54, vol. 5,
1120–22.
332. Wall, *The United States and the Making of Post-war France*, 287–90.
333. Minutes of the 216th Meeting of the NSC, October 6, 1954, *FRUS*, 1952–54, vol. 5,
1378–84; Memorandum of a conversation between Dulles and Greunther, September 27,
1954, *FRUS*, 1952–54, vol. 5, 1281–83.

under the EDC framework.[334] Ironically, despite the great disparity in power between the United States and France and all the Anglo-American pressure on France to accept the EDC, the French realized all of their ambitions: meaningful British participation in the European defense institution, an American commitment to maintain troops in Europe, national control of the French military, and adequate safeguards against German militarism. Rather than alienating their two more powerful allies, French leaders were able to exploit their domestic opposition masterfully to extract all the concessions they required from the Anglo-Saxons.

The agreements reached in London faced a final crisis when the French Assembly rejected German entry into the BT and NATO in a Christmas Eve ratification vote by a margin of 280 to 258. It required Anglo-American threats that there would be no renegotiation of these accords and a vote of confidence in the Assembly on December 29 to reverse the initial vote by a narrow margin (287 to 260) and put the matter of German rearmament to rest at long last.[335] Despite the safeguards and the Anglo-American troop commitments, however, the French public and many parliamentary deputies felt betrayed by the vote, which they interpreted as a sell-out to international pressure and German power. The final footnote to the whole affair was Mendès-France's dismissal in February 1955, in no small part for his sponsorship of the "new Wehrmacht."[336]

Conclusions: Anglo-American Independence, French Paralysis

The politics of German remilitarization after World War II reveals much about the impact of domestic opinion on policy in Great Britain, France, and the United States. On this particularly sensitive issue, the political leadership in all three countries proceeded cautiously until July 1950, despite the fact that their military establishments believed that Western defense would founder without German participation and despite Bevin's and Acheson's clear preference for eventual German rearmament. They were cautious in deference to Western public opinion, which was understandably concerned about a renaissance of German militarism. We can conclude,

334. For the agreements reached at the London conference, see *FRUS*, 1952–54, vol. 5, 1338–66.
335. Massigli, *Une comédie des erreurs*, 489–91; Eden, *Full Circle*, 170–71.
336. In fact, Mendès-France was defeated by an odd coalition of partisans of the EDC who resented him for killing the plan and opponents of German rearmament. See Large, *Germans to the Front*, 223; Massigli, *Une comédie des erreurs*, 495.

therefore, that even the most autonomous democratic executive must concern itself with domestic opinion and tread carefully rather than risk public outrage. Nonetheless, when the stakes of the German rearmament debate escalated as a result of the Korean War, Bevin and Acheson were able to adapt their policies rapidly in spite of public attitudes. In contrast, French policy conversion was a tortuously slow and uneven process because French leaders dared not provoke public opinion or upset their delicate parliamentary balance even when they were firmly convinced that German rearmament was necessary for French security. The French fear of domestic opposition thus caused a surprising five-year delay in the equipment of German troops, despite the overwhelming Soviet military advantage in Europe.

Table 11 illustrates the comparative ease with which British and American leaders ignored domestic opposition when they deemed it necessary to do so, as well as the immense difficulties French leaders had coping with public and parliamentary opposition. Shortly after the outbreak of the Korean War, both Truman and Bevin were able to declare themselves publicly in support of a German military contribution, despite domestic hostility to the idea. Conversely, when Bidault was denied the possibility of a secret agreement on the matter, the French government delayed a measure it believed to be crucial for national defense for a period of years. It is particularly striking in this regard that, after the Treaty was signed in May 1952, three successive pro-EDC premiers and two foreign ministers who desired its swift implementation nonetheless withheld it from the legislature because they feared it would be defeated by opponents of German rearmament.

This case study confirms, therefore, that the French executive, which was determined *a priori* to be considerably less autonomous than its British and

Table 11   Conflicts between domestic and leader preferences

Country	Year	Context	Victor
France	1950	September meetings	Domestic opinion
United Kingdom	1950	September meetings	Leaders
United States	1950	German rearmament	Leaders
France	1950	Pleven Plan	Leaders
France	early 1951	European army	Domestic opinion
France	late 1951	European army	Leaders
France	1952	EDC treaty	Mixed results
France	1952–54	EDC treaty	Domestic opinion
France	1954	Paris accords	Leaders

American counterparts in the realm of foreign security policy, was indeed more constrained by domestic opinion when it disagreed with government policy. Thus, my structural autonomy model hypothesis A1's predictions were highly accurate. Conversely, neorealist hypothesis N1's expectations were frustrated by the inability of French leaders to overcome domestic opposition to a military measure they deemed essential on national security grounds. Similarly, traditional realist hypothesis T1's predictions were undermined by the ease with which the American and British governments changed policy in 1950, ignoring domestic opposition as soon as they determined that German rearmament was an essential prerequisite for Western defense.

More so than any other issue area of the post–World War II peace settlement, the politics of German rearmament also demonstrate both the opportunities and the limits of the politics of deception for less autonomous governments. Although the French domestic arena was highly mobilized against the recreation of a German military, Schuman and Pleven, who accepted the logic of German rearmament, tried their best to commit to the policy incrementally while deceiving the public and the legislature as much as possible. Initially, Schuman issued categorical denials that France would ever consider or allow German rearmament, while indicating secretly to the Allies that he was willing to negotiate. Then he tried unsuccessfully to agree to the principle, provided it remained hidden from the public. Finally, at various stages, the government tried to sell the policy of a German military contribution to the legislature by arguing that the Americans left France no option. The mere fact that the French Assembly agreed initially to the Pleven Plan and then, in 1954, to German rearmament within NATO indicates the power of governmental blaming. Nonetheless, the failure of successive pro-EDC governments to ratify the EDC Treaty, together with Schuman's and Mendès-France's ousters, demonstrates that less autonomous governments cannot completely escape their domestic constraints through by hiding, misleading, and blaming.

This case also teaches us important lessons about negotiations between democratic states. Contrary to neorealist expectations (hypothesis N2), bargaining outcomes were not primarily determined by the relative power of the states involved, even on such important security matters as German rearmament and Western defense. Overwhelming American power and pressure was insufficient to secure either an early French ratification vote or French parliamentary approval of the EDC. Instead, the considerably weaker French were able to obtain a variety of concessions from the British and Americans because of their domestic difficulties.[337] Indeed, French leaders employed domestic constraint projection more successfully in the negotiations over German rearmament than they did in any other issue area, achieving almost everything they requested, including: delays, limited British association with the EDC, a number of amendments to the EDC Treaty after its signature, and, ultimately, German rearmament on Mendès-France's preferred terms with an extended Anglo-American commitment to Europe in order to protect France from German rearmament as well as from the Red Army.[338]

Yet, contrary to traditional liberal expectations (hypothesis T2), Dulles was unable either to influence the timing of the French EDC ratification vote or to introduce an element of supranationality into the final NATO solution by projecting domestic difficulties. His failure to extract concessions is all the more striking since he threatened to cut off much-needed military and economic assistance to France if it failed to comply. Table 12 illustrates this disjuncture between French success and American failure to induce concessions through domestic constraint projection. Furthermore, the French resorted to this bargaining tactic much more frequently than the Americans and the British, who did not employ it at all in this issue area of the postwar settlement, despite their inability to influence France by other means. This case, therefore, validates the predictions of my structural autonomy model (hypothesis A2).

Table 12   Domestic constraint projection in intergovernmental negotiations

Country	Year	Context	Outcome
France	1950	Fall meetings	Very limited success
France	1951–52	British association	Some success
United States	1953	French ratification vote	Failure
France	1953	British commitment and supplementary proposals	Some success
France	1954	After ratification vote	Success
United States	September 1954	Supranationality	Failure

337. Hitchcock similarly observes that the weaker French were able to subvert Washington's goals and advance their own interests in all aspects of the postwar settlement, despite overwhelming American power. See *France Restored*.

338. We may infer from Mendès-France's success that, paradoxically, nothing enhances a government's bargaining power internationally like a parliamentary defeat!

The politics of German rearmament from 1950 to 1954, therefore, supports both of my hypotheses about the impact of the domestic decision-making environment on democratic foreign security policies.

Final Considerations

The structural autonomy model of democratic foreign security policy developed in Chapter 1 clearly outperformed its neorealist and traditional competitors in all three issue areas of the post–World War II settlement. Nonetheless, two alternative explanations of British and American apparent independence and one alternative explanation of French paralysis must be considered before we can conclude with confidence that differences in structural autonomy explain these outcomes.

First, it is possible that the British and American governments faced cross-cutting domestic opinion to punish the Germans, but at the same time to reduce occupation costs; and to keep the Germans disarmed, but at the same time to contain the Soviet threat. Consequently, it is possible that their willingness to ignore domestic demands to punish the Germans constituted, rather than independence, deference to these other, countervailing domestic demands. While this is a plausible explanation, there are two key problems with it. To begin with, when the British and American executives made their decisions to revive the West German economy and avoid territorial amputations in 1945 and 1946, public opinion in both countries had not yet taken clear stands on either the need to avoid heavy occupation costs or the need to contain the Soviet Union.[339] In 1950, when both countries opted

---

339. In the United States, for example, while the vast majority disapproved of Russian policies in Europe (71 percent) and considered themselves less friendly toward Russia than in 1945 (62 percent), as late as 1947 more than half of decided respondents (52 percent) still believed that Russia would cooperate with the United States on foreign affairs and that the United States should continue to try to cooperate with Russia. Gallup, *The Gallup Poll: 1935–71*, 567, 591, 617, 649. This was hardly a strong public demand for containment at all costs. Moreover, neither the Gallup polls nor those of the NORC show American public pressure to reduce occupation costs in Germany. The British public was less hostile to the Soviet Union in 1946. Indeed, an April 1946 Gallup poll reported that 62 percent of decided respondents believed that Soviet foreign policy was motivated by "making certain of their security," rather than "imperialist expansion." Gallup, *The Gallup International Public Opinion Polls: Great Britain*, 132. There was, however, some British public sentiment in favor of reducing occupation costs. See, for example, "Anglo-U.S. Discussions on Germany," FO Minute by Franklin, September 3, 1946—FO371/55844.

for German rearmament despite public opposition, public opinion in both countries clearly opposed the Soviet Union and favored containment.[340] Nonetheless, when American pollsters explicitly linked rearming the Germans to Western defence against the Soviet Union, the public still rejected German rearmament until after their government's decision to proceed with it.[341] Furthermore, this line of argument overlooks the fact that at most cabinet meetings the British and American executives made their decisions on the basis of calculations of the national interest without reference to domestic preferences. This was especially true of the initial decisions to revive the German economy and the decisions on German rearmament.[342] Thus, while the French executive was preoccupied by public and legislative attitudes, the British and American executives reached key decisions largely without reference to domestic opinion, as we would expect autonomous executives to do.

340. In Great Britain, for example, Gallup polls in 1948 (70 percent) and 1950 (63 percent) revealed that the public feared that the Soviet Union desired to dominate the world. Gallup, *The Gallup International Public Opinion Polls: Great Britain*, 179, 227.

341. In May 1950, 55 percent of decided respondents rejected German rearmament "as a protection against Russia." Gallup, *The Gallup Poll: 1935–71*, 914.

342. In Bevin's 1946 memorandum to the cabinet on German economic recovery, for example, he explains British policy in terms of British national interests, and not in terms of domestic opinion on that or any other matter. "It involves avoiding measures which would permanently alienate the Germans and drive them into the arms of Russia. It involves again showing sufficient purpose not to let it appear that Russia, when it comes to the point, always gets her way in four-Power discussions about Germany. It involves showing ourselves to be no less constructive in our approach to the problems in our zone than the Russians loudly proclaim themselves to be in theirs. And, above all, it involves maintaining a sufficiently high standard of living in western Germany to prevent the Communists from exploiting to their advantage the economic hardships suffered by the population." CP (46) 186, May 3, 1946. See also CM 43 (46) 1, May 7, 1946; CP (46) 218, June 4, 1946; CM 56 (46) 3, June 6, 1946; CM (50) 58, September 14, 1950; and CM (50) 59, September 15, 1950.

In the July 6, 1950 NSC meeting, Truman similarly explained his decision to proceed with initial steps toward German rearmament in terms of national security interests—in this case, the Korean crisis and threats of similar Soviet-inspired moves in Western Germany. To the extent that domestic opinion was mentioned, it was cited only as a reason for proceeding secretly. Meeting summary of the sixtieth meeting of the NSC, July 8, 1950, PHST, HSTL, PSF, NSC files, meetings, meeting 60, July 6, 1950. See also NSC-71, June 8, 1950, HSTL, PSF, NSC files, meetings, meeting 60, July 6, 1950. The American decisions to rebuild the German economy and rehabilitate Germany politically were similarly made and explained behind closed doors as necessary to contain the spread of communism, rather than efforts to satisfy domestic opinion in any way, shape, or form. See, for example, Byrnes to Caffery, November 21, 1945, *FRUS, 1945*, vol. 3, 908; Stimson to Truman, *FRUS, 1945*, Potsdam, vol. 2, 990–91; Byrnes to Patterson, April 10, 1946, *FRUS, 1946*, vol. 5, 539–40; and Patterson to Byrnes, June 11, 1946, *FRUS, 1946*, vol. 2, 486–88.

A second plausible explanation is that, while the Anglo-Saxon executives acted independently of public and legislative opinion, they may have been beholden to powerful interest groups, both directly and through party cleavages. Such an explanation, however, is problematic. To begin with, while economic interests and organized interest groups weighed in on postwar issues, such as general rearmament and the economic reconstruction of Europe, where they had potential economic gains and losses directly at stake,[343] they played a far less salient role in the postwar settlements with Germany than public and legislative opinion. Most larger interest groups avoided taking stances on these issues.[344] The influence of those few larger organized interest groups that did wade into the political fray—such as the military and organized labor—followed the pattern of public and parliamentary opinion (i.e., those in autonomous states were largely ignored when state leaders thought it wise; those in more constrained states had more influence). For example, in 1946, the British Trades Unions Council called for a harsh and punitive economic settlement because "[t]he crimes of the German people have to be paid for."[345] Though it was discussed by the cabinet, their appeal did not sway even a British Labour Government that was heavily dependent on the trades unions for political and financial support. This indicates that the British cabinet, once insulated structurally, could ignore even the most powerful force in its governing coalition of interests. Conversely, the passionate appeals against German rearmament by the Force Ouvrière, the Socialist Trade Union Confederation in France— a highly constrained executive—were taken very seriously by the French government of the center.[346] Moreover, though the military establishments of all three Western powers lobbied for a German military contribution to Western defense, they had no impact on policy in any of the three democracies until after the outbreak of the Korean War. Thus, it does not appear that organized interest groups played a significant role in determining postwar peacemaking policies, especially in the more autonomous states.

343. See, for example, Benjamin O. Fordham, *Building the Cold War Consensus: The Political Economy of U.S. National Security Policy* (Ann Arbor: University of Michigan Press, 1998).

344. American documents I consulted in *FRUS* and at the Harry S. Truman Presidential Library, for example, make no mention of interest group pressure in favor of German political reconstruction or German rearmament. Only on the economic settlement and, in particular, industrial dismantling was there any real pressure to show leniency, largely from Congress, although it was probably influenced by broader economic interest groups.

345. "Report of TUC Delegation on Visit to Germany," Cabinet Note by the Chancellor of the Duchy of Lancaster, CP (46) 8, January 7, 1946.

346. Telegram 458 Saving from Harvey to FO, October 28, 1950, FO371/85089.

Finally, we should consider whether French governmental reluctance to rebuild and rearm postwar Germany truly stemmed from domestic opposition, or whether the government itself preferred a punitive peace—that is, perhaps domestic and governmental attitudes were not so far apart in France. On the surface, there is some support for this explanation, since the government's initial preference—the de Gaulle thesis—was in step with public goals. Moreover, at every step of the way after 1947, the cabinet was divided over German recovery, with some—such as Auriol—resisting almost every effort to ameliorate conditions in Germany. Nonetheless, after 1947, it is clear that the key French foreign policy officials—Bidault, Schuman, Pleven, and other leading figures in government and the Quai d'Orsay—viewed German recovery as a prerequisite for French recovery. After the outbreak of the Korean War, these same figures, together with every premier and a large group in the cabinet, viewed German rearmament as essential for French security.

Moreover, a comparison with the British experience reveals the limitations of this explanation. The British cabinet was also bitterly divided over German recovery, with such political heavyweights as Dalton and Bevin vigorously resisting the termination of industrial dismantling and German rearmament. Yet, when Bevin persuaded the majority that these measures were necessary, a more conciliatory policy carried the day. Conversely, when Bidault persuaded the cabinet in 1947 that a Western strategy was the only way to meet French economic and security objectives, and when Schuman and Pleven persuaded the cabinet of the need for German military units in 1950, French policy remained obstructionist. Thus, what paralyzed French policy was the public and parliamentary pressure on the government—which government documents frequently acknowledged—and the fragile cabinet structure in a multiparty Assembly, which gave dissenting ministers the ability to withdraw their parties from the cabinet and topple the government. In other words, it was the French foreign policy executive's comparative lack of structural autonomy that best explains French foot-dragging.

In the concluding chapter, we shall compare our case study findings for both postwar settlements, consider their implications for students of international politics, and discuss future avenues of research.

5 Structural Autonomy and Democratic Foreign Security Policy

Conclusions

and

Implications

The central argument in this book has been that the impact of public opinion and legislative processes on foreign security policy varies across democracies, depending on the institutional structures, decision-making procedures, and procedural norms that make up their domestic decision-making environments. Democratic executives that are granted a high degree of structural autonomy by their domestic decision-making environments will be better able to pursue unpopular policies in the face of domestic opposition than less autonomous executives. Weaker executives, however, will enjoy greater success at the international bargaining table when they project their domestic constraints as the basis of an appeal for concessions by their negotiating partners. In this regard, I disagree with the conventional treatment of "democracy" as a category of relatively homogeneous states that conduct foreign security policy in similar ways.

Specifically, this book tests my structural autonomy model against two competing models of democratic foreign security policy: the neorealist model, positing that the balance of power in the international system is the primary determinant of the foreign policies of all states, regardless of regime type; and the traditional realist/liberal consensus that democracies are necessarily constrained by domestic opposition. It does so by testing the explanatory power of hypotheses drawn from each model concerning the peacemaking policies of democratic states and the utility of democratic constraint projection in international negotiations. I shall now reconsider these hypotheses in light of my case studies.

Peacemaking after Two World Wars: Lessons

Structural Autonomy, Policy Independence,
and the Politics of Deception

Reflecting on peacemaking with Germany after both world wars, we can make a number of important observations about the impact of public opinion and legislative processes on the foreign security policy choices of democracies. To begin with, my assumptions about policy independence in democratic states are more consistent with the behavior of the states in this study than the traditional realist hypothesis T1, stating that all democratic leaders will be constrained from pursuing conciliatory settlements with former enemies even when they believe it is in the national interest to do so. As predicted by hypothesis A1, the executives of the two highly autonomous states in this study—the United States and Great Britain after World War II—acted with remarkable independence from domestic preferences. Almost immediately after the war, they opted to rebuild the German economy, to resist French demands for territorial amputation, and to create political stability in western Germany even though domestic opinion was bent on punishing the German people for the unspeakable atrocities they had committed during the war. Subsequently, when the outbreak of the Korean War highlighted the inadequacy of Western defense forces, the two governments took the dramatic and unpopular decision to rearm western Germany, despite widespread support for German demilitarization as the best means to keep German militarism in check. The British Government was slightly more attuned to domestic preferences than the American, particularly where the industrial dismantling program was concerned, but on the whole the two governments demonstrated remarkable policy independence.

Furthermore, hypothesis A1 also outperforms the neorealist hypothesis N1, stating that international rather than domestic factors determine national security policies. The three weak democratic governments of 1919 *were* constrained by public and, especially, legislative demands. In the face of persistent calls to make Germany pay, Lloyd George and his negotiators simply could not agree to a moderate reparations settlement, even though he believed that would be wise. All the prime minister could do to prevent the public from imposing an impracticably punitive indemnity was to delay the determination of the amount the Germans would have to pay and the terms of payment until later, when public sentiment would inevitably subside. Woodrow Wilson negotiated the Versailles Peace Treaty completely on his own, ignoring the wishes of the powerful Senate, but the Republican majority in that body punished him for doing so by declining to ratify it. This forcibly demonstrated what little independence the president actually had from Congress. Only the French foreign policy executive was able to take refuge from its constraining domestic decision-making environment, demonstrating some degree of policy independence. As I will argue, however, this was more a function of Clemenceau's skillful use of independence-enhancing strategies to bring the legislature to ratify the unpopular treaty.

The most powerful evidence against neorealist expectations comes from the experience of the structurally constrained French Fourth Republic, whose national security executive was completely paralyzed by domestic opposition. Even when Bidault was convinced that German economic and political stability was an essential prerequisite of both French receipt of Marshall Plan aid and French security from communism and the Soviet Union, he was forced to drag his feet on German recovery because the domestic reaction to such a policy could have toppled the government. Thus, for example, successive French governments fought bitterly to continue industrial dismantling and to maintain limits on German industry until the Schuman Plan provided a politically acceptable framework for German economic recovery. French resistance to German rearmament was even more indicative of its lack of policy independence. Even though both the military and political leadership in France determined that Western defenses were woefully underprepared to resist a Soviet invasion and that French security depended upon an immediate German military contribution, domestic opposition caused three successive pro-EDC governments to resist rearmament and delay an effective Western defense plan for four years. They thus displayed very little policy independence.

Thus, as represented in Table 13, there is a strong, although not perfect, correspondence between the actual policy independence from domestic pressures exhibited by the six states in this study and their structural autonomy as represented in Table 2 (reproduced as Table 14).

What accounts for the minor deviations from my expectations? Specifically, why did the United States executive in 1919—which had its entire program defeated by the Senate—display even less policy independence than Fourth Republic France? And why did Third Republic France in 1919 exhibit a significant degree of policy independence? As suggested in Chapter 3, the answer lies in the comparative willingness of the leaders of these weak executives to maximize their independence by practicing the politics of deception. The French governments in both periods were particularly willing to resort to deception. In 1919, Clemenceau hid behind the protective screen provided by the Council of Four's *in camera* sessions to the extent that the public and the Assembly had no clear idea what policies he was actually pursuing. This enabled him to mislead the Assembly during the ratification debate, where he claimed that he fought much harder than he actually did to achieve a permanent French military frontier on the Rhine and French sovereignty over the Saar. Therefore, he was able to blame Wilson and Lloyd George for any shortcomings in the treaty from the Assembly's point of view.

Bidault and Schuman of the Fourth Republic also tried to maximize their independence by hiding, misleading, and blaming. As much as possible, they tried to make their concessions secretly, whether they pertained to

Table 13   Demonstrated policy independence after both World Wars

Highly Independent	Somewhat Independent	Not Independent
United States, 1945–54 Great Britain, 1945–54 France, 1918–20	Great Britain, 1918–20	France, 1945–54 United States, 1918–20

Table 14   The relative autonomy of the three states after both World Wars

Highly Autonomous	Somewhat Autonomous	Not Autonomous
United States, 1945–54 Great Britain, 1945–54	Great Britain, 1918–20 France, 1918–20 United States, 1918–20	France, 1945–54

loosening the restrictions on the German economy or German rearmament. In 1947, Bidault consented to an Anglo-American increase in bi-zonal steel production, provided that the decision would not be announced immediately. At the 1950 foreign ministers' conference, Schuman tried unsuccessfully to convince Acheson and Bevin to keep their decision to rearm Germany secret, in which case the French government would be able to agree. Finally, successive postwar French governments sought to overcome domestic opposition by blaming Allied governments for the unpopular decisions they took. Bidault, for example, told the cabinet and the legislature that he could not stop the Allies from rebuilding a West German state in their zones. Thus, the best he could do was to participate and extract concessions, such as an international authority for the Ruhr, in order to control that state. Two years later, Pleven complained to the legislature that the Anglo-Saxons were adamant that Germany must participate in Western defense; therefore, all France could do was to control the process by proposing an EA formula.

At the other extreme, Woodrow Wilson refused to get his way through deception. It was anathema to his personality to stoop to such petty, manipulative tactics. Rather than appear that he was bowing to political foes such as Henry Cabot Lodge, he publicly scorned them, adhering only to policies that were consistent with what he believed to be morally superior. Even when he was forced to compromise with the European Allies in the bitter wrangling of Paris, he did not lay the blame for the shortcomings of the final treaty at their doorstep when he presented the treaty for ratification. Consequently, his entire treaty project was rebuffed by the Senate, making it appear that he had even less policy independence than the executive of the French Fourth Republic.

While the French governments employed deceptive strategies to enhance their policy independence, there were limits to their utility. Thus, for example, none of the pro-EDC governments from 1952 to 1954 was confident that these tactics could secure ratification of the treaty in a very hostile Assembly; consequently, they all withheld it from the legislature and tried in vain to modify the treaty before initiating a ratification vote. Moreover, deception frequently entailed significant political costs. While Clemenceau achieved a peace settlement that corresponded with his primary goal of an Anglo-American guarantee rather than the domestic demand for annexations, he was punished for it in the 1920 presidential election. Similarly, although Bidault convinced an unenthusiastic legislature to ratify the unpopular London Accords of 1948 by the barest of majorities, he undermined his own position in the process and lost his ministry as a direct result. Finally, Mendès-France won the ratification of the 1954 London and Paris Accords rearming Germany within NATO by blaming the Anglo-Americans, but he did so at the cost of his political survival. Thus, deception is a costly option that cannot fully enable weak democratic executives to overcome their structural constraints.

This study demonstrates, then, that democratic governments vary in the degree to which they must heed public and parliamentary demands when they construct national security policies. The degree of foreign security policy independence from domestic pressures that a democratic executive has is determined primarily by the structural autonomy it is granted by the institutional structures, decision-making procedures, and procedural norms that make up its domestic decision-making environment. Less autonomous governments, though, can expand their independence to some degree by engaging in the politics of deception when the secrecy of international negotiations grants them that opportunity and when they are willing to accept the political costs of deception.

Structural Autonomy and Inter-Governmental Negotiations

The case studies in this book also confirm that my structural autonomy model more accurately captures the ability of democratic states to invoke domestic opposition as a means of extracting concessions from other states in international negotiations than either of the traditional liberal or neorealist alternatives. Liberals assume that all democracies are nonautonomous states that are constrained by domestic politics; therefore, they conclude that all democratic governments should be able to employ this tactic successfully at the international bargaining table (traditional hypothesis T2). In these cases, however, the weaker executives enjoyed more success at domestic constraint projection than the more autonomous ones, and they attempted it more frequently, as my hypothesis A2 predicted.

Great Britain and France in 1919 and, especially, Fourth Republic France used domestic opposition to secure important concessions from their bargaining partners when negotiating the postwar settlements. Despite Wilson's commitment to restrict German reparations payments to the amount necessary to restore France and Belgium and to state the entire sum up front, Lloyd George convinced the president that British public opinion and, in particular, the Unionists in his coalition would withdraw their support from him if such a moderate settlement were initialed. Consequently, Wilson grudgingly agreed to include pensions as a category of damages that the Germans were to reimburse and, significantly, to postpone most of the major decisions until 1921. Similarly, the prime minister's refrain that British public opinion would not tolerate an extended British commitment to the continent caused Clemenceau to reduce both the length of the inter-Allied occupation of the Rhine, and the size of the British contingent on the Rhine.

Clemenceau used the vociferous Assembly demands for military security on the Rhine to secure both an Anglo-American treaty of guarantee against a future German attack and Anglo-American participation in a fifteen-year staged occupation of Rhine bridgeheads. In addition, the threat that his government could collapse motivated a frustrated Wilson to consent to Articles 429 and 430 of the Versailles Treaty, allowing France to extend the occupation if Allied security guarantees were deemed insufficient and to reoccupy the Rhineland if Germany defaulted on its reparations payments.

By far the most successful at securing concessions from other countries by invoking domestic opposition was the French Fourth Republic. By pointing to the obvious fragility of their governments, French Foreign Ministers Bidault, Schuman, and Mendès-France compelled the United States and Great Britain to make a number of considerable concessions. The two most important concessions the French won in this manner were the creation of an international authority for the Ruhr and the rearmament of Germany within NATO with adequate safeguards, a permanent British commitment to the continent, and an American guarantee of French security. In addition, the Allies frequently granted lesser concessions to the French, such as the acceptance of a provisional French regime in the Saar and delayed announcements of unpopular agreements.

The two highly autonomous democracies, however, did not attempt domestic constraint projection as much as their less autonomous counterparts. In the post–World War II period, American leaders tried to use congressional pressure to compel the Europeans to scale back the industrial dismantling program as well as to force a rapid French ratification vote for the EDC Treaty. They failed completely, as they did when they referred to the American public's preference for a supranational military framework in an effort to return to an EA formula for German rearmament in the autumn of 1954. In negotiating the post–World War II settlement with Germany, British representatives attempted domestic constraint projection only during negotiations over reparations and German industrial limitations. Each time, they were successful, but that appears to be more a function of the fact that the French supported these British pleas with references to their own instability.

Wilson invoked domestic opposition only once when negotiating the German provisions of the Versailles Treaty. He highlighted public opposition to an extended American military presence in Europe. Clemenceau accommodated both Wilson and Lloyd George to some extent on this occasion by reducing his demand to only a fifteen-year occupation and accepting only a token American force. It seems, however, that Wilson was reluctant to use the domestic politics ploy too often because it would not have been credible on account of both his defeat in the November 1918 congressional elections and the widespread desire for a punitive settlement amongst the American public. Thus, the president did not demonstrate much of an ability to project domestic constraints for international gains primarily because he did not try.

The predictions of hypothesis A2 are also more accurate than neorealist expectations. Neorealist hypothesis N2 assumes that international bargaining outcomes reflect the relative power of the participants and that domestic political concerns should be irrelevant, especially in matters of great importance. Therefore, neorealists would have expected that the United States should have been more successful in negotiations with the war-weary Europeans in 1919. Nonetheless, President Wilson was frequently stymied by Clemenceau and Lloyd George, particularly when they projected their domestic constraints. The post–World War II settlement, though, provides the most powerful evidence against the neorealist model. After all, since the United States was by far the preponderant power of the postwar Western alliance, and since the British and, in particular, the French were dependent on American economic, political, and military assistance, American leaders should have been able to impose their preferences regarding the German settlement on their much weaker allies. Yet, despite this overwhelming power disparity, French leaders were frequently able to secure significant concessions from the Americans in all issue areas of the settlement by highlighting their domestic instability. It is particularly noteworthy that, although American leaders were persuaded in 1950 that an immediate German military contribution was an essential requirement for a defense of Western Europe against the Soviet Union, the French were able to delay this contribution for five years, only to enlist it in 1955 on Mendès-France's preferred terms, rather than Dulles's terms.

The success of bargaining hypothesis A2 is illustrated in Table 15. It shows a strong inverse relationship between the level of structural autonomy afforded by domestic institutions, decision-making procedures, and procedural norms, on the one hand, and a democracy's ability to convert its

Table 15   Demonstrated ability to translate domestic opposition into political
concessions

High Ability	Moderate Ability	No Ability
France, 1945–54	Great Britain, 1918–20 France, 1918–20 Great Britain, 1945–54 United States, 1918–20	United States, 1945–54

domestic opposition into gains at the international bargaining table on the other. Clearly, the most autonomous executive, the United States from 1945 to 1954, had the least success in this regard, while the least autonomous executive, the French Fourth Republic, enjoyed the most success. The three democracies after World War I employed domestic constraint projection in a far more limited manner than the French Fourth Republic, but, by and large, they did so successfully. The minor deviation from my expectations may be attributable to the false manifestation of Bevin's success both times he used this ploy because he received French support.

One important caveat about hypothesis A2 is in order. The democracies in this study were able to attempt domestic constraint projection principally because their democratic negotiation partners placed a premium on continued multilateral cooperation in determining and enforcing the peace settlements. Since Wilson desired a departure from great power politics toward greater democracy, it would have been hypocritical for him to impose a solution on the weaker British or French governments. After World War II, when the threat of France succumbing to the French Communist Party was real and when, moreover, the precarious Cold War balance in Europe made it important for the United States to keep the French on side, the French were able to project domestic difficulties as a source of negotiating leverage. Under different circumstances, however, if no strong incentives exist to resolve problems cooperatively, it is likely that even less autonomous democracies would be unable to employ this tactic successfully.[1]

The case studies in this book, then, support my model of the domestic decision-making environment and democratic structural autonomy. It follows, then, that the impact of domestic opinion on the foreign security policies of democratic states is not comparable across democracies, as traditional theories assume. Instead, it varies across democracies, depending on the degree of structural autonomy afforded by their domestic decision-making

---

1. I am grateful to an anonymous reviewer for bringing this to my attention.

environments. Nor do all democracies construct foreign security policy strictly in accordance to the dictates of the international system, as neorealists assume. In this sense, my structural autonomy model identifies when the neorealist model or the traditional model of democratic foreign security policy is more appropriate. When leaders correctly identify systemic incentives, highly autonomous democracies should be able to adapt to the international environment as neorealists expect; weaker democracies, however, should display little actual policy independence, as traditional theorists claim.

Alternative Explanations

Before I conclude that variations in structural autonomy explain these findings, I must consider the possibility that they can be explained more efficiently with other, competing theories. In particular, I should consider whether the policies of the three states can be explained better by more parsimonious theories emphasizing the ability of states to learn from previous mistakes, a geopolitical explanation based on the geographic proximity of the victor to the former enemy, or, perhaps, by the intensity of domestic hostility in each country. I address each of these alternative explanations in turn.

Learning

Since states, like other institutions, possess institutional memory, they can learn over time and from event to event.[2] The process of learning allows states to derive valuable lessons from past mistakes, thereby changing their beliefs, goals, and, at times, future policy. The reader might wonder, therefore, whether changes in the level of punishment pursued by each of the three countries from World War I to World War II might be a function of institutional learning, rather than a product of structural changes in their domestic decision-making environments. Perhaps it would be reasonable to expect that, after the debacle of the Versailles Treaty and its direct contribution to the cataclysm of 1939, all three states learned the lesson that punitive settlements are counterproductive and inimical to stability. In that case, changes in the institutional structures, decision-making procedures,

2. James G. March and Johan P. Olsen, "The Uncertainty of the Past: Organizational Learning Under Ambiguity," in James G. March, *Decisions and Organizations* (New York: Basil Blackwell, 1988), 335–58; Lloyd S. Etheridge, *Can Governments Learn?* (New York: Pergamon, 1985); and Barbara Levitt and James G. March, "Organizational Learning,"

and procedural norms of these states would be incidental, rather than important factors that shaped their policies.

The main problem with this explanation is that French behavior in the 1940s is inconsistent with it. If French leaders learned anything from the interwar years, it was, quite the contrary, that the Versailles settlement failed to keep the peace because it was too lenient with Germany and, above all, it made the fatal error of leaving Germany intact. From 1945 to 1947, de Gaulle and Bidault were convinced that the only way to prevent a future German attack was to break up and decentralize the German state, while denying it the military and industrial means of waging war. It was only in 1947 that Bidault and others in the French cabinet realized that it was necessary to rebuild a stable Germany in order to receive American aid and Western support for French policy initiatives, as well as to create a Central European bulwark against communism and Soviet power. Their change of heart came not from an aversion to harsh peace terms, but from changes in the international environment that altered French strategic and economic interests. In addition, despite the conversion of French leaders to a more conciliatory program for Germany, they continued to drag their feet when it came to enacting that program due to their fear of public and legislative opposition. In order to explain why French leaders were unable to change policy as soon as their preferences changed, whereas American and British leaders were, we would have to refer to differences in the structures of their respective domestic decision-making environments and the autonomy that they consequently possessed.[3] Learning, therefore, does not explain the observed results as well as a structural autonomy model of democratic foreign security policy.

Geographical Proximity

Another plausible explanation would be that the content of Allied postwar peacemaking policies depended primarily upon their geographic proximity

---

Annual Review of Sociology 14 (1988): 324–34. For an excellent review essay on the effects of learning on foreign policy behavior, see Jack S. Levy, "Learning and Foreign Policy: Sweeping a Conceptual Minefield," *International Organization* 48, no. 2 (spring 1994): 279–312.

3. It is possible that French leaders learned from the experience of 1919 (particularly the immense outcry against Clemenceau during the ratification debates and his subsequent defeat in the presidential elections of January 1920) that they could only enact unpopular policies in a weak state at great political risk. In this case, however, the institutional learning would be epiphenomenal of the level of structural autonomy possessed by the French state and, therefore, hardly an alternative explanation. See Levy, "Learning and Foreign Policy," esp. 300–306.

to Germany. French reluctance to reintegrate Germany into international affairs after both world wars, for example, could easily be explained as a function of French geographical proximity to Germany. Certainly, Germany posed a greater menace to France than it did to Great Britain or to the United States, both of which were geographically removed from German power. Moreover, British policy after World War II, while more conciliatory overall than French policy, was more punitive than that of the United States, particularly regarding reparations and industrial limitations. Such a geopolitical explanation could, perhaps, rescue the neorealist model by explaining policy divergence not in terms of domestic politics, but as a product of differing systemic imperatives.

A geographical explanation is problematic, however, because of a Soviet threat after World War II that was a more formidable and more immediate concern than German militarism. After the war, the German war machine was shattered, the industrial juggernaut dismantled. Germany posed no short-term threat to France, but there was a very real threat that Soviet power could dominate the entire European continent. As French military and political leaders were well aware after 1947, the exposed French position on the continent made them far more dependent on a stable western Germany and, ultimately, a German military contribution than the Anglo-Saxons were. If Soviet troops swept through Germany, they would directly threaten France, while the British and the Americans would be secure across the water. Thus, in the late 1940s and early 1950s, geographical proximity should have compelled the French to foster German stability and recovery in order to create a stable strategic buffer between France and the Red Army. Indeed, since the Soviet Union represented an overwhelmingly superior power to defeated Germany, with vaunted offensive capabilities, both neorealist balance of power theory and balance of threat theory would have expected France to put aside its differences with Germany immediately in order to balance against the greater strategic threat.[4] Instead, successive French governments dragged their feet for seven years, obstructing the very measures that were most consistent with French security. In order to explain this dysfunctional international behavior, we must consider the French executive's lack of structural autonomy over national security policy. Therefore, proximity alone cannot explain my observed results.

---

4. Stephen M. Walt, *The Origins of Alliances* (Ithaca: Cornell University Press, 1987), 21–27; Kenneth N. Waltz, *Theory of International Politics* (New York: McGraw Hill, 1979).

Intensity of Public Opinion

A third possibility is that the ability of Allied governments to show leniency toward defeated Germany depended not on their domestic decision-making environments, but upon the intensity of public hostility toward the German people. It is reasonable to expect, for example, that due to the immense French suffering inflicted by Germany in three wars over seventy-five years, public hostility toward Germany after both world wars might have been of a greater order of magnitude in France than it was in the United States or Great Britain. It should hardly be surprising, therefore, that French leaders were forced to satisfy the French public's demand for vengeance. Conversely, since the United States entered both wars rather late and did not suffer casualties on the same scale as the Europeans, the American public might not have been as anti-German as their British and French counterparts. This might explain the more generous American policies. Therefore, my observed results could reflect the intensity of public emotions, rather than the relative structural autonomy of the three states.

The intensity of public opinion is a compelling alternative explanation and is, in fact, the most difficult to dismiss. Nonetheless, it ignores an important fact. The two world wars were bitter and protracted conflicts that imposed extraordinary deprivations and casualties on all sides. It would be wrong to assume that Americans and Britons who had been reluctantly galvanized to war because of the Germans and suffered immensely at German hands would bear appreciably less hostility toward their former enemy than the French. Indeed, as I show in Chapter 4, public opinion polls and other indicators in all three countries showed comparable levels of distrust of and hostility toward the Germans—who had committed monstrous atrocities against European Jews and other victims—in the aftermath of World War II and, in particular, comparable opposition to remilitarizing the Germans. In 1919, the outpouring of British hatred toward the German people was even more intense than that in France. Both the press and the legislature called upon the Government to "make the Hun pay" and even to expel enemy aliens, who presumably played no part in the war, from the British Isles. These are compelling reasons to conclude that differences in structural autonomy, rather than emotional intensity, explain my observed outcomes. Nonetheless, to ensure that my observed results are not an artifact of the case selection, additional case studies would be fruitful in order to control for the intensity of public emotion.

Theoretical Implications of This Study

Autonomy vs. Control

Since this book demonstrates that even democratic executives can vary in the structural autonomy they possess to conduct national security policy, it behooves us to consider when structurally autonomous national security executives are necessary and how much autonomy is warranted. Indeed, this is the more interesting and relevant aspect of the realist/liberal debate on democratic foreign policy presented in Chapter 1. Traditional realists and liberals do not disagree about whether or not democratic national security executives can be autonomous—they both agree, mistakenly, that democratic executives necessarily lack autonomy—but rather over whether domestic constraints are functional. Realists argue that they are dysfunctional because they prevent judicious and decisive action when the stakes are high. Liberals maintain that democratic constraints are useful because they prevent abuses of executive power and the pursuit of policies that conflict with the true national interest. In fact, these two positions are not contradictory or mutually exclusive. It is true that autonomy conveys certain distinct advantages to an executive that can assist it in responding to a hostile international environment. It is equally true that autonomy may enable a government to trample upon the democratic rights of its citizens. The challenge, therefore, is to square the circle by allowing enough autonomy to facilitate the pursuit of national security interests, while maintaining a level of public and legislative control over national leaders consistent with democratic values.[5]

This is the central dilemma of democratic control over foreign security policy. The solution, if one exists, is to delegate a level of autonomy to the national security executive commensurate with the degree of international threat that particular democratic states face. When the stakes of foreign security policy are high (because of a high-threat security environment or the need to make peace with neighboring rivals), traditional realists are correct that the dangers of allowing domestic interference in policymaking—at least in the realm of high politics—outweigh the benefits. Conversely, when democracies face a rather stable, low-threat security environment, the benefits of autonomy are negligible and are outweighed by the dangers of abuse identified by traditional liberals.

5. Robert A. Dahl similarly observes that a key challenge of democratic governance is to strike an appropriate balance between autonomy and democratic control. See *Dilemmas of Pluralist Democracy: Autonomy vs. Control* (New Haven: Yale University Press, 1982).

Unfortunately, because of the availability of independence-enhancing strategies of deception, we cannot guarantee that structural constraints will restrain democratic executives in a low-threat security environment. Leaders might be tempted to subvert democratic control, even in the absence of a compelling international reason for doing so, in order to advance their own personal interests. These dangers, however, are diminished by the costs of deception—the political repercussions of ignoring domestic opposition. While these costs are not automatic or even necessary consequences—Lloyd George, for example, was able to avoid them—the risk of incurring them should help counterbalance the temptation to resort to deception, except in extreme situations when leaders expect that obeying domestic demands will cause considerable harm to national interests abroad. Nonetheless, in times of low international threats, the public, the legislature, and the media must guard their power jealously to defeat governmental attempts to be deceptive.

Building Better Theories

This book concludes that foreign security policy analysts must look beyond simplistic characterizations of democratic states as homogenous and weak, or as fundamentally interchangeable with other regimes. They must consider the unique institutional, procedural, and normative contexts of each democracy in order to distinguish between democracies and generate more accurate predictions about the national security policy choices of particular democratic states. In this book, I have presented a framework for analyzing the domestic decision-making environments of democratic states to assist scholars in this task.

Careful attention to relative autonomy may help to explain anomalous behavior by democratic states and surprising instances of democratic divergence. For example, it might help to explain why British leaders quickly liquidated their colonial possessions after World War II, but their French colleagues were unwilling or unable to follow suit. Furthermore, it can help to refine existing theories, such as the democratic peace theory, by elucidating the conditions under which democracies are unlikely to go to war.[6] Miriam Fendius Elman, for example, has argued that presidential and

6. For similar points, see Susan Peterson, "How Democracies Differ: Public Opinion, State Structure, and the Lessons of the Fashoda Crisis," *Security Studies* 5, no. 1 (autumn 1995): 3–37; and T. Clifton Morgan and Sally Howard Campbell, "Domestic Structure, Decisional Constraints, and War: So Why Kant Democracies Fight?" *Journal of Conflict Resolution* 35, no. 1 (June 1991): 187–211.

majoritarian democracies, which she terms "strong democracies," are less likely to be subject to the logic of the democratic peace theory than "weak" parliamentary states.[7] The research in this book suggests that it would be fruitful to consider other distinguishing factors beyond the presidential/parliamentary divide, since various procedural and normative factors can yield both autonomous and constrained forms of each type of democracy, just like Wilson's presidential executive was highly constrained while Truman's was remarkably autonomous. Moreover, it suggests that the few foreign security policy theorists who do consider domestic structures, such as Elman, Susan Peterson, Thomas Risse-Kappen, and Helen Milner, must include procedural norms as an integral part of domestic structure.[8] After all, without studying the prevailing security norms in the post–World War II United States, we would mistakenly conclude that the constitutional division of foreign relations powers between the president and Congress tied the executive's hands in foreign affairs.

Another avenue of inquiry would be to conduct empirical examinations of the relative structural autonomy of a sample of both democratic and non-democratic states. My research indicates that regime type alone is a poor predictor of foreign security policy, since the United States from 1945 to 1954 behaved like a prototypical "nondemocracy" in the traditional sense. Nonetheless, it would be worthwhile investigating if, on average, there are any group differences on the autonomy scale between democratic and non-democratic states even if they are nongeneralizable across the category.

My research also has important implications for the field of comparative politics. The conventional wisdom in comparative politics and comparative political economy states that France was a highly centralized and autonomous state after World War II and that the United States in the same period was fragmented and constrained.[9] This study, however, indicates

7. Miriam Fendius Elman, "Unpacking Democracy: Presidentialism, Parliamentarism, and Theories of Democratic Peace," *Security Studies* 9, no. 4 (summer 2000): 91–126. See also Miriam Fendius Elman, "Testing the Democratic Peace Theory," in Elman, *Paths to Peace: Is Democracy the Answer* (Boston: CSIA, 1997), 479–506, in which she identifies civil-military relations and the policy preferences of national leaders as important noninstitutional differences between democracies that affect the applicability of the democratic peace theory.

8. Elman, "Unpacking Democracy"; Peterson, "How Democracies Differ"; Thomas Risse-Kappen, "Public Opinion, Domestic Structure, and Foreign Policy in Liberal Democracies," *World Politics* 43, no. 4 (July 1991): 479–512; Helen V. Milner, *Interests, Institutions, and Information* (Princeton: Princeton University Press, 1997).

9. Peter J. Katzenstein, "Conclusion," in Peter J. Katzenstein, ed., *Between Power and Plenty: Foreign Economic Policies in Advanced Industrial States* (Madison: University of Wisconsin Press, 1978), 306–23; John Zysman, "The French State in the International Economy,"

that, in the field of foreign affairs, the structural autonomy of the French executive during this period was actually quite low, while the American executive was extremely independent of public and legislative constraints. Therefore, autonomy must be examined on an issue-by-issue basis, taking into account not only institutional and procedural inputs, but also the procedural norms that inform executive and legislative behavior in specific policy areas.

Policy Relevance

The principal policy-relevant implication of this research is that democratic states can and should tailor their foreign security apparatuses to fit their international environments. Those that face high threat environments or that have other compelling reasons to engineer executive autonomy should take steps to insulate their national security executives, while those facing relatively stable international environments may wish to reign in their executives. It is thus important, for example, for the American democracy to reconsider the autonomy of its foreign security apparatus in the wake of the Cold War. Following World War II, the American executive expanded its authority over foreign affairs and constructed a powerful national security state in order to meet the rising Soviet challenge. This was functional behavior, since executive autonomy over foreign affairs is essential in a hostile international environment. Now that the Soviet Union is no longer a serious threat to United States security interests, it is no longer clear that executive autonomy is still functional.

On the one hand, some will argue that the steady growth in power of the People's Republic of China will require a degree of vigilance that only the continued insulation of foreign security policymakers can assure.[10] These will, no doubt, bolster their claims with reference to the recent political clashes between Beijing and the new Bush administration. In a similar vein,

---

in Katzenstein, *Between Power and Plenty*, 255–93; and Stephen D. Krasner, "United States Commercial and Monetary Policy: Unraveling the Paradox of External Strength and Internal Weakness," in Katzenstein, *Between Power and Plenty*, 51–87.

10. On the potential Chinese threat to international security, see Richard Bernstein and Ross Munro, "China I: The Coming Conflict With America," *Foreign Affairs* 76, no. 2 (March/April 1997): 18–32; Aaron Friedberg, "Ripe for Rivalry: Prospects for Peace in a Multipolar Asia," *International Security* 18, no. 3 (winter 1993/4): 5–33; and Denny Roy, "Hegemon on the Horizon? China's Threat to East Asian Security," *International Security* 19, no. 1 (summer 1994): 149–68.

others will cite the terrorist attacks of September 11, 2001 as proof that the U.S. national security environment remains threatening. Consequently, they will conclude that the elements of the national security state that survived the backlash against Vietnam and Watergate should remain intact. There are, however, considerable costs inherent in such a course of action. As these two painful events of Cold War American history attest, an autonomous state is capable of monumental abuses of power. Moreover, less autonomous democratic states enjoy a number of advantages over their more autonomous counterparts when the level of international threat is comparatively low. Since the the threats posed both by China and Islamic fundamentalism—in terms of conventional military capability, nuclear capability, and economic resources—is, at this point, markedly less severe than the Soviet threat during the Cold War and does not directly menace American security to the same extent,[11] a powerful case can be made to reign in the American national security apparatus. Provided that the United States continues to monitor Chinese power and behavior, it might be more prudent to follow a policy of constructive engagement with China in the hope of overcoming any potential Chinese threat, while making the U.S. foreign security establishment more democratically accountable.[12] Similarly, the American war on terrorism may be able to proceed without keeping the national security state on a Cold War footing.

This book also has policy-relevant implications for the termination of ethnic and international conflicts in the democratizing regions of the globe. Edward D. Mansfield and Jack Snyder demonstrated that democratizing states are highly war-prone.[13] This problem should be particularly salient

---

11. On China, see Robert S. Ross, "China II: Beijing as a Conservative Power," *Foreign Affairs* 76, no. 2 (March/April 1997): 33–44. The terrorist threat is far less formidable. While it may be more likely for terrorists to strike against the United States in the future than for the United States and China to wage war against each other, the technology that terrorist groups have used presents only a limited threat to American national security. This could change, however, if terrorist groups were to acquire nuclear weapons or large supplies of chemical or biological weapons.

12. Kenneth Lieberthal, "A New China Strategy," *Foreign Affairs* 74, no. 6 (November/December 1995): 35–49; David Shambaugh, "Containment or Engagement of China? Calculating Beijing's Responses," *International Security* 21, no. 2 (fall 1996): 180–209; Paul A. Papayoanou and Scott L. Kastner, "Sleeping with the (Potential) Enemy: Assessing the U.S. Policy of Engagement with China," in Jean-Marc F. Blanchard, Edward D. Mansfield, and Norrin M. Ripsman, eds., *Power and the Purse: Economic Statecraft, Interdependence, and National Security* (London: Frank Cass, 2000), 157–87.

13. Edward D. Mansfield and Jack Snyder, "Democratization and the Danger of War," *International Security* 20, no. 1 (summer 1995): 5–38.

in contemporary Eastern Europe and the former Soviet Union—a region plagued by ethnic rivalries and nationalist conflict, in which many unstable states are experimenting with democracy. My research implies, however, that to the extent that many ethnic conflicts are driven by societal animosities, the construction of domestic political institutions that generate executive autonomy over foreign policy could facilitate conflict resolution and help to mitigate instability as many of the newly independent states in this region make the transition to democracy. At the same time, care must be taken to avoid granting similar structural autonomy to these executives in other less-essential issue areas in order to prevent these fledgling governments from trampling the rights of their electorates.

Institution-building is likely to be of only limited value, however, unless we are also able to foster procedural norms that will inspire patterns of decision making that allow for a broad range of executive power over foreign affairs within these institutions. That will not be an easy task. It will require an intensive and prolonged education program within these countries and will, consequently, require the active participation and assistance of the United States and the European Union. The effort and expense will undoubtedly be worthwhile if it helps to break the cycle of conflict in this important region.

Bibliography

Theory

Almond, Gabriel A. "The Return to the State." *American Political Science Review* 82, no. 3 (September 1988): 853–74.

Aron, Raymond. *The Century of Total War*. Garden City, N.Y.: Doubleday, 1954.

Auriol, Vincent. *Journal du Septennat*. 7 vols. Paris: Librarie Armand Colin, 1970.

Barbieri, Katherine. "Economic Interdependence: A Path Toward Peace or a Source of Interstate Conflict." *Journal of Peace Research* 33, no. 1 (1996): 29–49.

Barnett, Michael N. *Confronting the Costs of War*. Princeton: Princeton University Press, 1992.

Barnett, Michael N., and Jack S. Levy. "Domestic Sources of Alliances and Allignments: The Case of Egypt, 1962–1973." *International Organization* 45, no. 3 (summer 1991): 369–95.

Bernstein, Richard, and Ross Munro. "China I: The Coming Conflict With America." *Foreign Affairs* 76, no. 2 (March/April 1997): 18–32.

Blanchard, Jean-Marc F., Edward D. Mansfield, and Norrin M. Ripsman. "The Political Economy of National Security: Economic Statecraft, Interdependence and International Conflict." In *Power and the Purse: Economic Statecraft, Interdependence, and International Conflict*, edited by Jean-Marc F. Blanchard, Edward D. Mansfield, and Norrin M. Ripsman, 1–14. London: Frank Cass, 2000.

Block, Fred. "The Ruling Class Does Not Rule." In *The Political Economy*, edited by Thomas Ferguson and Joel Rogers, 32–46. Armonk, N.Y.: M. E. Sharpe, 1984.

Boyce, Brigitte. "The Democratic Deficit of the European Community." *Parliamentary Affairs* 46, no. 4 (October 1993): 458–77.

Bremer, Stuart A. "Democracy and Militarized Interstate Conflict, 1816–1965." *International Interactions* 18, no. 3 (1993): 231–50.

Brodie, Bernard. *Strategy in the Missile Age*. Princeton: Princeton University Press, 1959.

Burk, James. "Support for Peacekeeping in Lebanon and Somalia." *Political Science Quarterly* 114, no. 1 (spring 1999): 53–78.

Buzan, Barry. "Peoples, States, and Fear: The National Security Problem in the

Third World." In *National Security in the Third World*, edited by E. Azar and C. Moon, 14–43. Hants, U.K.: Edward Elger, 1988.

Callaghy, Thomas M. "Political Passions and Economic Interests: Economic Reform and Political Structure in Africa." In *Hemmed In: Responses to Africa's Economic Decline*, edited by Thomas M. Callaghy and John Ravenhill, 463–519. New York: Columbia University Press, 1993.

Caporaso, James A. *The European Union: Dilemmas of Regional Integration*. Boulder, Colo.: Westview Press, 2000.

Cohen, Bernard C. *The Public's Impact on Foreign Policy*. Boston: Little, Brown, 1973.

——— "The Influence of Special-Interest Groups and the Mass Media on Security Policy in the United States." In *Perspectives on American Foreign Policy*, edited by Charles W. Kegley Jr. and Eugene R. Wittkopf, 222–41. New York: St. Martin's Press, 1983.

Cohen, Raymond. "Pacific unions: a reappraisal of the theory that 'democracies do not go to war with each other'." *Review of International Studies* 20, no. 2 (April 1994): 207–23.

Collier, Ellen C., ed. *Bipartisanship and the Making of Foreign Policy*. Boulder, Colo.: Westview Press, 1991.

Cowhey, Peter F. "Domestic Institutions and International Commitments: Japan and the United States." *International Organization* 47, no. 2 (spring 1993): 299–326.

Crozier, Michael, Samuel P. Huntington, and Joji Watanuki. *The Crisis of Democracy*. New York: New York University Press, 1975.

Dahl, Robert A. *Dilemmas of Pluralist Democracy: Autonomy vs. Control*. New Haven: Yale University Press, 1982.

———. *Polyarchy: Participation and Opposition*. New Haven: Yale University Press, 1971.

Destler, I. M., Leslie H. Gelb, and Anthony Lake. *Our Own Worst Enemy: The Unmaking of American Foreign Policy*. New York: Simon & Schuster, 1984.

Deudney, Daniel. "The Philadelphian System: Sovereignty, Arms Control, and Balance of Power in the American States-Union, Circa 1787–1861." *International Organization* 49, no. 2 (spring 1995): 191–228.

Dixon, William J. "Democracy and the Peaceful Settlement of International Conflict." *American Political Science Review* 88, no. 1 (March 1994): 14–32.

Downs, Anthony. *An Economic Theory of Democracy*. New York: Harper & Row, 1957.

Doyle, Michael. "Kant, Liberal Legacies, and Foreign Affairs, part 1." *Philosophy and Public Affairs* 12, no. 3 (summer 1983): 205–35.

———. "Kant, Liberal Legacies, and Foreign Affairs, part 2." *Philosophy and Public Affairs* 12, no. 4 (autumn 1983): 323–53.

———. "Liberalism and World Politics." *The American Political Science Review* 80, no. 4 (1986): 1151–61.

Eichenberg, Richard. *Public Opinion and National Security in Western Europe*. Ithaca: Cornell University Press, 1989.

Eichengreen, Barry, and Marc Uzan. "The 1933 World Economic Conference as an

Instance of Failed Cooperation." In *Double-Edged Diplomacy: International Bargaining and Domestic Politics*, edited by Peter B. Evans, Harold K. Jacobson, and Robert D. Putnam, 171–206. Berkeley and Los Angeles: University of California Press, 1993.

Eisenhower, Dwight D. *Mandate for Change, 1953–1956.* Garden City, N.J.: Doubleday, 1963.

Elman, Colin. "Horses for Courses: Why *Not* a Neorealist Theory of Foreign Policy." *Security Studies* 6, no. 1 (autumn 1996): 7–53.

Elman, Miriam Fendius. "Unpacking Democracy: Presidentialism, Parliamentarism, and Theories of Democratic Peace." *Security Studies* 9, no. 4 (summer 2000): 91–126.

———. "Testing the Democratic Peace Theory." In *Paths to Peace: Is Democracy the Answer?*, edited by Miriam Fendius Elman, 473–506. Boston: CSIA, 1997.

Etheridge, Lloyd S. *Can Governments Learn?* New York: Pergamon, 1985.

Evangelista, Matthew. "The Paradox of State Strength: Transnational Relations, Domestic Structures, and Security Policy in Russia and The Soviet Union." *International Organization* 49, no. 1 (winter 1995): 1–38.

Evans, Peter B. "Building an Integrative Approach to International and Domestic Politics." In *Double-Edged Diplomacy: International Bargaining and Domestic Politics*, edited by Peter B. Evans, Harold K. Jacobson, and Robert D. Putnam, 397–430. Berkeley and Los Angeles: University of California Press, 1993.

Evans, Peter B., Dietrich Rueschemeyer, and Theda Skocpol. "On the Road to a More Adequate Understanding of the State." In *Bringing the State Back In*, edited by Peter B. Evans, Dietrich Rueschemeyer, and Theda Skocpol, 347–66. Cambridge: Cambridge University Press, 1985.

———. *Bringing the State Back In.* Cambridge: Cambridge University Press, 1985.

Fearon, James D. "Domestic Political Audiences and the Escalation of International Disputes." *American Political Science Review* 88, no. 3 (September 1994): 577–92.

Ferguson, Thomas. "From Normalcy to New Deal: Industrial Structure, Party Competition and American Public Policy in the Great Depression." *International Organization* 38, no. 1 (winter 1984): 41–94.

Fordham, Benjamin O. *Building the Cold War Consensus: The Political Economy of U.S. National Security Policy.* Ann Arbor: University of Michigan Press, 1998.

Friedberg, Aaron. "Why Didn't the United States Become a Garrison State?" *International Security* 16, no. 4 (spring 1992): 109–42.

———. "Ripe for Rivalry: Prospects for Peace in a Multipolar Asia." *International Security* 18, no. 3 (winter 1993/94): 5–33.

Frieden, Jeffry. "Sectoral Conflict and U.S. Foreign Economic Policy, 1914–1940." *International Organization* 42, no. 1 (winter 1988): 59–90.

Gaddis, John Lewis. "History, Science and the Study of International Relations." In *Explaining International Relations Since 1945*, edited by Ngaire Woods, 32–48. New York: Oxford University Press, 1996.

————. "History, Theory, and Common Ground," *International Security* 22, no. 1 (summer 1997): 75–85.

Gaubatz, Kurt Taylor. "Democratic States and Commitment in International Relations." *International Organization* 50, no. 1 (winter 1996): 109–39.

George, Alexander L. "Case Studies and Theory Development." In *Diplomacy*, edited by Paul Gordon Lauren, 43–68. New York: The Free Press, 1979.

————. "Domestic Constraints on Regime Change in U.S. Foreign Policy: The Need for Policy Legitimation." In *Change in the International System*, edited by Ole Holsti, Randolph M. Siverson, and Alexander L. George, 233–62. Boulder, Colo.: Westview Press, 1980.

————. "Knowledge for Statecraft: The Challenge for Political Science and History." *International Security* 22, no. 1 (summer 1997): 44–52.

————. and Timothy J. McKeown, "Case Studies and Theories of Organizational Decision Making." *Advances in Information Processes in Organizations* 2 (1985): 21–58.

Geva, Nehemia, Karl DeRouen, and Alex Mintz. "The Political Incentive Explanation of the 'Democratic Peace' Phenomenon: Evidence from Experimental Research." *International Interactions* 18, no. 3 (1993): 215–29.

Goldstein, Judith. *Ideas, Interests, and American Trade Policy*. Ithaca: Cornell University Press, 1993.

Goldstein, Judith, and Robert O. Keohane. "Ideas and Foreign Policy: An Analytical Framework." In *Ideas and Foreign Policy: Beliefs, Institutions, and Political Change*, edited by Judith Goldstein and Robert O. Keohane, 3–30. Ithaca: Cornell University Press, 1993.

Goodman, John B. *Monetary Sovereignty: The Politics of Central Banking in Western Europe*. Ithaca: Cornell University Press, 1992.

Gourevitch, Peter Alexis. "Breaking with Orthodoxy: The Politics of Economic Policy Responses to the Depression of the 1930s." *International Organization* 38, no. 1 (1984): 95–129.

Gowa, Joanne. "Democratic States and International Disputes." *International Organization* 49, no. 3 (1995): 511–22.

Hagan, Joe D. "Domestic Political Systems and War Proneness." *Mershon International Studies Review* 38 (October 1994): 186.

Hall, Peter A. *Governing the Economy*. New York: Oxford University Press, 1986.

————., and Rosemary C. R. Taylor. "Political Science and the Three New Institutionalisms." *Political Studies* 44, no. 5 (December 1996): 936–57.

Hamilton, Alexander, James Madison, and John Jay. *The Federalist Papers*. Edited by Clinton Rossiter. New York: Mentor Books, 1961.

Heclo, Hugh. *Modern Social Politics in Britain and Sweden*. New Haven: Yale University Press, 1974.

Hermann, Margaret G., and Charles W. Kegley Jr. "Rethinking Democracy and International Peace: Perspectives from Political Psychology." *International Studies Quarterly* 39, no. 4 (December 1995): 511–34.

————., Charles F. Hermann, and Joe D. Hagan. "How Decision Units Shape Foreign Policy Behavior." In *New Directions in the Study of Foreign Policy*, edited by Charles F. Hermann, Charles W. Kegley Jr., and James N. Rosenau, 309–36. Boston: Allen & Unwin, 1987.

Hermann, Tamar. "Grassroots Activism as a Factor in Foreign Policy-Making." In *The Limits of State Autonomy*, edited by David Skidmore and Valerie M. Hudson, 127–47. Boulder, Colo.: Westview Press, 1993.

Hinckley, Ronald H. *People, Polls, and Policymakers: American Public Opinion and National Security*. New York: Lexington Books, 1992.

Holsti, Ole R. *Public Opinion and American Foreign Policy*. Ann Arbor: University of Michigan Press, 1996.

Ikenberry, G. John. "The Irony of State Strength: Comparative Responses to the Oil Shocks in the 1970s." *International Organization* 40, no. 1 (winter 1986): 105–38.

———. *Reasons of State: Oil Politics and the Capacities of American Government*. Ithaca: Cornell University Press, 1988.

Jentleson, Bruce W. "The Pretty Prudent Public: Post Post-Vietnam American Opinion on the Use of Military Force." *International Studies Quarterly* 36, no. 1 (March 1992): 49–74.

Jervis, Robert. *Perception and Misperception in World Politics*. Princeton: Princeton University Press, 1976.

Kant, Immanuel. *Perpetual Peace: A Philosophical Essay*. Translated by M. Campbell Smith. New York: Garland Press, 1972.

Katzenstein, Peter J. "Conclusion: Domestic Structures and Strategies of Foreign Economic Policy." In *Between Power and Plenty: Foreign Economic Policies in Advanced Industrial States*, edited by Peter J. Katzenstein, 295–336. Madison: University of Wisconsin Press, 1978.

———. *Between Power and Plenty: Foreign Economic Policies in Advanced Industrial States*. Madison: University of Wisconsin Press, 1978.

Kegley, Charles W., Jr., and Eugene R. Wittkopf. *American Foreign Policy: Pattern and Process*. New York: St. Martin's Press, 1991.

Kennan, George F. *The Cloud of Danger*. Boston: Little, Brown & Co., 1977.

———. "Foreign Policy and the Professional Diplomat." In *Foreign Policy and the Democratic Process: The Geneva Papers*, edited by Louis J. Halle and Kenneth W. Thompson, 14–26. Lanham: University Press of America, 1978.

———. *American Diplomacy, 1900–1950*. Chicago: University of Chicago Press, 1951.

Keohane, Robert O. "International Liberalism Reconsidered." In *The Economic Limits to Modern Politics*, edited by John Dunn, 165–94. Cambridge: Cambridge University Press, 1990.

Key, V. O. *Public Opinion and American Democracy*. New York: Alfred A. Knopf, 1961.

Kiraly, Béla K. "Total War and Peacemaking." In *Essays on World War I*, edited by Béla K. Kiraly, Peter Pasto, and Ivan Sanders, 15–21. New York: Brooklyn College Press, 1982.

Kircheimer, Otto. "The Transformation of Western European Party Systems." In *Political Parties and Political Development*, edited by Joseph LaPalombara and Myron Weiner, 177–200. Princeton: Princeton University Press, 1966.

Kissinger, Henry A. *A World Restored*. Boston: Houghton-Mifflin, 1973.

Knopf, Jeffrey W. "How Rational is 'The Rational Public'?" *Journal of Conflict Resolution* 42, no. 5 (October 1998): 544–71.

Kowert, Paul, and Jeffrey Legro. "Norms, Identity, and Their Limits: A Theoretical Reprise." In *The Culture of National Security: Norms and Identity in World Politics*, edited by Peter J. Katzenstein, 451–97. New York: Columbia University Press, 1996.

Krasner, Stephen D. *Defending the National Interest*. Princeton: Princeton University Press, 1978.

———. "Structural Causes and Regime Consequences: Regimes as Intervening Variables." In *International Regimes*, edited by Stephen D. Krasner, 1–21 Ithaca: Cornell University Press, 1983.

———. "United States Commercial and Monetary Policy: Unravelling the Paradox of External Strength and Internal Weakness." In *Between Power and Plenty: Foreign Economic Policies in Advanced Industrial States*, edited by Peter J. Katzenstein, 51–87. Madison: University of Wisconsin Press, 1978.

Kratochwil, Friedrich V. *Rules, Norms and Decisions*. Cambridge: Cambridge University Press, 1989.

Lake, David A. "Powerful Pacifists: Democratic States and War." *American Political Science Review* 86, no. 1 (March 1992): 24–37.

Layne, Christopher. "Kant or Cant: The Myth of the Democratic Peace." *International Security* 19, no. 2 (fall 1994): 5–49.

Lehman, Howard P., and Jennifer L. McCoy. "The Dynamics of the Two-Level Bargaining Game: The 1988 Brazilian Debt Negotiations." *World Politics* 44, no. 4 (July 1992): 600–644.

Levering, Ralph B. *The Public and American Foreign Policy, 1918–1978*. New York: Morrow Press, 1978.

Levitt, Barbara, and James G. March. "Organizational Learning." *Annual Review of Sociology* 14 (1988): 324–34.

Levy, Jack S. "Domestic Politics and War." *Journal of Interdisciplinary History* 18, no. 4 (spring 1988): 653–73.

———. "Learning and Foreign Policy: Sweeping a Conceptual Minefield." *International Organization* 48, no. 2 (spring 1994): 279–312.

Liddell Hart, Sir Basil H. *Strategy*. New York: Praeger, 1954.

Lieberthal, Kenneth. "A New China Strategy." *Foreign Affairs* 74, no. 6 (November/December 1995): 35–49.

Lijphart, Arend. "Comparative Politics and the Comparative Method." *American Political Science Review* 65, no. 2 (September 1971): 682–93.

———. *Democracies: Patterns of Majoritarian and Consensus Government in Twenty-One Countries*. New Haven: Yale University Press, 1984.

Linz, Juan J. "Presidential or Parliamentary Democracy: Does It Make a Difference?" In *The Failure of Presidential Democracy: Comparative Perspectives*, vol. 1, edited by Juan J. Linz and Arturo Valenzuela, 3–87. Baltimore: Johns Hopkins University Press, 1994.

Lippmann, Walter. *Essays in the Public Philosophy*. Boston: Little, Brown & Co., 1955.

Lowi, Theodore J. "American Business, Public Policy, Case Studies, and Political Theory." *World Politics* 16, no. 4 (July 1964): 676–716.

———. "Four Systems of Policy, Politics, and Choice." *Public Administration Review* 32, no. 4 (July/August 1972): 298–310.

Mann, Michael. "The Autonomous Power of States: Its Origins, Mechanisms, and Results." In *States in History*, edited by John A. Hall, 109–36. London: Basil Blackwell, 1986.

Mansfield, Edward D., and Jack Snyder. "Democratization and the Danger of War." *International Security* 20, no. 1 (summer 1995): 5–38.

Maoz, Zeev, and Nasrin Abdolai. "Regime Types and International Conflict, 1816–1976." *Journal of Conflict Resolution* 33, no. 1 (1989): 3–35.

March, James G., and Johan P. Olsen. "The Uncertainty of the Past: Organizational Learning Under Ambiguity." In *Decisions and Organizations*, edited by James G. March, 335–58. New York: Basil Blackwell, 1988.

Marwick, Arthur, ed. *Total War and Social Change*. New York: St. Martin's Press, 1988.

Matthews, Donald R. *U. S. Senators and Their World*. New York: Vintage Books, 1960.

Migdal, Joel S. *Strong States and Weak Societies: State-Society Relations and State Capabilities in the Third World*. Princeton: Princeton University Press, 1988.

Milbrath, Lester W. "Interest Groups and Foreign Policy." In *Domestic Sources of Foreign Policy*, edited by James N. Rosenau, 231–51. New York: The Free Press, 1967.

Miller, Benjamin. *When Opponents Cooperate*. Ann Arbor: University of Michigan Press, 1995.

Milner, Helen V. *Interests, Institutions, and Information*. Princeton: Princeton University Press, 1997.

Mintz, Alex, and Nehemia Geva. "Why Don't Democracies Fight Each Other? An Experimental Assessment of the 'Political Assessment' Explanation." *Journal of Conflict Resolution* 37, no. 3 (1993): 484–503.

Montesquieu, Baron de. *Spirit of the Laws*. Translated and edited by Anne M. Cohler, Basia Carolyn Miller, and Harold Samuel Stone. Cambridge: Cambridge University Press, 1989.

———. *The Political Theory of Montesquieu*. Edited by Melvin Richter. Cambridge: Cambridge University Press, 1977.

Moravcsik, Andrew. "Introduction: Integrating International and Domestic Theories of International Bargaining." In *Double-Edged Diplomacy: International Bargaining and Domestic Politics*, edited by Peter B. Evans, Harold K. Jacobson, and Robert D. Putnam, 3–42. Berkeley and Los Angeles: University of California Press, 1993.

———. "Why the European Community Strengthens the State: International Cooperation and Domestic Politics." Center for European Studies Working Paper Series No. 52. Cambridge: Harvard University Press, 1994.

Morgan, T. Clifton, and Sally Howard Campbell. "Domestic Structure, Decisional Constraints, and War: So Why Kant Democracies Fight?" *Journal of Conflict Resolution* 35, no. 1 (June 1991): 187–211.

Morgenthau, Hans J. *Dilemmas of Politics*. Chicago: University of Chicago Press, 1958.

———, and Kenneth W. Thompson. *Politics Among Nations,* 6th ed. New York: McGraw-Hill, 1985.

Niebuhr, Reinhold. *The Structure of Nations and Empires*. New York: Scribner, 1959.
———, and Paul E. Sigmund. *The Democratic Experience: Past and Prospects*. New York: Frederick A. Praeger, 1969.
Nincic, Miroslav. *Democracy and Foreign Policy*. New York: Columbia University Press, 1992.
Nordlinger, Eric A. *On the Autonomy of the Democratic State*. Cambridge: Harvard University Press, 1981.
Oneal, John R., and Bruce M. Russett. "The Classical Liberals Were Right: Democracy, Interdependence, and Conflict, 1950–1985." *International Studies Quarterly* 41, no. 2 (June 1997): 267–94.
———. "The Kantian Peace: The Pacific Benefits of Democracy, Interdependence, and International Organizations, 1885–1992." *World Politics* 52, no. 1 (October 1999): 1–37.
Owen, John M. "How Liberalism Produces Democratic Peace." *International Security* 19, no. 2 (fall 1994): 87–125.
Page, Benjamin I., and Robert Y. Shapiro. "Effects of Public Opinion on Policy." *American Political Science Review* 77, no. 1 (1983): 175–90.
Papayoanou, Paul A., and Scott L. Kastner. "Sleeping with the (Potential) Enemy: Assessing the U.S. Policy of Engagement with China." In *Power and the Purse: Economic Statecraft, Interdependence, and National Security*, edited by Jean-Marc F. Blanchard, Edward D. Mansfield, and Norrin M. Ripsman, 157–87. London: Frank Cass, 2000.
Peterson, Susan. *Crisis Bargaining and the State*. Ann Arbor: University of Michigan Press, 1996.
———. "How Democracies Differ: Public Opinion, State Structure, and the Lessons of the Fashoda Crisis." *Security Studies* 5, no. 1 (autumn 1995): 3–37.
Powell, G. Bingham. *Contemporary Democracies*. Cambridge: Harvard University Press, 1982.
Putnam, Robert D. "Diplomacy and Domestic Politics: The Logic of Two-Level Games." *International Organization* 42, no. 3 (summer 1988): 427–60.
Radway, Laurence I. *The Liberal Democracy in World Affairs: Foreign Policy and National Defense*. Glenview, Ill.: Scott, Foresman & Co., 1969.
Revel, Jean-François. *How Democracies Perish*. Translated by William Bighorn. Garden City, N.J.: Doubleday, 1984.
Ripsman, Norrin M. "The Conduct of Foreign Policy by Democracies: A Critical Review." Paper presented at the 1994 Annual Meeting of the American Political Science Association, New York, September 1–4, 1994.
———. "The Politics of Deception: Weak Democratic Governments, Domestic Opposition, and Foreign Security Policy." Unpublished ms: Concordia University, 2002.
———, and Jean-Marc F. Blanchard. "Commercial Liberalism Under Fire: Evidence from 1914 and 1936." *Security Studies* 6, no. 2 (winter 1996/97): 4–50.
———. "Contextual Information and the Study of Trade and Conflict: The Utility of an Interdisciplinary Approach." In *Beyond Boundaries? Disciplines, Paradigms, and Theoretical Integration in International Studies*, edited by Rudra Sil and Eileen M. Doherty, 57–85. Albany: SUNY Press, 2000.

Risse-Kappen, Thomas. *Cooperation Among Democracies*. Princeton: Princeton University Press, 1995.
———. "Public Opinion, Domestic Structure, and Foreign Policy in Liberal Democracies." *World Politics* 43, no. 4 (July 1991): 479–512.
Rogowski, Ronald. "Trade and the Variety of Democratic Institutions." *International Organization* 41, no. 2 (spring 1987): 203–23.
Root, Elihu. "A Requisite for the Success of Popular Diplomacy." *Foreign Affairs* 1 (September 1922): 3–10.
Ross, Robert S. "China II: Beijing as a Conservative Power." *Foreign Affairs* 76, no. 2 (March/April 1997): 33–44.
Roy, Denny. "Hegemon on the Horizon? China's Threat to East Asian Security." *International Security* 19, no. 1 (summer 1994): 149–68.
Russett, Bruce. *Controlling the Sword: the Democratic Governance of National Security*. Cambridge: Harvard University Press, 1990.
———. *Grasping the Democratic Peace*. Princeton: Princeton University Press, 1993.
———. "International Behavior Research: Case Studies and Cumulation." In *Approaches to the Study of Political Science*, edited by Michael Haas and Henry S. Kariel, 425–43. San Francisco: Chandler, 1970.
Shambaugh, David. "Containment or Engagement of China? Calculating Beijing's Responses." *International Security* 21, no. 2 (fall 1996): 180–209.
Shugart, Matthew Soberg, and John M. Carey. *Presidents and Assembles*. Cambridge: Cambridge University Press, 1992.
Sinclair, Barbara. *The Transformation of the U.S. Senate*. Baltimore: Johns Hopkins University Press, 1989.
Skocpol, Theda. "Bringing the State Back In: Strategies of Analysis in Current Research." In *Bringing the State Back In*, edited by Peter B. Evans, Dietrich Rueschemeyer, and Theda Skocpol, 3–37. Cambridge: Cambridge University Press, 1985.
———. "Political Response to Capitalist Crisis: Neo-Marxist Theories of the State and the Case of the New Deal." *Politics and Society* 10, no. 2 (1980): 155–201.
———. *States and Social Revolutions: A Comparative Analysis of France, Russia, and China*. Cambridge: Cambridge University Press, 1979.
Skowronek, Stephen. *Building a New American State: the Expansion of National Administrative Capacities, 1877–1920*. Cambridge: Cambridge University Press, 1982.
Snyder, Jack. *Myths of Empire*. Ithaca: Cornell University Press, 1991.
———. *Ideology of the Offensive*. Ithaca: Cornell University Press, 1984.
Steinmo, Sven. "Political Institutions and Tax Policy in the United States, Sweden, and Britain." *World Politics* 41, no. 4 (July 1989): 500–535.
Stepan, Alfred C. "State Power and the Strength of Civil Society in the Southern Cone of Latin America." In *Bringing the State Back In*, edited by Peter B. Evans, Dietrich Rueschemeyer, and Theda Skocpol, 317–43. Cambridge: Cambridge University Press, 1985.
Stepan, Alfred C., and Cindy Skach. "Constitutional Frameworks and Democratic Consolidation: Parliamentarism versus Presidentialism." *World Politics* 46, no. 1 (October 1993): 1–22.

Swenson, Peter. "Arranged Alliance: Business Interests in the New Deal." *Politics and Society* 25, no. 1 (March 1997): 66–116.

Telhami, Shibley. *Power and Leadership in International Bargaining*. New York: Columbia University Press, 1990.

de Tocqueville, Alexis. *Democracy in America*. 2 vols. New York: Vintage Books, 1954.

Trubowitz, Peter. *Defining National Interests: Conflict and Change in American Foreign Policy*. Chicago: University of Chicago Press, 1998.

Ullmann-Margolit, Edna. *The Emergence of Norms*. Oxford: Clarendon Press, 1977.

Van Evera, Stephen. *A Guide to Methodology for Students of Political Science*. Ithaca: Cornell University Press, 1997.

———. "The Cult of the Offensive and the Origins of the First World War." *International Security* 9, no. 1 (summer 1984): 58–108.

Walt, Stephen M. *The Origins of Alliances*. Ithaca: Cornell University Press, 1987.

Waltz, Kenneth N. *Foreign Policy and Democratic Politics, the American and British Experience*. Boston: Little, Brown & Co. 1967.

———. *Theory of International Politics*. New York: McGraw-Hill, 1979.

Weiler, J. H. H., Ulrich R. Haltern, and Franz C. Mayer. "European Democracy and its Critique." *West European Politics* 18 (July 1995): 4–39.

Weir, Margaret, and Theda Skocpol. "State Structures and the Possibilities for 'Keynesian' Responses to the Great Depression in Sweden, Britain and the United States." In *Bringing the State Back In*, edited by Peter B. Evans, Dietrich Rueschemeyer, and Theda Skocpol, 107–68. Cambridge: Cambridge University Press, 1985.

Williams, Robin M. Jr. "The Concept of Norms." In *International Encyclopedia of the Social Sciences*, vol. 11, edited by David L. Sills, 204–8. New York: Macmillan & Co. Ltd., 1968.

Yee, Albert S. "The Causal Effects of Ideas on Politics." *International Organization* 50, no. 1 (winter 1996): 69–108.

Zakaria, Fareed. "Realism and Domestic Politics: a Review Essay." *International Security* 17, no. 1 (summer 1992): 177–98.

Zysman, John. "The French State in the International Economy." In *Between Power and Plenty: Foreign Economic Policies in Advanced Industrial States*, edited by Peter J. Katzenstein, 255–93. Madison: University of Wisconsin Press, 1978.

The Domestic Decision-Making Environments in Great Britain, France, and the United States

Acheson, Dean. *Present at the Creation*. New York: Norton, 1969.

Brodie, Bernard. *Strategy in the Missile Age*. Princeton: Princeton University Press, 1959.

Buell, Raymond L. *Contemporary French Politics*. New York: Appleton, 1920.

Bullock, Allan. *Ernest Bevin: Foreign Secretary, 1945–1951*. London: Heinemann, 1983.

Butler, David E. *The British General Election of 1951.* London: Macmillan & Co. Ltd., 1952.

———, and Jennie Freeman. *British Political Facts.* London: MacMillan & Co. Ltd., 1969.

Capelle, Russell B. *The MRP and French Foreign Policy.* New York: Praeger, 1963.

Carstairs, Charles, and Richard Ware, eds. *Parliament and International Relations.* Buckingham, England: Open University Press, 1991.

Clarke, Michael. "The Policy-Making Process." In *British Foreign Policy: Tradition, Change and Transformation,* edited by Michael Smith, Steve Smith, and Brian White, 71–95. London: Unwin Hyman, 1988.

Corwin, Edward S. *The President: Office and Powers, 1787–1957.* New York: University Press, 1957.

Craig, Gordon A. "The British Foreign Office from Grey to Austen Chamberlain." In *The Diplomats, 1919–1939,* edited by Gordon A. Craig and Felix Gilbert, 15–48. Princeton: Princeton University Press, 1965.

Dearlove, John, and Peter Saunders. *Introduction to British Politics: Analysing a Capitalist Democracy.* 2nd ed. Cambridge: Polity Press, 1991.

Eden, Sir Anthony. *Full Circle: the Memoirs of Sir Anthony Eden.* London: Cassell, 1960.

Finegold, Kenneth, and Theda Skocpol. *State and Party in America's New Deal.* Madison: University of Wisconsin Press, 1995.

Foster, H. Schuyler. *Activism Replaces Isolationism.* Washington: Foxhall Press, 1983.

Furniss, Edgar S., Jr. *Weaknesses in French Foreign Policy-Making.* Princeton: Center for International Studies, Princeton University Press, 1954.

———. *France, Troubled Ally.* New York: Harper & Row, 1960.

Grosser, Alfred. *Affaires Extérieures: La Politique de la France, 1944–1984.* Paris: Flammarion, 1984.

Guinsburg, Thomas N. *The Pursuit of Isolationism in the United States Senate from Versailles to Pearl Harbor.* New York: Garland, 1982.

Hayne, Mark B. "The Quai d'Orsay and the Formation of French Foreign Policy in Historical Context." In *France in World Politics,* edited by Robert Aldrich and John Connell, 194–218. London: Routledge, 1989.

Henkin, Louis. *Foreign Affairs and the Constitution.* New York: Norton, 1975.

Howard, John Eldred. *Parliament and Foreign Policy in France.* London: Cresset, 1948.

Ikenberry, G. John. *Reasons of State: Oil Politics and the Capacities of American Government.* Ithaca: Cornell University Press, 1988.

Jeffreys-Jones, Rhodri. *The CIA and American Democracy.* New Haven: Yale University Press, 1989.

Jones, Bill, and Dennis Kavanagh. *British Politics Today.* 6th ed. Manchester: Manchester University Press, 1998.

Katzenstein, Peter J. "Conclusion: Domestic Structures and Strategies of Foreign Economic Policy." In *Between Power and Plenty: Foreign Economic Policies in Advanced Industrial States,* edited by Peter J. Katzenstein, 295–336. Madison: University of Wisconsin Press, 1978.

Krasner, Stephen D. "United States Commercial and Monetary Policy: Unraveling the Paradox of External Strength and Internal Weakness." In *Between Power and Plenty: Foreign Economic Policies in Advanced Industrial States*, edited by Peter J. Katzenstein, 51–87. Madison: University of Wisconsin Press, 1978.

Lauren, Paul Gordon. *Bureaucrats and Diplomats*. Stanford: Hoover Institution Press, 1976.

Leuchtenburg, William E. *Franklin D. Roosevelt and the New Deal, 1932–1940*. New York: Harper Colophon, 1963.

Leyret, Henry. *Le Président de la République*. Paris: A. Cohn, 1973.

Linz, Juan J. "Presidential or Parliamentary Democracy: Does it Make a Difference?" In *The Failure of Presidential Democracy: Comparative Perspectives*, vol. 1, edited by Juan J. Linz and Arturo Valenzuela, 3–87. Baltimore: Johns Hopkins University Press, 1994.

Lloyd George, David. *Memoirs of the Peace Conference*. 2 vols. New York: Howard Fertig, 1972.

Paterson, Thomas G. "Presidential Foreign Policy, Public Opinion, and Congress: The Truman Years." *Diplomatic History* 7 (1983): 14–17.

Peterson, Susan. *Crisis Bargaining and the State*. Ann Arbor: University of Michigan Press, 1996.

Pickles, Dorothy. *French Politics: The First Years of the Fourth Republic*. London: RIIA, 1953.

Powaski, Ronald E. *Toward an Entangling Alliance: American Isolationism, Internationalism, and Europe, 1901–1950*. New York: Greenwood, 1991.

Ransom, Harry Howe. *Central Intelligence and National Security*. Cambridge: Harvard University Press, 1965.

Raskin, Marcus G. *Essays of a Citizen: From National Security State to Democracy*. Armonk, N.Y.: Sharpe, 1991.

Richards, Peter G. *Parliament and Foreign Affairs*. London: George Allen & Unwin, 1967.

de Saint-Mart, Pierre. *Etude Historique et Critique sur les Interpellations en France*. Paris: Societé de Recueil Sirey, 1912.

Schuman, Frederick L. *War and Diplomacy in the French Republic*. New York: AMS Press, 1970.

Skocpol, Theda. "Political Response to Capitalist Crisis: Neo-Marxist Theories of the State and the Case of the New Deal." *Politics and Society* 10, no. 2 (1980): 155–201.

Steiner, Zara. *The Foreign Office and Foreign Policy, 1898–1914*. (Cambridge: Cambridge University Press, 1969.

Turner, John. *British Politics and the Great War*. New Haven: Yale University Press, 1992.

United States National Security Council. *Organizational History of the National Security Council during the Truman and Eisenhower Administrations*. Washington: National Security Council, 1988.

Vital, David. *The Making of British Foreign Policy*. London: George Allen & Unwin, 1968.

Ware, Richard. "Parliament and Treaties." In *Parliament and International Relations*, edited by Carstairs and Ware, 37–48. Buckingham, England: Open University Press, 1991.

Yergin, Daniel. *Shattered Peace*. Boston: Houghton Mifflin, 1977.

Zysman, John. "The French State in the International Economy." In *Between Power and Plenty: Foreign Economic Policies in Advanced Industrial States*, edited by Peter J. Katzenstein, 255–93. Madison: University of Wisconsin Press, 1978.

Unpublished Sources for Case Studies

a) France:

Archives Nationale (AN), rue des Archives, Paris.
* 560 AP, The Papers of René Pleven.
* 563 AP, The Papers of René Mayer.

Ministère des Affaires Etrangères (MAE), Quai d'Orsay, Paris.
* EU: Series EU, Europe, 1949–1955.
* Y: Series Y, Internationale, 1944–1949.
* Z: Series Z, Europe, 1944–1949.

b) Great Britain:

Public Records Office (PRO), Kew Gardens, England.
* CAB 128: Cabinet Minutes (CM) (after October 26, 1951, CC).
* CAB 129: Cabinet Papers (CP) (after October 26, 1951, C.).
* DEFE 4: Chiefs of Staff (COS) Papers.
* FO 371: Foreign Office Correspondence.
* FO 800: Foreign Office Private Paper Collections.

c) United States:

Dwight D. Eisenhower Presidential Library (DDEL), Abilene, Kansas.
* Papers of Dwight D. Eisenhower as President.
    - Administration Series (AS).
        European Defense Community.
        General Alfred Gruenther.
    - Dulles-Herter Series.
        John Foster Dulles.

Harry S. Truman Presidential Library (HSTL), Independence, Missouri.
* Papers of Dean Acheson (PDA).
    - Memoranda of Conversations.
    - Princeton Seminars.
* Presidential Papers.
    - President's Secretary's File (PSF).
        CIA Files.

- Intelligence File.
    ORE Reports.
    Central Intelligence Agency Reports (CIA).
- National Security Council Files.
- White House Central File (WHCF).
    Confidential File.
    Official File.
    Public Opinion Mail.

National Archives (NARA), College Park, Maryland.
* State Department Central File.
* State Department Decimal File.

Seeley G. Mudd Manuscript Library, Princeton University, Princeton, New Jersey.
* John Foster Dulles Papers.
* John Foster Dulles Oral History Collection.

Roper Center at the University of Connecticut, "Public Opinion On-Line" (*POO*).

Case Study I: Peacemaking 1919

Adamthwaite, Anthony. *Grandeur and Misery: France's Bid for Power in Europe,
    1914–1940.* London: Arnold, 1995.
Ambrosius, Lloyd E. *Woodrow Wilson and the American Diplomatic Tradition: the
    Treaty Fight in Perspective.* Cambridge: Cambridge University Press, 1987.
Bailey, Thomas A. *Woodrow Wilson and the Lost Peace.* Chicago: Encounter Paper-
    backs, 1963.
Baker, Ray Stannard. *Woodrow Wilson and World Settlement.* 3 vols. Gloucester,
    Mass.: Peter Smith, 1960.
———, and William E. Dodd, eds. *The Public Papers of Woodrow Wilson.* 6 vols.
    New York: Kraus Reprint Co., 1970.
Bourne, Kenneth, and D. Cameron Watt, eds. *British Documents on Foreign Affairs*
    (*BDFA*). 15 vols. Part 2, Series 1, The Paris Peace Conference of 1919, edited
    by Michael Dockrill. Frederick, Md.: University Publications of America,
    1989.
Briault, Edouard. *La paix de la France, les traités de 1918–1921.* Paris: Librairie de
    Recueil Sirey, 1937.
Bunselmeyer, Robert E. *The Cost of the War, 1914–1919: British Economic War
    Aims and the Origins of Reparation.* Hamden, Conn.: Archon Books, 1975.
Burnett, Philip Mason. *Reparation at the Paris Peace Conference from the Stand-
    point of the American Delegation.* New York: Columbia University Press,
    1940.
Cienciala, Anna M. "The Battle of Danzig and the Polish Corridor at the Paris Peace
    Conference of 1919." In *The Reconstruction of Poland, 1914–23,* edited by
    Paul Latawski, 71–94. New York: St. Martin's Press, 1992.

Clemenceau, Georges. *Grandeur and Misery of Victory*. New York: Harcourt, Brace & Co., 1930.

Clementel, Etienne. *La France et la Politique Économique Interalliée*. Paris: Presses Universitaires de France, 1931.

Duroselle, Jean-Baptiste. *Clemenceau*. Paris: Fayard, 1988.

France—Assemblée Nationale. *Journal Officiel de la République Française, Débats Parlementaires, Chambre des Députés* (JO). Paris: Imprimerie Nationale.

France—Ministère des Affaires Etrangères. *Documents Diplomatiques Français*. Paris: Imprimerie Nationale.

Gatzke, Hans Wilhelm. *European Diplomacy Between Two Wars, 1919–1939*. Chicago: Quadrangle Books, 1972.

George, Alexander L., and Juliette L. George. *Woodrow Wilson and Colonel House*. New York: Dover Publications, 1964.

Great Britain. *Parliamentary Debates*. *Hansard*.

Great Britain—Foreign Office. *Documents on British Foreign Policy, 1919–1939*. Edited by E. L. Woodward. London: H. M. Stationery Office.

Heckscher, August. *Woodrow Wilson*. New York: Scribner, 1991.

Karski, Jan. *The Great Powers and Poland, 1919–1945*. Lanham, Md.: University Press of America, 1985.

Keynes, John Maynard. *The Economic Consequences of the Peace*. London: Macmillan, 1920.

King, Jere Clemens. *Foch Versus Clemenceau: France and German Dismemberment, 1918–1919*. Cambridge: Harvard University Press, 1960.

Lentin, A. *Lloyd George, Woodrow Wilson and the Guilt of Germany*. Leicester: Leicester University Press, 1984.

Lentin, Antony. "Several Types of Ambiguity: Lloyd George at the Paris Peace Conference." In *Ethics and Statecraft: The Moral Dimension of International Affairs*, edited by Cathal J. Nolan, 109–34. Westport, Conn.: Greenwood, 1995.

Link, Arthur S., ed. *The Deliberations of the Council of Four (DCF)*. 2 vols. Princeton: Princeton University Press, 1992.

———, et al., eds. *The Papers of Woodrow Wilson (PWW)*. 69 vols. Princeton: Princeton University Press, 1966–92.

Lippmann, Walter. *Essays in the Public Philosophy*. Boston: Little, Brown and Co., 1955.

Lloyd George, David. *Memoirs of the Peace Conference*. 2 vols. New York: Howard Fertig, 1972.

Lundgreen-Nielsen, Kay. "Aspects of American Policy towards Poland at the Paris Peace Conference and the Role of Isaiah Bowman." In *The Reconstruction of Poland, 1914–23*, edited by Paul Latawski, 95–116. New York: St. Martin's Press, 1992.

———. *The Polish Problem at the Paris Peace Conference*. Odense: Odense University Press, 1979.

Mantoux, Étienne. *The Carthaginian Peace; or, The Economic Consequences of Mr. Keynes*. New York, Scribner, 1952.

Marks, Sally. *The Illusion of Peace*. New York: St. Martin's Press, 1976.

———. *Politics and Diplomacy of Peacemaking: Containment and Counterrevolution at Versailles 1918–1919*. New York: Alfred A. Knopf, 1967.

McCrum, Robert. "French Rhineland Policy at the Paris Peace Conference, 1919." *Historical Journal* 21, no. 3 (1978): 623–48.

McDougall, Walter A. *France's Rhineland Diplomacy, 1914–1924*. Princeton: Princeton University Press, 1978.

Miller, David Hunter. *My Diary at the Conference of Paris*, with documents [microform]. New York: Printed for the author by the Appeal printing company, 1924.

Miquel, Pierre. *Clemenceau: La guerre et la paix*. Paris: Tallandier, 1996.

———. *La paix de Versailles et l'opinion publique Française*. Paris: Flammarion, 1972.

Morgan, Kenneth O. *Lloyd George*. London: Weidenfeld and Nicolson, 1983.

Morgenthau, Hans J., and Kenneth W. Thompson. *Politics Among Nations*. 6th ed. New York: McGraw-Hill, 1985.

Nelson, Harold I. *Land and Power: British and Allied Policy on Germany's Frontiers*. London: Routledge & Kegan Paul, 1963.

Nelson, Keith L. *Victors Divided: America and the Allies in Germany, 1918–1923*. Berkeley and Los Angeles: University of California Press, 1975.

Nicolson, Harold. *Peacemaking 1919*. New York: Grosset & Dunlop, 1974.

Rowland, Peter. *Lloyd George*. London: Barrie & Jenkins, 1975.

Schwabe, Klaus. *Woodrow Wilson, Revolutionary Germany, and Peacemaking, 1918–1919: Missionary Diplomacy and the Realities of Power*. Translated by Rita and Robert Kimber. Chapel Hill: University of North Carolina Press, 1985.

Seymour, Charles, ed. *The Intimate Papers of Colonel House*. 4 vols. New York: Houghton Mifflin, 1928.

Sharp, Alan. *The Versailles Settlement: Peacemaking in Paris*. New York: St. Martin's Press, 1991.

Sontag, Raymond J. *A Broken World, 1919–1939*. New York: Harper & Row, 1971.

Soutou, Georges-Henri. "L'Allemagne et la France en 1919." *La France et l'Allemagne entre les Deux Guerres Mondiales*, edited by J. Bariéty, A. Guth and J. M. Valentin, 9–20. Nancy: Presses Universitaires de Nancy, 1987.

Tardieu, André. *The Truth About the Treaty*. Indianapolis: Bobbs-Merrill, 1921.

Taylor, A. J. P. *The Origins of the Second World War*. New York: Atheneum, 1961.

Tillman, Seth P. *Anglo-American Relations at the Paris Peace Conference of 1919*. Princeton: Princeton University Press, 1961.

Trachtenberg, Marc. *Reparation in World Politics: France and European Economic Diplomacy, 1916–1923*. New York: Columbia University Press, 1980.

United States Congress. *Congressional Record*.

United States Department of State. *Foreign Relations of the United States (FRUS)*. Washington, D.C.

Watson, David Robin. *Georges Clemenceau*. New York: McKay, 1974.

Widenor, William C. *Henry Cabot Lodge and the Search for an American Foreign Policy*. Berkeley and Los Angeles: University of California Press, 1980.

Yates, Louis A. R. *United States and French Security*. New York: Twayne, 1957.

Case Study II: Peacemaking After World War II

Acheson, Dean. *Present at the Creation: My Years in the State Department*. New York: Norton, 1969.

Adenauer, Konrad. *Memoirs 1945–53*. Chicago: Henry Regnery, 1965.

Alphand, Hervé. *L'étonnement d'être: Journal, 1939–1973*. Paris: Fayard, 1977.

Ambrose, Stephen. *Eisenhower*. 2 vols. New York: Simon and Schuster, 1988.

Auriol, Vincent. *Journal de Septennat*. 7 vols. Paris: Librarie Armand Colin, 1970.

Backer, John H. *Winds of History: The German Years of Lucius DuBignon Clay*. New York: Van Nostrand Reinhold, 1983.

Bullen, Roger, and M. E. Pelly, eds. *Documents on British Policy Overseas* (DBPO). London: Her Majesty's Stationery Office.

Bullock, Alan. *Ernest Bevin, Foreign Secretary 1945–1951*. London: Heinemann, 1983.

Burridge, Trevor D. *British Labour and Hitler's War*. London: Deutsch, 1976.

Byrnes, James F. *All In One Lifetime*. New York: Harper & Brothers, 1958.

Cairncross, Alec. *The Price of War*. Oxford: Basil Blackwell, 1986.

Calvocoressi, Peter. *Survey of International Affairs, 1949–1950*. London: Oxford University, 1953.

Carden, Robert W. "Before Bizonia: Britain's Economic Dilemma in Germany." *Journal of Contemporary History* 14, no. 3 (July 1979): 535–55.

Chauvel, Jean. *Commentaire: d'Alger à Berne*. Paris: Fayard, 1972.

Churchill, Winston S. *Defending the West*. Westport, Conn.: Arlington House, 1981.

Crossman, R. H. S. "Open Letter." *The Times*, April 10, 1950.

Dallek, Robert. *Franklin D. Roosevelt and American Foreign Policy, 1932–1945*. New York: Oxford University Press, 1995.

Dalloz, Jacques. *Georges Bidault: Biographie Politique*. Paris: L'Harmattan, 1992.

Dalton, Hugh. *The Political Diary of Hugh Dalton, 1918–40, 1945–60*. Edited by Ben Pimlott. London: Jonathan Cape, 1986.

Debré, Michel. *Trois Républiques pour une France: Mémoires, 1946–58*. Paris: A. Michel, 1988.

Deighton, Anne. *The Impossible Peace: Britain, the Division of Germany, and the Origins of the Cold War*. Oxford: Clarendon, 1990.

———. "Towards a 'Western' Strategy: The Making of British Policy Towards Germany, 1945–46." In *Britain and the First Cold War*, edited by Anne Deighton, 53–70. New York: St. Martin's Press, 1990.

Diebold, William, Jr. *The Schuman Plan*. New York: Praeger, 1959.

Dockrill, Saki. *Britain's Policy for West German Rearmament, 1950–55*. (Cambridge: Cambridge University Press, 1991.

Eden, Sir Anthony. *Full Circle: The Memoirs of Anthony Eden*. Boston: Houghton Mifflin, 1960.

Eisenberg, Carolyn Woods. *Drawing the Line: The American Decision to Divide Germany, 1944–1949*. Cambridge: Cambridge University Press, 1996.

Eisenhower, Dwight D. *Mandate for Change, 1953–1956: The White House Years*. Garden City, N.J.: Doubleday & Co., 1963.

Elgey, Georgette. *La République des Contradictions, 1951–1954*. Paris: Fayard, 1968.

———. *La République des Illusions, 1945–1951.* Paris: Fayard, 1965.

Fauvet, Jacques. "Birth and Death of a Treaty." In *France Defeats EDC,* edited by Daniel Lerner and Raymond Aron, 128–64. New York: Praeger, 1957.

Foot, Michael. *Aneurin Bevan.* vol. 2. London: Davis-Poynter, 1973.

Fordham, Benjamin O. *Building the Cold War Consensus: The Political Economy of U.S. National Security Policy.* Ann Arbor: University of Michigan Press, 1998.

France. *L'Année Politique, 1948.* Paris: Éditions du Grand Siècle.

———. Assemblée Nationale. *Journal Officiel de la République Française, Débats Parlementaires, Chambre des Députés.* Paris: Imprimerie Nationale.

———. Ministère des Affaires Etrangères. *Documents Diplomatiques Français.* Paris: Imprimerie Nationale.

———. *Documents Français Relatifs à l'Allemagne* (DFRA). Paris: Imprimerie Nationale, 1947.

Freymond, Jacques. *The Saar Conflict.* New York: Praeger, 1960.

Gallup, George H. *The Gallup International Public Opinion Polls: France, 1939, 1944–1975.* 2 vols. New York: Random House, 1976.

———. *The Gallup International Public Opinion Polls: Great Britain, 1937–1975.* 2 vols. New York: Random House, 1976.

———. *The Gallup Poll: Public Opinion 1935–71.* 2 vols. New York: Random House, 1972.

de Gaulle, Charles. *Lettres Notes et Carnets.* 12 vols. Paris: Plon, 1984.

———. *War Memoirs.* 5 vols. New York: Simon and Schuster, 1960.

Gimbel, John. *The American Occupation of Germany.* Stanford: Stanford University Press, 1968).

———. *The Origins of the Marshall Plan.* Stanford: Stanford University Press, 1976.

Gottlieb, Manuel. *The German Peace Settlement and the Berlin Crisis.* New York: Paine Whitman, 1960.

Great Britain. *Parliamentary Debates.* Hansard.

Guillen, Pierre. "Les Chefs Militaires Français, le Réarmement de l'Allemagne et la CED, 1950–1954." *Revue d'histoire de la Deuxième Guerre Mondiale et des Conflits Contemporains* 33 (1983): 3–33.

Hardach, Karl. *The Political Economy of Germany in the Twentieth Century.* Berkeley and Los Angeles: University of California Press, 1976.

Hillel, Marc. *L'occupation française en Allemagne.* Paris: Balland, 1983.

Hitchcock, William I. *France Restored: Cold War Diplomacy and the Quest for Leadership in Europe, 1944–1954.* Chapel Hill: University of North Carolina Press, 1998).

Institut Français d'Opinion Publique. *Sondages.*

Ireland, Timothy P. *Creating the Entangling Alliance: The Origins of the North Atlantic Treaty Organization.* Westport, Conn.: Greenwood, 1981.

Jonas, Manfred. *The United States and Germany.* Ithaca: Cornell University Press, 1984.

Kimball, Warren F. *Swords or Ploughshares? The Morgenthau Plan for Defeated Nazi Germany, 1943–1946.* Philadelphia: Lippincott, 1976.

Kuklick, Bruce. *American Policy and the Division of Germany.* Ithaca: Cornell University Press, 1972.

Lapie, Pierre-Olivier. *De Léon Blum à de Gaulle*. Paris: Fayard, 1971.

Large, David Clay. *Germans to the Front: West German Rearmament in the Adenauer Era*. Chapel Hill: University of North Carolina Press, 1996.

Leffler, Melvyn P. *A Preponderance of Power: National Security, the Truman Administration, and the Cold War*. Stanford: Stanford University Press, 1992.

Lerner, Daniel, and Raymond Aron, eds. *France Defeats EDC*. New York: Praeger, 1957.

Marchand, Jean José. "A Tableau of the French Press." In *France Defeats EDC*, edited by Daniel Lerner and Raymond Aron, pp. 102–23. New York: Praeger, 1957.

Massigli, René Lucien Daniel. *Une comédie des erreurs, 1943–1956: Souvenirs et réflexions sur une étape de la construction européenne*. Paris: Plon, 1978.

Mayer, Herbert Carleton. *German Recovery and the Marshall Plan*. Bonn: Edition Atlantic Forum, 1969.

McGeehan, Robert. *The German Rearmament Question: American Diplomacy and European Defense after World War II*. Urbana: University of Illinois Press, 1971.

Mendès-France, Pierre. *Oeuvres Complètes*. Paris: Gallimard, 1984.

Mioche, Philippe. *Le Plan Monnet: Genèse et élaboration*. Paris: La Sorbonne, 1986.

Monnet, Jean. *Memoirs*. Translated by Richard Mayne. London: Collins, 1978.

Montgomery of Alamein, Viscount Bernard Law. *The Memoirs of Field-Marshal the Viscount Montgomery of Alamein, K. G.* New York: Da Capo, 1958.

Paterson, Thomas G. *Meeting the Communist Threat: Truman to Reagan*. New York: Oxford University Press, 1988.

Poidevin, Raymond. *Robert Schuman*. Paris: Imprimerie Nationale, 1986.

Ratchford, Benjamin U., and William D. Ross. *Berlin Reparations Assignment*. Chapel Hill: University of North Carolina Press, 1947.

Rostow, Walt W. *The Division of Europe after World War II: 1946*. Austin: University of Texas Press, 1981.

Ruhm von Oppen, Beate, ed. *Documents on Germany under Occupation, 1945–54* (DGO). London: Oxford University Press, 1955.

Schwartz, Thomas Alan. *America's Germany: John J. McCloy and the Federal Republic of Germany*. Cambridge: Harvard University Press, 1991.

Seldon, Anthony. *Churchill's Indian Summer: The Conservative Government, 1951–1955*. London: Hodder & Stoughton, 1981.

Seydoux, François. *Mémoires d'Outre-Rhin*. Paris: B. Grasset, 1975.

Smith, Jean Edward. *The Papers of General Lucius D. Clay*. 2 vols. Bloomington: Indiana University Press, 1974.

Soutou, Georges-Henri. "France and the German Rearmament Problem, 1945–1955." In *The Quest for Stability: Problems of West European Security, 1918–1957*, edited by R. Ahmann, A. M. Birke, and M. Howard, 487–512. London: Oxford University Press, 1993.

———. "La France et les notes soviétiques de 1952 sur l'Allemagne," *Revue d'Allemagne* 20 (1988): 261–73.

Stoetzel, Jean. "The Evolution of French Opinion." In *France Defeats EDC*, edited by Daniel Lerner and Raymond Aron, 72–101. New York: Praeger, 1957.

Trachtenberg, Marc. *A Constructed Peace: The Making of the European Settlement, 1945–1963*. Princeton: Princeton University Press, 1999.

Truman, Harry S. *The Autobiography of Harry S. Truman*. Boulder, Colo.: Associated University Press, 1980.

United States Department of State. *Foreign Relations of the United States (FRUS)*. Washington, D.C.

United States National Security Council. *Documents of the National Security Council, 1947–1977 (DNSC)*. Maryland: a Microfilm Project of University Publications of America Inc., 1980.

Wall, Irwin. *The United States and the Making of Post-War France, 1945–54*. Cambridge: Cambridge University Press, 1991.

Watt, D. C. *Britain Looks to Germany*. London: Oswald Wolff, 1965.

Werth, Alexander. *Lost Statesman: The Strange Case of Pierre Mendès-France*. Ann Arbor: University Microfilms, 1980.

Willis, Frank Roy. *The French in Germany*. Stanford: Stanford University Press, 1962.

Yergin, Daniel. *Shattered Peace*. Boston: Houghton Mifflin, 1977.

Young, John W. *Britain, France and the Unity of Europe*. Leicester: Leicester University Press, 1984.

———. *France, the Cold War and the Western Alliance, 1944–49: French Foreign Policy and Postwar Europe*. New York: St. Martin's Press, 1990.

———. "German Rearmament and the European Defence Community." In *The Foreign Policy of Churchill's Peacetime Administration*, edited by John W. Young, 81–107. Leicester: Leicester University Press, 1988.

Index